Convergences:
Inventories of the Present

_____

Edward W. Said, General Editor

Dominance
without
Hegemony

*History and Power in
Colonial India*

RANAJIT GUHA

Harvard University Press

CAMBRIDGE, MASSACHUSETTS
LONDON, ENGLAND

Library of Congress Cataloging-in-Publication Data

Guha, Ranajit.
   Dominance without Hegemony : history and power in colonial India /
Ranajit Guha.
      p.   cm. — (Convergences)
   Includes index.
      ISBN 0-674-21482-X (cloth : alk. paper). — ISBN 0-674-21483-8
(paper : alk. paper)
      1. India — History — British occupation, 1765–1947.   2. Civil
service — India.   3. India — Politics and government — 1765–1947.
I. Title. II. Series: Convergences (Cambridge, Mass.)
DS463.G837   1997   97-15888
954 — dc21   CIP

This book has been digitally reprinted. The content remains
identical to that of previous printings.

To my colleagues of the *Subaltern Studies* project,
1974–1989

Contents

Preface

This book is made up of modified versions of three essays written in 1986–87 and published between 1988 and 1992. All three connect with our project, *Subaltern Studies,* and refer back to and develop certain positions I have taken up there. That project made its debut by announcing its revisionist aims for studies on colonial India. However, in doing so, it did not claim any novelty. Ours was not the first or only intervention to express discontent about the state of South Asian historiography and social sciences and provoke debates about it. Debates of this kind had already started in the nineteenth century, when Indian intellectuals put on record their first public, though cautious and loyalist, criticism of the colonial administration and have continued ever since as one variety or another of a whole range of liberal-imperialist and liberal-nationalist tendencies. In spite of their differences in other respects, these tendencies have been unanimous in the assumption that the power relations of colonial rule were contained in an integrated and unified field with all the ideologies and political practices of the period articulated within a single domain.

Subaltern Studies made its debut by questioning that assumption and arguing that there was no such unified and singular domain of politics and the latter was, to the contrary, structurally split between an elite and a subaltern part, each of which was autonomous in its own way. Much of what we have to say has indeed been concerned with documenting the existence of these two distinct but interacting parts as well as with arguing why such a structural split between them was historically necessary.

However, by questioning that monistic conception we immediately and inevitably raised a question about the nature of the colonial state itself. For all those tendencies I have mentioned had proceeded from a thoroughly unexamined belief that the so-called unitary character of politics was nothing other than the effect of the homogenizing function of colonialism.

This notion of colonialism as a homogenizing force is fundamental to both of the dominant historiographies—neocolonialist and nationalist. The former characterizes it in positive terms as either a cultural or an institutional force. According to one of its versions, the colonial regime politicized India by the introduction of liberal education, and the ideas and activities of a Western-educated elite in the course of its collaboration with the raj were all that was there to Indian politics. According to another version, which superseded the first, it was not so much the metropolitan liberal culture as the colonial administration itself which created a political arena for the natives by involving them in a scramble for rewards in the form of privileges and power in governmental institutions developed by the raj.

Whichever version one takes, it is the civilizing or institutionalizing function of the regime that figures as the generative impulse of Indian politics and its unifying force in this neocolonialist view. The nationalist standpoint shares the same assumption, but turns it to its own advantage by defining the content and character of politics simply in terms of the indigenous elite's response to colonial rule and the sum of all the ideas and activities by which it dealt with the government of the day.

Between these two interpretations the question of power was reduced to an elite contest with no room left in it for the South Asian people except as an inert mass deployed by the dominant elements to serve their own ends according to strategies of their own invention. We took notice of this omission in an inaugural statement in *Subaltern Studies I* (Delhi: Oxford University Press, 1982) thus:

> What is clearly left out of this un-historical historiography is the *politics of the people.* For parallel to the domain of elite politics there existed throughout the colonial period another domain of Indian politics in which the principal actors were not the dominant groups of the indigenous society or the colonial authorities but the subaltern classes and groups constituting the mass of the labouring population and the intermediate strata in town and country—that is, the people. This was an *autonomous* domain, for

it neither originated in elite politics nor did its existence depend on the latter.

Underlying the exclusive and elitist approach is an idea which has prevailed in historiography since the rise of the Italian city-states and has continued through the Enlightenment until the emergence of the modern nation-states nearer our time. This is the idea that with the ascendancy of the bourgeoisie in Western Europe all of the power relations of civil society have everywhere been so fully assimilated to those of the state that the two may be said to have coincided in an undifferentiated and integrated space where alone such relations have situated and articulated themselves ever since. It has been possible therefore for historical scholarship that has fed on this theorem for centuries and made it into the stuff of academic common sense to represent power in its most generalized form as Civil Society = Nation = State.

To say and demonstrate, as we have done, that the domain of politics is not unitary but structurally split is of course to spoil the elegance of this equation at once. However, by doing so, we take it upon ourselves to redefine how these three terms relate to each other in such a domain. Our attempt to face up to that task leads directly, as indicated above, to the question: "What is colonialism and what is a colonial state?"

Questions like these have of course been asked before. An answer to one or another of them is indeed presupposed in all that has ever been written about British rule in South Asia. This has been so since the first histories of the subcontinent were published by the East India Company's servants as early the 1770s and has continued to be the case until today with the imperial theme established firmly as an object of academic research and teaching. Yet the progress of scholarship during the last two hundred years has done little to challenge or even seriously interrogate such presuppositions. In fact, they have hardly moved from where Bolts and Verelst had left them standing as a set of necessary, if invisible, prejudices which the passage of time has allowed to merge unobtrusively in the background of historical discourse. Thanks to an amazing oversight characteristic of academic work of all kinds irrespective of their points of view, the notion of a unitary political domain has survived until now even the mutually opposed readings of the Indian past from imperialist and nationalist points of view.

We take the enigma of that oversight common to both of those rival ideologies as our point of departure and go on to suggest that the colonial state in South Asia was very unlike and indeed fundamentally different from the metropolitan bourgeois state which had sired it. The difference consisted in the fact that the metropolitan state was hegemonic in character with its claim to dominance based on a power relation in which the moment of persuasion outweighed that of coercion, whereas the colonial state was nonhegemonic with persuasion outweighed by coercion in its structure of dominance. Indeed, we have argued that the originality of the South Asian colonial state lay precisely in this difference: a historical paradox, it was an autocracy set up and sustained in the East by the foremost democracy of the Western world. And since it was nonhegemonic, it was not possible for that state to assimilate the civil society of the colonized to itself. We have defined the character of the colonial state therefore as a *dominance without hegemony.*

The consequence of this paradox for the political culture of colonial India was to generate an original alloy from the fusion and overdetermination of two distinct paradigms — an originality which has been witness to the historic failure of capital to realize its universalizing tendency under colonial conditions, and the corresponding failure of the metropolitan bourgeois culture to dissolve or assimilate fully the indigenous culture of South Asia in the power relations of the colonial period. We have followed up these considerations by reflecting on the character of colonialist historiography and shown how it has sought to endow colonialism with a spurious hegemony denied it by history.

Dominance without hegemony has a nationalist aspect as well. This follows from the structural split in politics and the coexistence of its two domains. As it has been put in the statement cited above, "The co-existence of these two domains or streams, which can be sensed by intuition and proved by demonstration as well, was the index of an important historical truth, that is, the *failure of the Indian bourgeoisie to speak for the nation.* There were vast areas in the life and consciousness of the people which were never integrated into their hegemony."

That failure is self-evident from the difficulty which has frustrated the bourgeoisie in its effort so far at winning a hegemonic role for itself even after half a century since the birth of a sovereign Indian nation-state. The predicament continues to grow worse, and by current showing should keep students of contemporary South Asia busy for years to come. For our part we have concentrated, in what follows, on two important moments of its career under the raj which anticipated its accession to power by mobilization and by historiography. What was at issue in both respects was its desire for recognition in its claim to speak for the people constituted as a nation and to challenge thereby any pretensions the alien rulers had to represent the colonized. A rivalry between an aspirant to power and its incumbent, this was in essence a contest for hegemony.

Our approach to these problems picks its way through historiography, as the readers will notice no doubt from the signs displayed all over the text and the arguments these refer to. We have taken this particular course not out of any conviction that this is the only possible way of asking questions about colonialism and the colonial state. One could have formulated the same or very similar questions deductively following the classical models of political philosophy (whose influence, especially that of Hobbes, Machiavelli, and Montesquieu, on the development of our own argument should be obvious to all) or any of their latter-day adaptations in academic work on the modern state-systems. But we have decided on the historiographical approach primarily because it helps us to combine the advantages of the classical theories with a consideration of history as writing.

The importance of the latter for our problematic is hard to exaggerate. For at a certain level the question of power in colonial South Asia or anywhere else in a land under foreign occupation can be phrased succinctly as "Who writes the history of the subjugated people?" In the Indian instance that question resonates with one that agitated the very first architects of the empire as they asked, "Who is the king of Bengal?" As Warren Hastings and Philip Francis were both thoughtful enough to declare in response, the East India Company's claim to such "kingship" derived entirely from the right of conquest. For all that was involved in such a claim, ranging from the assumption of statutory authority to act as *Diwan* to grabbing the produce of the land and converting it by the most predatory means into mercantile wealth, rested simply and exclusively on the power of the sword.

What we have tried to point out here is how that sword conferred a "right" on the pen as well. It was conquest which empowered the conquerors to impose on the colonized a past written from the colonizer's point of view and uphold that writing as foundational to the law of the land. Our attempt to inform this study of colonialism by the pathos of a purloined past is therefore not so much a matter of professional convenience as a strategy to situate the writing of a conquered people's history by conquerors at the very heart of the question of one nation's oppression by another.

To think the colonial condition of rulership and historiography together in this manner is of course to think of the second term too as a force. To do so would not be to raise the power of the pen to that of the gun by *utprekṣā*—the figure of Sanskrit poetics which allows a thing to be elevated fancifully, if absurdly on occasions, to the likeness of something superior to it. Rather, it would be to put on record the effect of an *atideśa*—a metonymic extension by which statist concerns forced their way into historical interpretation, allowing a colonial dominance to overflow and appropriate a writing culture of the colonized.

But such extension did not come about as a simple laterality. The force of that writing culture was destined to acquire a vertical thrust as well. For it enlisted the colonized too as interpreters of their own past and created the conditions for an Indian historiography of India. However, as discussed in these pages, such an agenda for the reclamation of an appropriated past could in no way be adequate to its concept without wrenching itself away from its liberal-imperialist armature, without in fact arming itself with a genuinely anti-imperialist critique for which it did not, alas, have either the strength or the motivation yet. It was precisely such debility that frustrated whatever was there as a desire for power underlying the first historical discourses informed by an Indian point of view. Insofar as any nationalist claim to speak for a people's past was hegemonic by implication, it would be sometime yet for that claim to be fully upheld by historiography.

My thanks are due to the Centre for Studies in Social Sciences (Calcutta) for permission to use the text of my Sakharam Ganesh

Deuskar Lectures, "An Indian Historiography of India : A Nineteenth-century Agenda and Its Implications" published by the Centre in 1988, and to Oxford University Press (India) for permission to reproduce the earlier versions of my essays "Dominance Without Hegemony and Its Historiography" and "Discipline and Mobilize" published respectively in *Subaltern Studies VI* (1989) and *Subaltern Studies VII* (1992).

I am grateful to the following institutions for encouraging and promoting collective discussions amongst its members on parts of this work in previous versions at seminars, conferences, and other academic gatherings: Centre for Studies in the Social Sciences, Calcutta; Merrill College, University of California at Santa Cruz; Department of Humanities, California Institute of Technology; Department of Anthropology, University of Chicago; Centre for Asian Studies, Amsterdam School for Social Research; and Department of Anthropology, Australian National University.

I am particularly grateful to a number of scholars who encouraged me either by sponsoring such discussions and/or by their comments on some of these writings. My thanks are due in this regard to Dilip Basu, Jan Breman, Edmund Burke III, James Clifford, Bernard S. Cohn, Nicholas Dirks, Christopher Gregory, Tejaswini Niranjana, Gyan Prakash, and James Scott. I thank Edward Said and Amartya Sen for their support; Sugata Bose and Partha Chatterjee for their help in choosing a name for the volume; and Lindsay Waters, scholar-editor at Harvard University Press, and his colleagues for their advice and cooperation.

The members of the *Subaltern Studies* editorial team were closely associated with my work during a period of about fifteen years when some of the ideas which have gone into the making of this book took shape. I thank them for their cooperation and kindness.

As always, Mechthild Guha has shared all the anxieties and excitement of this writing as only a co-author can.

Note on Transliteration

Certain words of Indian origin have been italicized throughout the text. Many of these are in Sanskrit and distinguished by diacritical marks from others taken from the vernacular languages of the subcontinent. If no diacritical marking is shown for a Sanskrit word as required by grammar and convention, this should be understood as evidence of its vernacularization in the context in which it occurs. The style of diacritical markings followed here is the same as used in the Harvard Oriental Series for such texts as *The Dhvanyāloka of Ānandavardhana with the Locana of Abhinavagupta* edited by Daniel H. H. Ingalls (Cambridge, Mass.: Harvard University Press, 1990).

From this arises the following question: whether it is better to be loved than feared, or the reverse. The answer is that one would like to be both the one and the other; but because it is difficult to combine them, it is far better to be feared than loved if you cannot be both . . .

The prince should nonetheless make himself feared in such a way that, if he is not loved, at least he escapes being hated. For fear is quite compatible with absence of hatred . . .

Niccolò Machiavelli, The Prince

1

Colonialism in South Asia

A Dominance without Hegemony and Its Historiography

I. Conditions for a Critique of Historiography

Dominance and Its Historiographies

There was one Indian battle that Britain never won. It was a battle for appropriation of the Indian past. It began with the East India Company's accession to *Diwani* in 1765. The duties of that office required that its incumbent should know the structure of landed property in Bengal, Bihar, and Orissa well enough to be able to collect the revenues on behalf of the Nawab. But since the intricacies of proprietorship could hardly be understood without a grasp of the relations of power which had accumulated to it over time, the *Diwan* had to undertake the function of the historian as well. Consequently, many of the local histories to be written in English during these early days had the concerns of a hard-pressed but still rather inexperienced bureaucracy branded on them. Meant primarily to help the administration to determine inheritance along the lines of descent within the leading landlord families of a district, these are among the first specimens of elitist bias in British Indian historiography.

A bias of that order was clearly expressed in the assumption that the local aristocracies were the "natural proprietors" of land in India. Based entirely on contemporary Whig doctrines about law and society in Britain, that assumption was soon to be dressed up

1

as a fact of Indian history and used as an argument in favor of a
zamindari settlement. The past acquired its depth in these accounts
from elaborately constructed genealogies going back to (an often
mythical) antiquity in some cases and from (genuine or fabricated)
Mughal charters as evidence of proprietary right. This had the
effect of conferring a sense of spurious continuity on what was a
total rupture brought about by the intervention of a European
power in the structure of landed property in South Asia. The
illusion of continuity was reinforced further by global histories
which drew copiously on medieval chronicles in order to situate
the British dominion in a line of conquests that had begun with the
Turko-Afghans and within a tradition that allowed the conquerors
to extract tribute from the conquered.

These preliminary exercises in colonialist historiography,
whether done on a local or a global scale, abetted thus in laying the
foundations of the raj. Nothing illustrates this better than the way
the Indian past was mobilized by the various contending parties in
the debates within the Company's administration during the last
three decades of the eighteenth century. The history of the subject
population was reconstructed there over and over again as the
central question of the relation of property to empire became the
subject of controversies between Hastings and Francis in the
1770s, between Grant and Shore in the 1780s, and between Shore
and Cornwallis in 1788–1792 on the eve of the Permanent Settlement. The outcome of such attempts at appropriation was to provide legal and administrative support for those measures which in
the course of time set up British rule in the subcontinent eventually
as a rule of property.

This rudimentary historiography was soon followed up by a
more mature and sophisticated discourse when the time came for
the growing colonial state, already secure in its control of the
wealth of the land, to reinforce its apparatus of ideological control
as well. All the energies and skills of nineteenth-century British
scholarship were harnessed to this project. It investigated, recorded, and wrote up the Indian past in a vast corpus which,
worked by many hands during the seventy years between Mill's
History of British India (1812) and Hunter's *Indian Empire* (1881),
came to constitute an entirely new kind of knowledge. A colonialist
knowledge, its function was to erect that past as a pedestal on

which the triumphs and glories of the colonizers and their instrument, the colonial state, could be displayed to best advantage.

Indian history, assimilated thereby to the history of Great Britain, would henceforth be used as a comprehensive measure of difference between the peoples of these two countries. Politically that difference was spelled out as one between rulers and the ruled; ethnically, between a white *Herrenvolk* and blacks; materially, between a prosperous Western power and its poor Asian subjects; culturally, between higher and lower levels of civilization, between the superior religion of Christianity and indigenous belief systems made up of superstition and barbarism — all adding up to an irreconcilable difference between colonizer and colonized. The Indian past was thus painted red.

However, the appropriation of a past by conquest carries with it the risk of rebounding upon the conquerors. It can end up by sacralizing the past for the subject people and encouraging them to use it in their effort to define and affirm their own identity. This, no doubt, was what happened in the instance under discussion, and the appropriated past came to serve as the sign of the Other not only for the colonizers but, ironically, for the colonized as well. The colonized, in their turn, reconstructed their past for purposes opposed to those of their rulers and made it the ground for marking out their differences in cultural and political terms. History became thus a game for two to play as the alien colonialist project of appropriation was matched by an indigenous nationalist project of counter-appropriation.

The two have been locked in an indecisive battle ever since. The contradictions of colonialism which have inspired this contest in the first place lingered on at the ideological level even after their resolution, in constitutional terms, by the Transfer of Power. The cultural regime of colonialism clearly outlived the raj in the study of the Indian past, as was obvious from the influence which continued to be exerted on it by the more recent avatars of colonialist historiography. What made it possible, indeed necessary, for that influence to persist was a fundamental agreement between the Indian bourgeoisie and the British whom they replaced as rulers about the nature of colonialism itself — that is, what it was and what constituted its power relations. Both proceeded from the stand-

point of liberalism to regard the colonial state as an organic extension of the metropolitan bourgeois state and colonialism as an
adaptation, if not quite a replication, of the classical bourgeois
culture of the West in English rendering. Generally speaking, that
phenomenon was regarded by both as a positive confirmation of
the universalizing tendency of capital—a point to which we shall
soon return.

The rivalries of the two bourgeoisies and their representations
in colonialist and nationalist discourses did little to diminish the
importance of this essential agreement. On the contrary, all transactions between the two parties which made up the stuff of elite
politics followed from an understanding to abide by a common set
of rules based on the British constitutionalist parliamentary model.
It was a matter of playing cricket. If a nationalist agitation ran into
difficulty, the bureaucracy would gloat that Gandhi was on a poor
wicket, and he would, on his part, condemn the administration as
"un-British" whenever he felt outraged by the harshness of official
violence.

Neither side appears to have realized the absurdity of accusing
each other of deviating from norms which were displayed as ideals
but prevented in fact from realizing themselves to any significant
extent at all in the dominant idioms of political practice. This
incomprehension, so symptomatic of the malaise of a liberalism
grafted on to colonial conditions, informed historical discourses
corresponding to both the points of view and underscored their
common failure to discern the anomalies that made colonialism
into a figure of paradox.

The paradox consists of the fact that the performance of the elite
groups whose careers have provided both these historiographies
with their principal themes was widely at variance with their historic competence. Thus there were the metropolitan bourgeoisie
who professed and practiced democracy at home, but were quite
happy to conduct the government of their Indian empire as an
autocracy. Champions of the right of the European nations to
self-determination, they denied the same right to their Indian subjects until the very last phase of the raj and granted it without grace
only when forced to do so under the impact of the anti-imperialist
struggles of the subject population. Their antagonism to feudal
values and institutions in their own society made little difference

(in spite of the much publicized though rather ineffective campaigns against *sati*, child marriage, and so on) to their vast tolerance of pre-capitalist values and institutions in Indian society.

Their opposite numbers, the indigenous bourgeoisie, spawned and nurtured by colonialism itself, adopted a role that was distinguished by its failure to measure up to the heroism of the European bourgeoisie in its period of ascendancy. Pliant and prone to compromise from their inception, they lived in a state of happy accommodation with imperialism for the greater part of their career as a constituted political force between 1885 and 1947. The destruction of the colonial state was never a part of their project. They abjured and indeed resolutely opposed all forms of armed struggle against the raj, and settled for pressure politics as their main tactical means in bargaining for power. Compromise and accommodation were equally characteristic of their attitude to the semi-feudal values and institutions entrenched in Indian society. The liberalism they professed was never strong enough to exceed the limitations of the half-hearted initiatives for reform which issued from the colonial administration. This mediocre liberalism, a caricature of the vigorous democratic culture of the epoch of the rise of the bourgeoisie in the West, operated throughout the colonial period in a symbiotic relationship with the still active and vigorous forces of the semi-feudal culture of India.

How come that liberal historiography of both kinds fails to take notice of such paradoxes? Why is it that on those rare occasions when it does take notice, it still makes no serious attempt to explain them? Why, on the contrary, is the discrepancy between competence and performance in the record of the metropolitan bourgeoisie trivialized so often by liberal-imperialism and its intellectual representatives merely as an exceptional and aberrant instance of malfunctioning in the administrative apparatus of the raj? Why does liberal-nationalism, in its turn, tend to account for discrepancies of the same order in the record of the indigenous bourgeoisie simply as local difficulties generated by some weak survivals of a precapitalist culture and destined to be overcome by the leaders of the nation on their march to progress? How is it that no real effort is ever made by historians on either side to link these paradoxes to any structural fault in the historic project of the bourgeoisie?

6 Dominance without Hegemony

Containment of Historiography in a Dominant Culture

None of these questions can be answered without dispelling, first of all, the myth of ideological neutrality which is central to liberal historiography. For it is not possible to write or speak about the past without the use of concepts and presuppositions derived from one's experience and understanding of the present, that is, from those ideas by which the writer or speaker interprets his own times to himself and to others. As Hayden White has observed:

> There does, in fact, appear to be an irreducible ideological component in every historical account of reality . . . the very claim to have discerned some kind of formal coherence in the historical record brings with it theories of the nature of the historical world and of historical knowledge itself which have ideological implications for attempts to understand "the present," however this "present" is defined. To put it another way, the very claim to have distinguished a past from a present world of social thought and praxis, and to have determined the formal coherence of that past world, *implies* a conception of the form that knowledge of the present world also must take, insofar as it is *continuous* with that past world. Commitment to a particular *form* of knowledge predetermines the *kinds* of generalizations one can make about the present world, the kinds of knowledge one can have of it, and hence the kinds of projects one can legitimately conceive for changing that present or for maintaining it in its present form indefinitely.

> The ideological dimensions of a historical account reflect the ethical element in the historian's assumption of a particular position on the question of the nature of historical knowledge and the implications that can be drawn from the study of past events for the understanding of present ones. By the term "ideology" I mean a set of prescriptions for taking a position in the present world of social praxis and acting upon it (either to change the world or to maintain it in its current state).[1]

To change the world *and* to maintain it in its current state have indeed been the dual functions of liberal historiography performed on behalf of the class for which it speaks. A bourgeois discourse par excellence, it helped the bourgeoisie to change or at least significantly to modify the world according to its class interests in the period of its ascendancy, and since then to consolidate and perpetuate its dominance. As such, this historiography may be said not only to share, but actively to propagate, all the fundamental ideas by which the bourgeoisie represents and explains the world both as it is and as it was. The function of this complicity is, in short, to make liberal historiography speak from within the bourgeois consciousness itself.

To commit a discourse to speak from within a given consciousness is to disarm it insofar as its critical faculty is made inoperative thereby with regard to that particular consciousness. For no criticism can be fully activated unless its object is distanced from its agency. This is why liberal historiography, cramped as it is within the bourgeois consciousness, can never attack it vigorously enough as the object of its criticism. Since the paradoxes characteristic of the political culture of colonialism testify to the failure of the bourgeoisie to acknowledge the structural limitations of bourgeois dominance itself, it is hardly surprising that the liberal historical discourse too should be blind to those paradoxes. This is a necessary, one could say congenital, blindness which this historiography acquires by virtue of its class origin.

However, such blindness is by no means limited to bourgeois discourse alone. The knowledge systems that make up any dominant culture are all contained within the dominant consciousness and have therefore the latter's deficiencies built into their optics. The light of criticism emitted by such systems can, under no circumstances, be strong enough to penetrate and scan some of the strategic areas of that consciousness where dominance stores the spiritual gear it needs to justify and sustain itself.

It is notorious, for instance, that the historic cultures of the European antiquity, those of Greece in the fifth and fourth centuries B.C. and of Rome during a period of four hundred years until the second century A.D., were not merely tolerant but positively supportive of slavery. Aristotle justified slavery both in psychological and institutional terms when he observed in *The Politics* "that by nature some are free, others slaves, and that for these it is both right and expedient that they should serve as slaves."[2] Herodotus, the historian, believed, according to Finley, "that—barring the inevitable exceptions—slaves as a class were inferior beings, inferior in their psychology, by their nature."[3] And yet another historian, Xenophon, was the author, we are told, of a plan to set up a state fund of public slaves large enough to provide three of them for every Athenian citizen.[4]

It was thus that a dominant culture spoke up for a dominance based on the exploitation of slaves. There is no critical distance separating the intellectual here from the ruler in his understanding of the basic power relations of a slave society. On the contrary, the knowledge philosophers and historians had of slavery was clearly a component of the same consciousness that made the slave-owner knowledgeable about his slaves. Together, the two knowledges constituted the polar ends of an epistemological system in which, as Anderson has so incisively remarked, an ideal of absolute juridical freedom and that of absolute unfreedom came to form a dyad and provide an "ideological correlate" for the material prosperity generated by a slave mode of production.[5] It is not surprising therefore that the historiography which was itself an instance of this ideological correlate was unable to break away from its moorings in slavery and deal critically with it.

Feudal historiography, too, was identified with the ruling culture and situated snugly within the relations of dominance and subordination specific to feudal society. As a result, the voice of the historian in such a society was often indistinguishable from that of the panegyrist, the courtier, and the apologist speaking for gods, kings, and noblemen. Historical discourse was indeed so completely integrated here in the discourse of power that some fundamental aspects of the authority structure were never questioned even by the most questioning of writers. One such distinguished writer was Kalhaṇa, the author of the *Rājataraṅginī*, the twelfth-century chronicle of Kashmir.

It is generally agreed that Kalhaṇa was outstanding, indeed exceptional, in his critical acumen amongst the historians of the pre-Sultanate period of medieval India. The range of his source material and the sophistication with which he used it have evoked the admiration and to some extent the amazement of modern scholars.[6] His evidence included not only the information he gathered from some of the older chronicles and *purāṇas*, but also a good deal of oral tradition. To these he added, anticipating the

historian's craft of later times, a reading of epigraphic and nu-
mismatic data. On that basis he proceeded to scrutinize as many
as eleven royal chronicles written before his time and challenged
effectively the work of the prestigious eleventh-century author
Kṣemendra by identifying some gross inaccuracies in his "List of
Kings." By such a procedure, he claimed, "all wearisome error
has been set at rest."[7]

What is even more important for the present discussion is that
he was centuries ahead of his own age in attributing the function
of a judge to his ideal historian. "That man of merit alone deserves
praise," he wrote, "whose language, like that of a judge, in re-
counting the events of the past has discarded bias as well as prejudice."[8] This was an exceptionally high standard for a medieval
annalist to set for himself. There was nothing in the material and
spiritual conditions of twelfth-century Kashmir, a feudal state
racked, according to Kosambi, by "a war of extermination" between kings and barons *(ḍāmaras)*, to enable historical discourse
to speak with judicial impartiality about royalty and aristocracy.[9]
For a feudal culture which had no use for genuine social criticism
left the historian with no choice other than bias or prejudice in
writing about the elite groups—bias in favor of those who offered
him patronage and prejudice against those who were opposed to
his patrons.

It is all the more remarkable therefore that Kalhaṇa's historiographical practice should have approximated his ideal to a certain
degree. Neither Lalitāditya Muktāpīḍa, a king he admired in many
respects, nor Harṣa, his father's patron, was spared his criticism.[10]
And even though his impartiality seems to have been strained to
the utmost in his account of the reign of Jayasiṃha, the ruling
prince, he did not pass over the ruler's misdeeds in silence.[11] The
faint praise addressed to the monarch fell appreciably short of the
conventional *praśasti*, the panegyric composed by a court
poet—and the chronicle was written as a *kāvya*—for his patron as
an obligatory feudal due. All this is no mean achievement for a
medieval chronicler, and it has led Majumdar to credit Kalhaṇa
with "the supreme merit of possessing a critical mind and that spirit
of skepticism which is the first virtue of a historian."[12]

But how far does this skepticism go, how deep is the thrust of
this critical mind? Judging by what Majumdar himself has to say

about Kalhaṇa's "belief in witchcraft and magic feats, occasional explanation of events as due to the influence of fate or wrath of gods rather than to any rational cause, and a general didactic tendency inspired by Hindu views of doctrines of *karma* and transmigration,"[13] it is clear that criticism was confined within the bounds of a feudal consciousness even in this outstanding instance of a historical discourse which had set out so bravely to try "in this narrative of past events to repair by all means where there is error."[14] Since the error was branded on the dominant consciousness itself, historiography, unable to jump out of its skin, was forced to work from within the ruling culture.

The verse with which Kalhaṇa concludes his account of the murderous rule of Mihirakula may be cited here as one of many possible illustrations of such containment. "Thus although [he was] wicked," it reads, "that the king had not been assassinated by the people in an uprising, was because he was protected by the very gods who had urged him to do that act."[15] In an age when *rājabhakti* was a principal component of political philosophy, the historian seems to have relied in equal degrees on his own doubts about the record of the Kashmir rulers and on the experience of frequent baronial revolts to ask why there were no popular uprisings and no regicide.

But the question fails to explode. Its skeptical charge is neutralized by a dominant ideology according to which the destiny of kings and kingdoms is governed not by the will of the people but by that of the gods. It is precisely such critical failure — the failure of criticism to exceed the limits of its conceptual universe — that, in the event, reduces Kalhaṇa with all his questioning into an apologist for the feudal polity of his times. Basham is by no means unduly harsh in his judgement when he observes that "In fact the *Rājataraṅginī* is in part a work of political propaganda, written for the purpose of persuading the ruling classes of Kashmir to put their house in order."[16] The author himself came close to assigning such a role to his *kathā* when, at the very beginning of the chronicle, he defined its function as that of entertaining and instructing his royal readership.[17] A witness to the internecine strife of the elite which was undermining the very foundations of this feudal principality, the historian, with all his skepticism, managed after all to secure a comfortable place for his discourse within the ruling ideology. Or, to phrase it according to the taxonomy of ancient Indian knowledge systems, one could say that Itihasa had become an accomplice here to Arthaśāstra.

Where Does Historical Criticism Come From?

All of this goes to show that no discourse can oppose a genuinely uncompromising critique to a ruling culture so long as its ideological parameters are the same as those of that very culture. Where then does criticism come from? From outside the universe of dominance which provides the critique with its object, indeed, from another and historically antagonistic universe, as should be evident even from a cursory look at the criticism that has been addressed to the slave-owning and feudal discourses mentioned above. Consider, for instance, two classic comments on Aristotle's justification of slavery. One of these comes from Montesquieu as he writes in *De l'Esprit des Lois* (1748)[18]: "Aristote veut prouver qu'il y a des esclaves par nature, et ce qu'il dit ne le preuve guère . . . Mais, comme tous les hommes naissent égaux, il faut dire que l'esclavage est contre la nature" (livre xv, ch. vii). ("Aristotle wants to prove that there are slaves by nature, and what he says scarcely proves it . . . But as all men are born equal, one must say that slavery is against nature.") A little later in the same work he denounces helotry in almost identical terms: "cette *ilotie* est contre la nature des choses" (livre xv, ch.x). ("This helotism is contrary to the nature of things.") It is illuminating for our purpose to read this together with Hegel's observations on the same subject in the Second Draft (1830) of his *Lectures on the Philosophy of World History — Introduction: Reason in History:*

The consciousness of freedom first awoke among the Greeks, and they were accordingly free; but, like the Romans, they only knew that Some and not all men as such, are free. Plato and Aristotle did not know this either; thus the Greeks not only had slaves, on which their life and the continued existence of their esteemable freedom depended, but their very freedom itself was on the one hand only a fortuitous, undeveloped, transient and limited efflorescence, and on the other, a harsh servitude of all that is humane and proper to man.[19]

In these two texts, both eminently representative of the ideology of the bourgeoisie in the period of its ascendancy in Western Europe, the critique of slavery proceeds from ideas which were clearly hostile to concepts and values that made up the slave-owner's attitude to slaves in Classical Antiquity. Written at equidistant points in time from the fall of Bastille, one of them comes before that event to denounce slavery in the name of the natural equality of men, while the other follows in its wake and rejects slavery in the name of an unlimited freedom, a universal liberty. Equality and Liberty — two words which heralded the advent of a new ruling class and a new ruling culture — are hallmarks here of a pure externality. They leave the reader in no doubt that this philosophical criticism stands outside the paradigm of slave-owning ideology and has its feet planted firmly in another paradigm, that of the ideology of "wage slavery."

Feudal historiography too is separated from its critique by a paradigmatic distance. Here again criticism arms itself with two well-known devices taken from the arsenal of bourgeois ideology. One of these is rationalism. Even Majumdar with all his admiration for Kalhaṇa feels obliged to reproach him for his belief in witches and magic, in karma and transmigration, and above all for his tendency to explain events by fate and divine will rather than "any rational cause."[20] Nothing heralds more eloquently the advent of a ruling culture that requires the past to be read as an unfolding of Reason rather than Providence and insists on causality rather than faith as the key to historical understanding. Foil to this abstract rationalism is an equally abstract humanism which serves as a second device to oppose feudal ideas, and Basham finds fault with the Kashmir chronicler for his failure to acknowledge man as the maker of his own history and master of his own destiny. "Nowhere does he explicitly state," says this humanist critic, "that man is wholly incapable of moulding in some measure his own history, but superhuman forces or beings evidently have the biggest part in the destiny of man."[21]

The critique in all these instances has come from liberal ideology — the ideology of the bourgeoisie in dominance — which is, by definition, hostile to and destructive of slave-owning and feudal cultures. It is, without doubt, a critique which speaks from outside the ideological domains of the objects criticized. But that, in turn, raises a question of fundamental importance for our inquiry. Where then, one may ask, does the critique of liberalism itself come from? It comes from an ideology that is antagonistic towards the dominant culture and declares war on it even before the class for which it speaks comes to rule. In rushing thus in advance of the conquest of power by its class, this critique demonstrates, all over again, a historic décalage characteristic of all periods of great social transformation when a young and ascendant class challenges the authority of another that is older and moribund but still dominant. The bourgeoisie itself had dramatized such décalage during the Enlightenment by a relentless critique of the *ancien régime* for decades before the French Revolution and anticipating it in effect. And yet, for all the appearance of being in a hurry and arriving before its time, that critique was true to the real contradictions of the epoch in seizing on the feudal mode of production and its power relations as the object of its criticism.

In much the same way, the critique of the dominant bourgeois culture arises from the real contradictions of capitalism and anticipates its dissolution. This too spans a long period of transition during which the ruling culture comes increasingly under attack from a historic opposition invested with such ideals, values and ways of interpreting the world as constitute a challenge to liberalism. Insofar as this challenge precedes the actual dissolution of the material basis of bourgeois dominance and the corresponding social and political structures, the critique is by its very nature still rather precocious, incomplete, and generally endowed with all the immaturity of a thing in its formative stage. But it is this very want of maturity that drives the critique audaciously, if not prudently in every instance, to probe those fundamental contradictions of the existing system which prefigure its demise.

The Universalizing Tendency of Capital and Its Limitations

One of such contradictions which serves as a basis for the critique of a bourgeois culture in dominance relates to the *universalizing tendency of capital.* This tendency derives from the self-expansion of capital. Its function is to create a world market, subjugate all antecedent modes of production, and replace all jural and institutional concomitants of such modes and generally the entire edifice of precapitalist cultures by laws, institutions, values, and other elements of a culture appropriate to bourgeois rule.

"The tendency to create the *world market*," writes Marx in the *Grundrisse*, "is directly given in the concept of capital itself. Every limit appears as a barrier to overcome." For capital to overcome such limits means, "Initially, to subjugate every moment of production itself to exchange and to suspend the production of direct use values not entering into exchange, i.e. precisely to posit production based on capital in place of earlier modes of production, which appear primitive [*naturwüchsig*] from its standpoint."[22] It is thanks to this tendency that capital strives constantly to go beyond the spatial and temporal limits to its "self-realization process [*Selbstverwertungsprozess*]" for

> while capital must on one side strive to tear down every spatial barrier to intercourse, i.e. to exchange, and conquer the whole earth for its market, it strives on the other side to annihilate this space with time, i.e., to reduce to a minimum the time spent in motion from one place to another. The more developed the capital, therefore, the more extensive the market over which it circulates, which forms the spatial orbit of its circulation, the more does it strive simultaneously for an even greater extension of the market and for greater annihilation of space by time.[23]

The radical implications of this tendency for the circulation of capital are matched by its bearing on the production aspect as well. It is indeed "the universalizing tendency of capital, which distinguishes it," says Marx, "from all previous stages of production."[24] Unlike its historic antecedents it is a mode characterized, on one side, by a "universal industriousness" generating surplus labor, "value-creating labour," and on the other by "a system of general exploitation of the natural and human qualities, a system of general utility, utilising science itself just as much as all the physical and mental qualities."[25] What an immense perspective of human development is opened up thereby, what a vista of receding horizons over an endless cultural space. To quote from the *Grundrisse* again:

> Thus capital creates the bourgeois society, and the universal appropriation of nature as well as of the social bond itself by the

members of society. Hence the great civilizing influence of capital; its production of a stage of society in comparison to which all earlier ones appear as mere *local developments* of humanity and as *nature idolatry* . . . In accord with this tendency, capital drives beyond national barriers and prejudices as much as beyond nature worship, as well as all traditional, confined, complacent, encrusted satisfactions of present needs, and reproductions of old ways of life. It is destructive towards all this, and constantly revolutionizes it, tearing down all the barriers which hem in the development of the forces of production, the expansion of needs, the all-sided development of production, and the exploitation and exchange of natural and mental forces.[26]

This eloquent passage, taken in isolation from the great body of its author's critique of capital, would make him indistinguishable from any of the myriad nineteenth-century liberals who saw nothing but the positive side of capital in an age when it was growing from strength to strength and there seemed to be no limit to its expansion and capacity to transform nature and society. One need not have been the founder of scientific socialism to compose such a paean, and some of Marx's writings—certain passages from his well-known articles on India, for instance—have indeed been read in isolation and distorted to the point of reducing his evaluation of the historic possibilities of capital into the adulation of a technomaniac.

Read in its proper context, however, the passage quoted above is to be understood as nothing but the initial movement of a critique developed, point counter-point, in two clear steps. For the argument rounds off emphatically to suggest that it is not about expansion alone, but about an expansion predicated firmly and inevitably on limitations capital can never overcome; not simply about a project powered by the possibility of infinite development, but a project predicated on the certainty of its failure to realize itself. Witness how the paragraph which, in the *Grundrisse*, describes the force of capital's universalizing tendency, is followed up immediately by another where the author states in no uncertain terms the restrictive conditions operating on it.

But from the fact [he writes] that capital posits every such limit [e.g. "national barriers and prejudices," "nature worship," "tradi-

tional, confined, complacent, encrusted satisfactions of present
needs," "reproductions of old ways of life," and so on] as a barrier
and hence gets *ideally* beyond it, it does not by any means follow
that it has *really* overcome it, and, since every such barrier con-
tradicts its character, its production moves in contradictions
which are constantly overcome but just as constantly posited.
Furthermore, the universality towards which it irresistibly
strives encounters barriers in its own nature, which will, at a
certain stage of its development, allow it to be recognized as
being itself the greatest barrier to this tendency, and hence will
drive towards its own suspension.[27]

Nothing could be more explicit and indeed more devastating
than this critique of the universalist pretensions of capital. It is a
critique which distinguishes itself unmistakably from liberalism by
a perspective extended well beyond the rule of capital. The continuity of the latter is a fundamental presupposition in every variety
of liberal thought, whereas the text cited above envisages the
development of capital's universalist tendency to a stage where it
"will drive towards its own suspension." Such prescience is particularly remarkable in view of the fact that it was contemporane-
ous with an ascendant and optimistic phase in the career of
liberalism when, as Russell has observed, it was still secure in the
belief that "it represented growing forces which appeared likely to
become victorious without great difficulty, and to bring by their
victory great benefits to mankind."[28]

Marx did not subscribe to this illusion at all. On the contrary,
the discrepancy between the universalizing tendency of capital as
an ideal and the frustration of that tendency in reality was, for him,
a measure of the contradictions of Western bourgeois societies of
his time and the differences which gave each of them its specificity.
He used this measure to define and explain the uneven character
of material development in the contemporary bourgeois world, as
illustrated by the clearly differentiated moments of that development in Germany, France, England, and the United States, considered in an ascending order. He used it also to throw light on many
of the anomalies and inconsistencies of bourgeois thought and
activity. In each instance he identified and defined its distinctive
features in terms of the extent and manner of their inadequacy with
regard to the universalist ideal.

Since the universalist claim rested largely on the recent series of historic defeats inflicted by the bourgeoisie on the forces of feudalism entrenched in the *anciens régimes* of continental Europe, Marx designed a litmus test for that claim by an examination of the tolerance for feudalism in the most representative aspect of nineteenth-century bourgeois thought, namely political economy. What emerged from this test, beyond doubt, was that even so typically bourgeois a body of knowledge had not quite transcended the limits of feudal thought. On the contrary, some of its theoretical tensions arose directly from the compromise forced on it by varying degrees of proximity to feudalism in time and space.

Thus Petty, Cantillon, and "in general the writers who are *closer to feudal times*" are distinguished from their successors in one important respect: unlike the latter, they "assume that ground-rent is the normal form of surplus-value, whereas profit to them is still vaguely combined with wages, or at best looks to them like a portion of surplus-value filched by the capitalist from the landlord."[29] Again, the differences between Bastiat and Carey in their attitudes towards the expansionist thrust of British capital, their respective preferences for free trade and protection, and even the dissimilarities of structure and style in their arguments are shown to have been the effect of a spatial difference within the history of Western feudalism: one originated in France, a country with a long record of feudal impediment to the progress of capital, and the other in the United States, "a country where bourgeois society did not develop on the foundation of the feudal system, but developed rather from itself."[30]

The triumph of the universalist tendency was not obvious in bourgeois practice either. The failure of the Prussian revolution of 1848 to achieve the comprehensive character of the English and French revolutions respectively of 1648 and 1789 inspired a series of brilliant but bitter reflections on this theme from Marx in the *Neue Rheinische Zeitung.* The performance of the nineteenth-century German bourgeoisie is distinguished here from that of their class in seventeenth-century England and eighteenth-century France in terms of their respective records in overcoming the old order. Both in 1648 and 1789, he writes, the victory of the bourgeoisie was, for its time, "*the victory of a new social order,* the victory of bourgeois ownership over feudal ownership, of nationality over provincialism, of competition over the guild, of the division of land over primogeniture, of the rule of the landowner over the domination of the owner by the land, of enlightenment over superstition, of the family over the family name, of industry over heroic idleness, of bourgeois law over medieval privileges."[31] Compared to that, in 1848, "it was not a question of establishing a new society" in Germany. The bourgeoisie there was from the outset "inclined to betray the people and to compromise with the crowned representative of the old society, for it itself already belonged to the old society; it did not represent the interests of a new society against an old one, but renewed interests within an obsolete society."[32]

This tendency to compromise with elements of the old order was, for Marx, "the most striking proof" that the German revolution of 1848 was "merely a parody of the French revolution of 1789." In an attack on the failure of the Prussian government to abolish feudal obligations, he contrasted its vacillation in this respect to the vigor and decisiveness of the French bourgeoisie in their struggle against feudalism in 1789. Thus,

> On August 4, 1789, [he wrote] three weeks after the storming of the Bastille, the French people, in a *single* day, got the better of the feudal obligations.
>
> On July 11, 1848, four months after the March barricades, the feudal obligations got the better of the German people . . .
>
> The French bourgeoisie of 1789 never left its allies, the peasants, in the lurch. It knew that the abolition of feudalism in the countryside and the creation of a free, landowning peasant class was the basis of its rule.
>
> The German bourgeoisie of 1848 unhesitatingly betrays the peasants, who are its *natural allies*, flesh of its own flesh, and without whom it cannot stand up to the aristocracy.
>
> The perpetuation of feudal rights and their endorsement in the form of the (illusory) commutations—such is the result of the German revolution of 1848.[33]

The relevance of this critique for the study of colonialism can hardly be overestimated. For the representation of the colonial project of the European bourgeoisie as a particularly convincing example of the universalist mission of capital has for long been a matter of routine in academic teaching and research, as witness the importance of the rubric "Expansion of Europe" in the curricula of liberal education. The constant play on this theme in text-books, dissertations and learned journals, its propagation by many of the most powerful pedagogic instruments wherever English serves as the medium of learning, has "normalized" it, in a Kuhnian sense, as an integral part of the paradigm of liberal culture.

The effect of all this has been to generate an illusion about the power of capital and promote its universalist pretensions by liberal discourse, as exemplified, among others, by the liberal-colonialist and liberal-nationalist histories of the raj. These show beyond doubt how historiography has got itself trapped in an abstract universalism thanks to which it is unable to distinguish between the ideal of capital's striving towards self-realization and the reality of its failure to do so. That is why the anomalies and contradictions which give colonialism its specific character in India are not central to either of the dominant modes of writing about British rule. For to construct a problematic based on the recognition of such anomalies, which are after all nothing but an unmistakable evidence of the frustration of the universalizing tendency of capital, would be to challenge the liberal paradigm itself. As a component of that paradigm, historiography can hardly afford to do so.

It is this critical failure which has been primarily responsible for a serious misrepresentation of the power relations of colonialism in historical discourse. The essential point about that misrepresentation is that dominance under colonial conditions has quite erroneously been endowed with hegemony. This is so because liberal historiography has been led to presume that capital, in its Indian career, succeeded in overcoming the obstacles to its self-expansion and subjugating all precapitalist relations in material and spiritual life well enough to enable the bourgeoisie to speak for all of that society, as it had done on the occasion of its historic triumphs in England in 1648 and France in 1789. Resistance to the rule of capital has been made to dissolve ideally into a hegemonic dominance.

In other words, there is no acknowledgment in either of the dominant modes of historical discourse that in reality the universalist project we have been discussing hurtled itself against an insuperable barrier in colonialism. Hence the attempt, in colonialist writings, to make the rule of British capital in India appear as a rule based on the consent of the subject population — that is, as hegemonic — and cor-

respondingly to construct, in nationalist writings, the dominance of
the Indian bourgeoisie as the political effect of a consensus representing all of the will of the people — that is, as hegemonic again.

There is little in this sweet and sanitized image of dominance
to expose or explain the harsh realities of politics during the raj.
On the contrary, the presumption of hegemony makes for a seriously distorted view of the colonial state and its configuration of
power. It is important, therefore, that the critique of historiography should begin by questioning the universalist assumptions of
liberal ideology and the attribution of hegemony taken for granted
in colonialist and nationalist interpretations of the Indian past. It
must begin, in short, by situating itself outside the universe of
liberal discourse.

The General Configuration of Power in Colonial India

In colonial India, where the role of capital was still marginal in the
mode of production and the authority of the state structured as an
autocracy that did not recognize any citizenship or rule of law,
power simply stood for a series of inequalities between the rulers
and the ruled as well as between classes, strata, and individuals.
These unequal relationships, in spite of the bewildering diversity
of their form and character and their numerous permutations, may
all be said to have derived from a general relation — that of Dominance (D) and Subordination (S). These two terms imply each
other: it is not possible to think of D without S and vice versa. As
such, they permit us to conceptualize the historical articulation of
power in colonial India in all its institutional, modal, and discursive
aspects as the interaction of these two terms — as D/S in short.

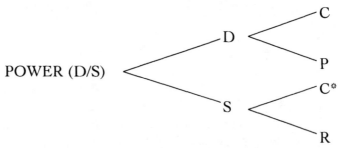

Figure 1. General Configuration of Power

While these two terms, in their interaction, give power its substance and form, each of them, in its own turn, is determined and
indeed constituted by a pair of interacting elements—D by Coercion (C) and Persuasion (P), and S by Collaboration (C*) and
Resistance (R), as shown in Figure 1. However, the relation between the terms of each of the constitutive pairs is not quite the
same as that between the terms of the parent pair. D and S imply
each other just as do C and P on the one hand, and C* and R on
the other. But while D and S imply each other logically and the
implication applies to all cases where an authority structure can be
legitimately defined in those terms, the same is not true of the other
dyads. There the terms imply each other contingently. In other
words, the mutual implication of D and S has a universal validity
for all power relations informed by them, whereas that of C and P
or of C* and R is true only under given conditions.

The mutual implication of D and S is logical and universal in the
sense that, considered at the level of abstraction, it may be said to
obtain wherever there is power, that is, under all historical social
formations irrespective of the modalities in which authority is
exercised there. Yet nothing in this abstract universality contra-
dicts the truth of the contingency of power relations arising from
the reciprocity of C and P in D and that of C* and R in S. On the
contrary, such contingency must be recognized as the site where
"human passion"—Hegel's name for the determinate aspects of
socially significant human activity[34]—mediates the concept of
power and turns it into a history of dominance and subordination.
Indeed, it is this interplay of the universal and the contingent, the
logical and the empirical aspects of D/S, that makes up "the warp
and the weft in the fabric of world history."[35]

This is why the necessity of contingency is recognized even in
the ideals of absolute authority constructed by classical political
philosophy, although the very notion of absolutism requires that
necessity to make its appearance in the guise of exceptions to the
prescribed norms of power. In other words, the contingent and the
empirical stand for a zero sign even in those discourses that make
the concept of power coincide ideally with its history. It is a
shadow which no body politic, however authoritarian, can manage
to shake off. Witness, for instance, how "Soveraignty . . . the Soule
of the Common-wealth," that Hobbesian paradigm of pure Domi-

nance and an apparently "immortall" figure of power, is "subject to violent death" from the contingency of "Intestine Discord" caused by "the ignorance and passions of men."[36]

The specificities of event and experience which provide historiography with its *matériel* are all a function of this interplay of the universal and the contingent. For it is precisely the force of this mutuality which distributes the constituent elements of D and S in varying moments to make up those characteristic variations in power relations that distinguish one society from another and one event from another. It can be said, borrowing a concept from political economy, that the power relation D/S differs from society to society and from event to event according to the *organic composition* of D and S. Just as the character of any fund of capital—its capacity to reproduce and expand itself—and its difference from any other fund in these respects depend on its organic composition, that is, on the weight of its constant part relative to that of its variable part, so does the character of D/S, in any particular instance, depend on the relative weightage of the elements C and P in D and of C^* and R in S—on the organic composition of that power relation in short.

What determines that organic composition of power is of course a host of factors and their combinations, circumstantial as well as structural. Insofar as these factors are not quite the same in all articulations of C and P on the one hand, and of C^* and R on the other, and insofar as the presence of such factors and their combinations is specific to the societies where they obtain and helps thereby to determine their individuality, the organic composition of D and S is, of necessity, contingent. Considered thus, there can be no ideal structure of power that is not subject to and modified by the contingencies of history: no Nazi fantasy of total force that is not disturbed by nightmares of dissent, no populist utopia of total consent that is not traversed by a constable's beat, if not trodden by army jackboots.

Considered thus, again, some of the vocabulary of politics which has been turned into antique hoards by the enthusiasm of collectors or debased by indiscriminate use, can return to circulation. For instance, the important word "hegemony"—which is crucial to our argument—may now be relocated at that point where its notion intersects with the trajectory of real historical power relations.

As used in this work, *hegemony stands for a condition of Dominance (D), such that, in the organic composition of D, Persuasion (P) outweighs Coercion (C).* Defined in these terms, hegemony operates as a dynamic concept and keeps even the most persuasive structure of Dominance always and necessarily open to Resistance. At the same time, it avoids the Gramscian juxtaposition of domination and hegemony (a term sometimes used in the *Prison Notebooks* synonymously with leadership) as antinomies.[37] This has, alas, provided far too often a theoretical pretext for the fabrication of a liberal absurdity—the absurdity of the idea of an uncoercive state—in spite of the basic drive of Gramsci's own work to the contrary.

Since hegemony, as we understand it, is a particular condition of D and the latter is constituted by C and P, it follows that there can be no hegemonic system under which P outweighs C to the point of reducing it to nullity. Were that to happen, there would be no Dominance, hence no hegemony. In short, hegemony, deduced thus from Dominance, offers us the double advantage of pre-empting a slide towards a liberal-utopian conceptualization of the state and of representing power as a concrete historical relation informed necessarily and irreducibly both by force and by consent. We shall use this term in the sense discussed above as an aid to our study of the paradoxes of power which made the constituent elements of D and S entail each other in the manner they did in Indian politics under colonial rule.

II. Paradoxes of Power

Idioms of Dominance and Subordination

The articulation of D and S and their constituent elements at the purely phenomenal level of Indian politics should be evident even to unreflective observation. It will notice, from the corner of its lazy eye, that there was nothing in the nature of authority which, under British rule, was not an instance of these elements operating singly or, as was most often the case, in combination. To try and list up all such instances in an inventory would, of course, be futile. Since the field of politics, taken as a whole, was not bounded and these elements constituted that field, their number was necessarily

beyond count. Also, the distribution of these instances was not
definitive either in a structural or a diachronic sense. Since the
elements were mutually interactive, each of their instances was
subject to the overdetermining effects of other instances both
within and outside the province of its primary affiliation. And,
again, the sheer force of contingency could, from time to time, prise
any particular instance out of an originating province and assign it
to another, so that what might have begun its career as an issue of,
say, C or C*, would end up by being attributed, respectively, to P
or R and vice versa.

The flux of such fusion and displacement as well as the sheer
immeasurability of occurrence in an unbounded field call for an
approach that would enable us to understand the operation of
these elements without constructing an inventory of all their instances. For such an approach one can do no better than to start
by recognizing that a principle of differentiation between two idioms is at work within each of the four constituents of D and S. One
of these idioms derives from the metropolitan political culture of
the colonizers, the other from the precolonial political traditions of
the colonized. They derive, in short, from two distinct paradigms,
one of which is typically British and the other Indian. It is the
coalescence of these two idioms and their divergence which determine the tensions within each element and define its character.

Order and Daṇḍa

To turn first to D and its constituents, it is clear that C comes
before P and indeed before all the other elements. This precedence
accrues to it by the logic of colonial state formation. For there can
be no colonialism without coercion, no subjugation of an entire
people in its own homeland by foreigners without the explicit use
of force. Insofar as the raj was an autocracy—a description with
which even some of its apologists have found it hard to dis-
agree—C prevails in D as its crucial defining element. Its precedence in the order of elements is equally justified by the temporal
development of British power in the subcontinent. For that power
had established itself initially by an act of conquest, as some of the
first colonialists themselves acknowledged without hesitation.
They used the power of the sword effectively to cut through the

maze of conflicting jurisdictions exercised by a moribund Mughal Emperor, an effete Nawab, and a company of foreign merchants officiating as tax collectors. "There was no power in India," said Philip Francis, "but the power of the sword, and that was the British sword, and no other." And in saying so, he confirmed his famous rival, Warren Hastings, who also had spoken of the sword as the most valid title the British had to sovereignty in India.[38]

However, the justification of Britain's occupation of India by the right of conquest was subjected before long to a dialectical shift as colonialism outgrew its predatory, mercantilist beginnings to graduate to a more systematic, imperial career. What was acquired haphazardly by conquest developed, in the course of this transition, into a carefully "regulated empire." Corresponding to that change, the exclusive reliance on the sword, too, gave way to an orderly control in which force (without losing its primacy in the duplex system of D) had to learn to live with institutions and ideologies designed to generate consent. In other words, the idiom of conquest was replaced by the idiom of Order.

Within the British tradition, as indeed in bourgeois politics in general, Order is enforced by the coercive apparatus of the state. That apparatus was well on display under the raj, which boasted one of the largest standing armies of the world, an elaborate penal system, and a highly developed police force. Its bureaucracy was armed with powers which could and often did muzzle free speech and censor the press, curb the individual's freedom of movement, and deny the right of assembly to the people—all in the name of Order. It is no wonder then that Order came to be identified with some of the most repugnant aspects of colonial rule and helped to designate it as an autocracy. What, however, made the imprimatur of colonialism particularly remarkable was that in India the official concern for Order extended to matters which were regarded in Western Europe, since the end of the absolute monarchies, as having little to do with the state or to do, at the most, with its non-coercive functions alone.

Instances abound. Thus it is clearly on record that Order was made to preside over public health, sanitation, and municipalization in the large urban centers from the very beginning of the raj. Some of the first medical reports on Calcutta were produced by the law-enforcing agencies of that city, while the operations of the army to fight the plague in Pune testified to the readiness with which official violence could step in to tackle problems of disease control. And as Veena Talwar Oldenburg tells us in her remarkable work,[39] the authority of the sword in urban development was unmistakable in the purely military considerations introduced by the British into the municipalization of Lucknow after the Mutiny.

In rural India the coercive intervention of the state was allowed to encroach on a domain which was jealously guarded by the instruments and ideology of bourgeois law in metropolitan Britain. This was the domain of the body, made inviolable by habeas corpus and the individual's right to the security of his or her own person. But the body of the colonized person was not so secure under the rule of the same bourgeoisie in our subcontinent, as the uses of Order to mobilize manpower demonstrated again and again. A step had already been taken in the early days of the East India Company's rule towards drafting *begar* (forced labor) for public works. The memory of press gangs used to force villagers to build roads for the Company's army under the administration of Hastings continued to be evoked in folklore well into the nineteenth century, as, for example, in the ballad *Rastar Kavita* of 1836.[40] Discontinued as official practice in the central parts of British India under late colonialism, the drafting of *paharis, adivasis,* and in general the rural poor for porterage and similar services demanded by visiting bureaucrats continued for much longer in the outlying hilly and forest regions. In one such region, the Kumauns,[41] landholders were required to provide labor and services for the benefit of touring government officials and European sportsmen. They had also to supply labor for an entire range of public works. This was supposed to be paid for. But in practice the villagers were made to carry civilian and army baggage, set up rest huts *(chappars)*, prepare sites for buildings and roads, and transport iron and timber needed for the construction of bridges—all for no remuneration at all.

Some of these aspects of forced labor, known locally as *coolie utar*, had been taken over by the British from chieftains who ruled these hills before them. But it is one of the characteristic paradoxes of colonialism that such feudal practices, far from being abolished or at least reduced, were in fact reinforced under a government representing the authority of the world's most advanced bourgeoisie. What had been a matter of custom under the hill rajas acquired a sort of statutory dignity under the raj and was systematized by its forest department into an administrative routine. The result was to convert the management of forced labor increasingly into a concern for Order as the people became more and more resolute in their resistance to it.

The idiom of Order helped also to mobilize labor for plantations owned by Europeans. The collusion between the indigo factories of nineteenth-century Bengal and the guardians of order was such an obvious and salient feature of the local administration that even Torap, the leading peasant character of Dinabandhu Mitra's *Neel-Darpan*, failed to convince his fellow *ryots* about the district magistrate's innocence in this respect. It would be true, however, to say that government policy had, by this time, turned decisively against the indigo planters, so that the support they received from the local administration did not necessarily have the approval of the higher authorities.[42]

But no such distinction could be made in the case of the tea plantations. The utterly oppressive system of labor recruitment for the Assam tea estates was sanctioned by the law of the central government and administered faithfully, even enthusiastically, by its regional representatives. At both levels this was done as a conscious measure of official solidarity with planters, even if it meant the perpetuation of inhumanity towards coolies. No less a person than the Law Member of the Government of India admitted that the labor contract authorized by the law was designed to commit a person to employment in Assam even before he knew what he was doing and hold him to his promise for some years on pain of arrest and imprisonment. "Conditions like these have no place in the ordinary law of master and servant," he said. "We made them part of the law of British India at the instance and for the benefit of the planters of Assam." And for quite some time, until his celebrated change of heart was to occur, Henry Cotton himself lent his authority, as the Chief Commissioner of Assam, to suppress the evidence of planters' oppression in official reports and used the powers of his office to apprehend runaway coolies and return them to their masters.[43]

In one vital respect the mobilization of coolies for tea plantations differed little from the mobilization of cannon-fodder for the First

World War. In both cases, it was a matter of C being articulated in the idiom of Order. As recruitment for active service was made into an essential part of the Government of India's contribution to Britain's war efforts, all the coercive organs of the state—from the army through the judiciary to the police and village watch—were brought into operation in order to rob the vast mass of the subaltern population of its manpower. The thrust of this offensive penetrated to the deepest levels of rural society—perhaps the only imperial initiative ever to do so—especially in the regions inhabited by what the British called "the martial races."

In Punjab, the most important of such martial regions, recruitment was conducted more vigorously than elsewhere and yielded the largest haul. All the agencies of Order, at all levels from Lieutenant-Governor to *lambardars*, combined here to bribe and bully the peasantry into surrendering their able-bodied men to the army, and would beat, torture, and sometimes shoot them for refusing to comply. How the horrors of war on the Western Front and the Middle East were thus brought home to the Punjab villages by official intervention in what was supposed to be voluntary enlistment has been documented amply enough by the Hunter Committee and the Congress Inquiry Committee of 1919–20 not to require any discussion here. The most important lesson to draw from that massive body of evidence for the purpose of our present argument is that Order, as an idiom of state violence, constituted a distinctive feature of colonialism primarily in one respect: that is, in colonial India, it was allowed to intrude again and again into many such areas of the life of the people as would have been firmly kept out of bounds in metropolitan Britain. In other words, the specificity of D in the power relations of the raj derived to a significant degree from the structuring of C by Order.

But the idiom of Order did not function all by itself. It interacted with another idiom to make C what it was under colonial conditions. That was an *Indian* idiom—the idiom of Daṇḍa, which was central to all indigenous notions of dominance. All the semi-feudal practices and theories of power which had come down intact from the precolonial era or were remolded under the impact of colonialism without being radically altered fed in varying degrees on this idiom. The private feudal armies and levies, caste and territorial *panchayats* governed by local elite authority, caste sanctions imposed by the elite and religious sanctions by the priesthood, bonded labor and begar, the partial entitlement of landlords to civilian and criminal jurisdiction over the tenantry, punitive measures taken against women for disobeying patriarchal moral codes, elite violence organized on sectarian, ethnic and caste lines, and so on are all instances of C framed in the idiom of Daṇḍa. They represent only a small sample taken from a large area of indigenous politics, where almost any superordinate authority that sought support from an Indian tradition of coercion tended inevitably to fall back on the concept of Daṇḍa.

That concept is central to ancient Indian polity, based in its classical form on monarchical absolutism, and it extends far beyond "punishment" (which is how it is usually translated into English) to stand for all that is implied by dominance in that particular historical context. It represents, as Gonda has observed, an ensemble of "power, authority and punishment."[44] It emphasizes force and fear as the fundamental principles of politics. Source and foundation of royal authority, Daṇḍa is regarded as the manifestation of divine will in the affairs of the state.

There are no shastric discourses on dharma and *nīti* which are indifferent to this theme, but the *Laws of Manu* may be said to speak for all of them.[45] Daṇḍa is described in that text as an emanation of the supreme generative deity Brahman himself, indeed as "his own son" (VII, 14) — a red-eyed, dark-skinned god (VII, 25), "through fear of [whom] all created beings, both the immoveable and moveable, allow themselves to be enjoyed and swerve not from their duties" (VII, 15). Daṇḍa is identified as the universal authority: "Daṇḍa is (in reality) the king and the male, that [is] the ruler, and that is called the surety for the four orders' obedience to the law" (VII, 17). Any deviation from Daṇḍa would turn the world upside down: "If the king did not, without tiring, inflict daṇḍa on those worthy to be punished, the stronger would roast the weaker, like fish on a spit; the crow would eat the sacrificial cake and the dog would lick the sacrificial viands, and ownership would not remain with anyone, the lower ones would (usurp the place of) the higher ones" (VII, 20–21).

This harsh concept of power served, in the colonial period, to legitimize all exercises of coercive authority by the dominant over the subordinate in every walk of life that was outside the jealously guarded realm of official Order. The sacral aspect of the idiom allowed such exercise to justify itself by a morality conforming fully to the semi-feudal values still pronounced in our culture. "In this emphasis on the role of punishment in maintaining order," writes a distinguished student of ancient Indian polity, "some statements on the interdependence of dharma and danda come dangerously close to identifying the legal and the moral, to assuming (at least for the lower strata of society) that moral behaviour is possible only through coercion and conformity. In this view there can be no real moral choice on the part of the masses, and fear of punishment replaces positive allegiance to dharma."[46]

Armed with this doctrine, every landlord could indeed play "maharaj" to his tenants in extracting begar from them or setting his lathi-wielding myrmidons on them if they refused to oblige. Again, according to this principle, the use of violence by upper-caste elites against untouchables and adivasis or the instigation of sectarian strife by a dominant local group against the subaltern adherents of a faith other than its own, could pass as a meritorious act modeled on a sovereign's defense of dharma. And since, as noticed above, Daṇḍa is depicted as a male (Manu: VII, 17), there could be nothing wrong about exploiting women by force either for labor or for the sexual gratification of men. Indeed, punitive sanctions imposed on women for disregarding a code of sexual morality constructed entirely from a male point of view could be justified as essential for the maintenance of an undifferentiated moral order. In short, Daṇḍa was there to uphold a putative king's authority in every little kingdom constituted by D and S in all relationships of gender, age, caste, and class.

Improvement and Dharma

There were two distinct idioms at work within the element P as well. One of these was the British idiom of Improvement, which informed all efforts made by the colonial rulers to relate nonantagonistically to the ruled. These included among others the introduction of Western-style education (siksha) and English as the language of administration and instruction; official and quasi-official patronage for Indian literary, theatrical, and other artistic productions; Christian missionary efforts at ameliorating the conditions of lower-caste and tribal populations; Orientalist projects aimed at exploring, interpreting, and preserving the heritage of ancient and medieval Indian culture; constitutional and administrative measures to accommodate the Indian elite in a secondary position within the colonial power structure; paternalistic *(ma-baap)* British attitude towards the peasantry; tenancy legislations; legal (if often ineffective) abolition of feudal impositions; legal and institutional measures to promote a subcontinental market consistent with colonial interests by removing precapitalist impediments to its development at the local and regional levels as well as by positive interventions in favor of monetization, standardization of weights and measures, and the modernization of instruments of credit and means of transport; enactment of factory laws (however inadequately enforced); partial standardization of wages in certain industries; official inquiries into the conditions of workers, peasants, untouchables, and adivasis, legal (though not fully effective) prohibition of widow-burning, child marriage, female infanticide, and Hindu polygamy, and so on.

The idea of Improvement which informed these and other measures so often displayed by colonialist historiography as evidence of the essentially liberal character of the raj was a cardinal feature of the political culture of England for the greater part of a century beginning with the 1780s.[47] There was hardly anything in that country's economic and technological progress, its social and political movements, or in the intellectual trends of the period, which was not a response, in one sense or another, to the urge for Improvement—that big thrust of an optimistic and ascendant bourgeoisie to prove itself adequate to its own historic project. Since this era of Improvement coincided with the formative phase of colonialism in India, it was inevitable that the raj, too, would be caught up in some of the enthusiasm radiating from the metropolis. Indeed, India figured almost obsessively in the metropolitan discourse on Improvement, precisely because of its importance as a limiting case. Consequently, during these decades, says Asa Briggs,

different "schools" of Englishmen as well as great individuals tested their theories and tried out their ideas on Indian soil.

Whigs, Evangelicals, even men of the Manchester School were drawn or driven to concern themselves with Indian as well as with English questions, with the balance sheet of commitment and responsibility, with the serious issues of freedom, authority, plan and force, above all with questions of "scale" which did not always arise in the development of improvement in England itself.[48]

The idea of Improvement made its debut in India with the administration of Lord Cornwallis. The verb "improve" and adjectival and noun phrases based on it occurred frequently in his correspondence and official pronouncements—something like nineteen times in his two famous minutes of 18 September 1789 and 3 February 1790 written in defence of his plan for an immediate introduction of Permanent Settlement.[49] The plan, an echo, fifteen years later, of Philip Francis's physiocratic doctrines, was intended to bestow permanent proprietary rights in land on the zamindars of Bengal in order to convert them into "economical landlords and prudent trustees of public interest" who would transform agriculture by bringing wastelands into cultivation, building irrigation works, and generally enhancing the value of landed property to an extent "hitherto unknown in Hindoostan."[50]

But this vision of economic improvement was framed by considerations of power. Permanent Settlement was "indispensably necessary" not only "to restore this country to a state of prosperity" but "to enable it to continue to be a solid support to the British interests and power in this part of the world."[51] For the stability of that power was critically dependent on the collaboration of the propertied classes. "In case of a foreign invasion," wrote Cornwallis,

> it is a matter of the last [that is, ultimate] importance, considering the means by which we keep possession of this country, that the proprietors of the lands should be attached to us, from motives of self-interest. A landholder, who is secured in the quiet enjoyment of a profitable estate can have no motive for wishing for a change. On the contrary, if the rents of his lands are raised, in proportion to their improvement, . . . he will readily listen to any offers which are likely to bring about a change that cannot place him in a worse situation, but which hold out to him hopes of a better.[52]

In other words, Improvement was a political strategy to persuade the indigenous elite to "attach" themselves to the colonial regime.

Improvement as the means of political persuasion remained central to official policy throughout the formative period of the raj between Permanent Settlement and the Mutiny. The Governor-General who promoted this policy more vigorously and more successfully than anyone else was William Bentinck. He took over Cornwallis's legacy, nurtured and developed it with great authority, and bequeathed it to all subsequent administrations as an established principle of government. A Benthamite of sorts and admirer of James Mill, he too wrote and spoke obsessively about Improvement. An improving landlord himself in the Fenlands of his native England, he speculated about the benefits of a modest degree of capitalist development in Indian agriculture. He advocated, albeit unsuccessfully, a policy of opening up the subcontinent to British settlers with capital and skill, so that their enterprise could contribute to economic prosperity by exploiting its "singularly cheap supply of labour."[53] An enthusiast for Evangelicalism, he swung the weight of the government in favor of a number of initiatives for social reform. Deeply convinced of "the superiority which has gained us the dominion of India," he made English the principal language of government, promoted Western-style education, and generally encouraged the propagation of a liberal culture among the intelligentsia and the urban middle classes.

All this has made a historian describe him, with good reason, as a "liberal imperialist"[54]—that characteristic product of nineteenth-century British politics whose historical function was to persuade the colonized and the colonizer to coexist without mutual antagonism. However, any temptation to interpret Bentinck's success in this role as evidence of a pure and disinterested goodwill must be tempered by the recognition that his liberalism was the faithful and astute instrument of a hard-headed imperialism. For this was, in effect, his response to the fear which haunted so many of the more perceptive British observers during the second quarter of the nineteenth century—the fear that the regime's isolation from the people under its rule would gravely undermine its security.[55] "Is there anywhere the prospect of our obtaining, in a season of exigency," Bentinck wondered, "that co-operation which a community, not avowedly hostile, ought to afford to its rulers? Is it not rather true that we are the objects of dislike to the bulk of those classes who possess the influence, courage, and vigour of character which would enable them to aid us?"[56]

It is the attachment of these elite sections of Indian society to the raj which he sought to ensure, in the true Cornwallis tradition, by the politics of Improvement—a strategy of persuasion to make imperial dominance acceptable, even desirable, to Indians. All the initiatives which originated with the colonial state for educational, social, and generally cultural reform, all laws, regulations, and institutions by which it sought to ameliorate the material conditions of our people, all its measures to "civilize" us and contribute to our "happiness" in conformity to the doctrines of Evangelicalism and Utilitarianism were variations on the idiom of Improvement, a derivative of metropolitan liberalism which operated, under colonial conditions, as an active principle of the element P in D/S.

The success of that strategy can hardly be exaggerated. Combined with a fair amount of force, it helped Britain to keep the antagonism of the subject population well under control despite the two extensive rebellions of 1857 and 1942 and many local uprisings. That peace between the rulers and the ruled was mediated to no mean extent by the indigenous elite. Thanks to the propagation of western-style education, they had imbibed the ideology of liberal-imperialism well enough to believe that "dominion by the English would be conducive to the happiness of *projas*"—the prophecy which, at the conclusion of *Anandamath*, persuades its hero to withdraw from armed opposition to the raj. Nothing could demonstrate the power of that ideology more clearly than its author's notion of such happiness both as a benefit of positivist knowledge acquired from the West and as an outcome of the assimilation of Utilitarianism to the supposedly rational core of Hindu religious culture.[57]

What made such assimilation possible was the presence of an Indian idiom of politics—the idiom of Dharma—alongside the British idiom of Improvement in P. For it was to Dharma that the indigenous elite turned in order to justify and explain the initiatives by which they hoped to make their subordinates relate to them as nonantagonistically as possible. Even when an initiative was clearly liberal in form and intent, such as setting up a village school, its rationale was sought in Dharma, understood, broadly, as the quintessence of "virtue, the moral duty," which implied a social duty conforming to one's place in the caste hierarchy as well as the local power structures—that is, conforming to what Weber called the "organic" societal doctrine of Hinduism."[58] In this sense, any elite authority, whether exercised by an individual or a group, would model itself on *rājadharma,* the archetypal dominance of Hindu polity, and imply not only the prerogatives of coercion *(daṇḍa)* but also an obligation to protect, foster, support, and promote the subordinate. The ideal, consecrated both by myth, as in that of King Pṛthu, the primordial provider and protector, and by prescription as in the Saṃhitās and the Śāntiparva and Anuśāsani-kaparva of the Mahābhārata, could, under certain historical circumstances, act as a powerful instrument of class conciliation.[59] Kosambi comments on this with profound insight in his discussion of Aśokan *dhamma.*

The state [he writes] developed a new function after Aśoka, the reconciliation of classes. This had never been visualised by the *Arthaśāstra* . . . The special tool for this conciliatory action was precisely the universal *dhamma* in the new sense. King and citizen found common meeting-ground in freshly developed religion . . . It can even be said that the Indian national character received the stamp of *dhamma* from the time of Aśoka. The word soon came to mean something else than equity, namely religion—and by no means the sort of religion Aśoka himself professed. The most prominent future cultural developments thereafter would always bear the misleading outer cover of some *dharma.* It is altogether fitting that the present Indian national symbol is derived from what remains of the Aśokan lion-capital at Sarnath.[60]

Between the Aśokan and Nehruite phases of its career the concept is invoked by yet another generation of the elite in its endeavor to build neither a kingdom nor even a dynastic republic but a nation as the stepping stone for its access to power. Wanting both in the material conditions and the culture adequate for this task its attempt to speak for the nation relied heavily on the traditional idiom of Dharma, with the curious result that something as contemporary as nineteenth- and twentieth-century nationalism often made its appearance in political discourse dressed up as ancient Hindu wisdom. This is why even in its very first (if unsuccessful) attempt to mobilize the masses in a campaign of opposition to the raj, the nationalist elite, in the course of the Swadeshi Movement of 1903–1908, made Dharma into a unifying *(aikya)* and harmonizing *(samanjasya)* principle of politics, as witness the many writings of the great ideologue of that period, Rabindranath Tagore. Commenting on the patriotic upsurge against Curzon's plan to partition Bengal he observed: "What is it that lies at the root of all our miseries? It lies in our mutual isolation. It therefore follows that any serious application to the cause of our country's welfare must be addressed to the work of uniting the disparate Many of our land. What is it that can unify the disparate Many? Dharma."[61]

The idiom of Swadeshi politics which thus identified Dharma with patriotic duty on the one hand and with Hindu religiosity on the other, failed, in the event, to conciliate the mutually antagonistic interests with the body politic — especially the opposing interests of Hindu and Muslim sectarian politics. The more the Hindu middle classes united in a nationalism inspired by Dharma, the more the exclusive aspects of Hindu Dharma divided the nation, ranging the rural gentry against the peasantry, upper castes against Namasudras, and above all Hindus and Muslims against each other.

Subsequently, even after the Congress had emerged as a mass party under Mahatma Gandhi's leadership and the nationalist elite acquired a relatively broader base for itself in Indian politics, its urge to speak for the nation was still wanting in those material and spiritual conditions which alone would have made it possible to do so. As a result, the idiom of Dharma continued to influence elite political discourse, especially of that particular variety which refused to acknowledge class struggle as a necessary and significant instrument of the struggle against imperialism. Since Gandhism was, in this period, the most important of all the ideologies of class collaboration within the nationalist movement, it was also the one that had the most elaborate and most frequent recourse to the concept of Dharma.

This is documented so well in all that was significant about Gandhi's ideas and practice that it would do, for the economy of

the present discussion, to limit ourselves to his theory of trusteeship which epitomizes it. "It is the duty of the ruler," he wrote,

> to serve his people. What I have said about the ruler applies to
> all owners of wealth. Just as it is the duty of the ruler to be the
> trustee and friend of the people, so that of the latter is not to be
> jealous of the former. The poor man must know that to a great
> extent poverty is due to his own faults and shortcomings. So
> while the poor man must strive to improve his condition, let him
> not hate the ruler and wish his destruction . . . He must not want
> rulership for himself, but remain content by earning his own
> wants. This condition of mutual co-operation and help is the
> Swaraj of my conception.

Another name for that Swaraj is Dharmaraj, literally, the Rule
of Dharma: "A just administration is *Satyayuga* (Age of Truth),
Swaraj, Dharmaraj, Ramraj, people's government. In such government, the ruler will be the protector, trustee and friend of the
people."[62]

Gandhi made no secret of the practical uses he had in mind for
this theory. It was formulated and avowed in opposition to socialist
theory and in defense of landlordism. "I enunciated this theory," he
said, "when, the socialist theory was placed before the country in
respect to the possessions held by zamindars and ruling chiefs."[63]
To avoid class struggle in the countryside, he pleaded with the
landlords to "regard themselves, even as the Japanese nobles did
[!], as trustees holding their wealth for the good of their wards, the
ryots."[64] In his Dharmaraj, "a model zamindar" would help his
ryots to overcome their "ignorance of the laws of sanitation and
hygiene" and

> He will study the economic condition of the ryots under his care,
> establish schools in which he will educate his own children side
> by side with those of the ryots. He will purify the village well and
> the village tank. He will teach the ryot to sweep his roads and
> clean his latrines by himself doing this necessary labour. He will
> throw open without reserve his own gardens for the unrestricted
> use of the ryot. He will use as hospital, school or the like most of
> the unnecessary buildings which he keeps for his pleasure.

In general, Gandhi expected that "model zamindar" to "reduce himself to poverty in order that the ryot may have the necessaries of life." It is a measure of his commitment to this ideology of class conciliation based on tenants' subordination to landlords that these hopeful lines were published in *Young India* in December 1929 when the peasantry were being driven by the force of the Depression to rise against the zamindars and talukdars of the United Provinces (renamed Uttar Pradesh after Independence). These sentiments, he wrote, were inspired by the very positive impressions he had gained, during a recent tour of that province, of some young landlords who "had simplified their lives and fired by patriotic zeal were easing the burden of the ryots."

In the same article he also hoped that the capitalist class would "read the signs of the times" and voluntarily surrender its wealth before "the impending chaos into which, if the capitalist does not wake up betimes, awakened but ignorant, famishing millions will plunge the country and which not even the armed force that a powerful government can bring into play can avert." His appeal to the capitalists' fear of the consequences of class struggle and their sense of Dharma did not, apparently, go unheeded. For the article quoted above was followed exactly a fortnight later in the pages of the same journal by extracts from a speech delivered by a leading capitalist at the Maharashtra Merchants' Conference.[65] "Speaking on the duty of capitalists," wrote Gandhi in an editorial note, "he [the speaker] presented an ideal which it will be difficult even for a labour man to improve upon." It would be equally justified to say that the interpretation of the Gandhian theory of trusteeship in favor of capitalism could hardly have been bettered by Gandhi himself. Indeed, the speech testifies to the ingenuity with which the most advanced section of the bourgeoisie used the idiom of Dharma in order to promote class conciliation as well as to secure a place for its own interests within the developing ideology of elitist nationalism. The speaker was Ghanshyamdas Birla.

In his speech Birla deplored that the modern capitalist was treated as an alien "belonging to a separate class," which he felt was not in agreement with Indian tradition: "in the days of yore the situation was something quite different. If we analyse the functions of the Vaishya of the ancient times, we find that he was assigned the duty of production and distribution not for personal gain but for common good. All the wealth that he amassed, he held as a trustee for the nation."

Having assimilated thus the present to the past, capitalist to Vaishya, his social and economic role to the functionalism of *varṇā flramadharma*, his hunt for profit to a concern for common good, exploitation to trusteeship and above all his class interest to the national interest, Birla then goes on to exhort his audience of industrialists and traders to act up to their *swadharma* and "fulfil their real function . . . not as exploiters, but as servants of society," as those genuinely engaged in production and distribution "for the service of the community." All this, to ward off the spectre of class struggle and avert the chaos of popular violence about which Gandhi had warned the bourgeoisie. "No Communism or Bolshevism can thrive if we know and discharge our duty," said Birla. "If I may say so, it is we who provided a fertile soil for the development of Communism and Bolshevism by relegating our duty to the background. If we knew our duty and followed it faithfully, I am sure that we could save society from many evils." This identification of Communism and Bolshevism, the most radical of all the contemporary movements of class struggle, as "evils," that is *adharma*, corresponds to the dharmic function of trusteeship assigned by Gandhi to indigenous capitalism and is willingly accepted by Birla on its behalf.

Thus the penetration of elite nationalism by the interests of big business came to be mediated by the classical idiom of political conciliation—Dharma. Within the relation D/S, it invested the element P with a characteristically Indian ingredient to match the British ingredient of Improvement promoted by liberal-imperialism. The purpose served by each idiom, in its respective domain, was to assuage contradictions by making them mutually nonantagonistic and enable the engine of dominance to run on smoothly.

Obedience and Bhakti

We have noticed how the idea of Improvement had already been caught up in the drift of Utilitarianism even when it was still associated with Physiocracy and how it was eventually assimilated to the mainstream of Utilitarian thought in full by the 1820s under Bentinck. The British idiom which informs the element C* is also derived from the same source. This is the idiom of Obedience which is emphasized in early Benthamite thought and its rejection of Locke's theory of an "original contract" in favor of Hume's notion of authority.

The principle of utility does not deny the legitimacy of resistance in "exceptional cases"—a question to which we shall soon return—but maintains that "obedience is the rule,"[66] true to which Bentham thought it fit to side with the Crown both against Wilkes and the American rebels of 1776. In other words, the subjects owed loyalty to the government for the sake of their own happiness. The struggles for reform and republicanism, which frightened authority everywhere in Europe during the first half of the nineteenth century, helped merely to strengthen the idiom of Obedience in conservative political thinking and assimilate it, by the high-noon of mid-Victorian imperialism, to the concept of duty, as witness the writings of Samuel Smiles, whose highly influential *Self-Help* (1859) is said to have "voiced the dominant philosophy of his age."[67]

Smiles followed up the success of that initial work by three other equally popular publications—all on the ideals of social and political morality—culminating in one called *Duty* (1880). Here "obedience to duty" is identified as "the very essence of the highest civilized life." Regarded as "a larger creed and a loftier code" than what is involved in "the routine of worldly-wise morality," it approximates religiosity in so far as it involves conscience and "the cultivation of all the faculties which God has given us"[68]—a recipe for individualism which, as Briggs has observed, put him within the same Utilitarian lineage as John Stuart Mill.[69] For Smiles, Obedience and duty coincide with the entire domain of social and political morality—"obedience to the parent, to the master, to the officer" and "duty to God" followed by "duty to one's family; duty to our neighbours; duty of masters to servants, and of servants to master; duty to our fellow-creatures; duty to the State, which has also its duty to perform to the citizen." As such, Obedience must be inculcated in all members of the society in childhood and emphasized throughout their lives. That, according to Smiles, was a task specific to his own generation: "The task of our fathers has been to conquer right; be it the task of this generation to teach and propagate duty."[70]

In this insistence on duty rather than right one can see the continuity, indeed resurgence, of that authoritarian aspect of Utilitarian thought which was so conspicuous in Hume and the younger Bentham. It registers the spirit of a dominant bourgeoisie which had used the power of dissidence on its way to the top, but having arrived there found it easier to live with conformism. Smiles, for his part, does not deny that protest and resistance have a place in the Christian sentiment, but is firmly of the opinion that "obedience, self-restraint and self-government," rather than liberty, "are the conditions chiefly to be aimed at." Failure in this regard is, according to him, fraught with such negative consequences as "the mad riot in human life . . . among the Nihilists in Germany and Russia, and the fire and destruction of the Communists' war in Paris."

Nearer home, he deplores the suffragette movement as "the outcries of women who protest against their womanhood and wildly strain to throw off their most lovable characteristics . . . [who] want power—political power and the desire to be 'enfranchised,'" even though "St. Paul gave the palm to the women who were stayers and workers at home." He also regrets the "widening chasm which divides the various classes of society" as "the main evil of our time" when the rich and the poor "shrink back" from each other and sympathy seems to be dying out between employers and employed in the great manufacturing towns[71]—a remarkable though by no means solitary instance of a sentiment once so supportive of Chartism pulling up sharply as it comes face to face with the enduring force of class struggle.[72]

In all such deviation from obedience and duty Smiles saw the tragic decline of "the old principle that the world must be ruled by kind and earnest guardianship." However, there was still a place in the world where that "old principle" was very much alive and guardianship was earnestly, if not altogether kindly, exercised. That was India under British rule. It provided the book with a great many of its "Illustrations of Courage, Patience, and Endurance"—all based on the exploits of British officials of the Indian army. In general, the soldier was, for the author, the supreme exemplar of the virtues of obedience and duty: "We often connect the idea of Duty with the soldier's trust," and "Obedience, submission, discipline, courage—these are among the characteristics which make a man; they are also those which make the true soldier." The army could therefore be said to epitomize what an ideal society, governed by discipline, should be; for "discipline in the army is nothing but discipline in private life—that is, sense of duty, obedience to appointed superiors, respect for the principles of authority and established institutions."[73] That being so, where could one find duty, obedience, and respect for authority more thoroughly and more successfully practiced than in the army that had built up the Indian empire and saved it from destruction in 1857?

Produced during the two decades which immediately followed the Mutiny, all of Smiles's writings exude the heavy and—for his chauvinistic working-class and petty-bourgeois readership, endearing—smell of gunpowder. At a time when Britain was painting the map red in three continents, his "heroes" are mostly professional soldiers, with the pride of place going to those serving in the Indian subcontinent. About a dozen of them crowd into the pages of *Duty*. [74] "It is by the valour and honesty of such men," we are told, "that the Empire of India has been maintained. They have toiled at their duty, often at the risk of their lives." And the point is driven further home by martyrology, as Smiles quotes an inscription on the tombstone of one of the more notorious British army chiefs of 1857: "Here lies Henry Lawrence who tried to do his Duty!"

If duty performed in defence of the empire had to be invoked in order to reinforce the "old principle" of guardianship in metropolitan society, it was propagated all the more vigorously by the guardians of the raj to ensure the loyalty of their subjects. Protocols, codes, emblems, and rituals were elaborately worked out to promote a veritable cult of loyalism, as witness the ceremonies prescribed for royal, viceregal and provincial darbars, for official visits ranging from grand tours by members of the royal family to routine administrative rounds by magistrates and judges, for the celebration of the King's, Queen's, and Queen Mother's birthdays, and so on.[75] Above all, the cult was activated to induce collaboration whenever the regime felt insecure for political or military reasons. On such occasions, the appeal to loyalty would proceed by emphasizing the mutuality of interest between rulers and the ruled in, say, constitutional reforms or defence of the realm, with the former glorified as partnership, power sharing, self-government, and the latter as patriotism.

How the idiom of Obedience helped to shape Indian collaboration at such crises may be studied in the light of Gandhi's record during the Boer War when, as even the hagiographer D. G. Tendulkar admits, "his loyalty to the empire drove him to side with the British in the teeth of opposition from some of his countrymen."[76] His offer of help, made on behalf of the Indian community in South Africa, was at first treated by the British with almost undisguised contempt. However, they were eventually persuaded to accept it, and an Indian Ambulance Corps, made up of over 1,000 Indian stretcher-bearers, was formed and allowed to serve at the front.[77] The speeches and writings in which Gandhi justifies his offer and reflects on its outcome between October 1899 and April 1900 constitute a classic text of collaborationist nationalism. Here are some samples.

> We do not know how to handle arms. It is not our fault : it is perhaps our misfortune that we cannot, but it may be there are other *duties* . . . and, no matter of what description they may be, we would consider it *a privilege to be called upon to perform them* . . . If an unflinching *devotion to duty* and an extreme eagerness to serve our Sovereign can make us of any use on the field of battle, we trust we would not fail.
>
> The motive underlying this humble offer is to endeavour *to prove* that, in common with other subjects of the Queen-Empress in South Africa, the Indians, too, are *ready to do duty for their Sovereign* on the battlefield. The offer is meant to be *an earnest of the Indian loyalty.* (19 October 1899)

Some local English-speaking Indians met together a few days ago, and decided that because they were *British subjects, and as such demanded rights*, they ought to forget their domestic differences, and irrespective of their opinion on the justice of the war, render *some service, no matter how humble*, on the battlefield during the crisis, even if it were to act as bearers of the wounded . . . They have offered their *services without pay, unconditionally*, to the Government or the Imperial authorities, stating that they do not know how to handle arms, and that they would consider it a privilege if they could perform *some duty, even menial,* on the battlefield. (27 October 1899)

The English-speaking Indians came to the conclusion that they would offer their services, *unconditionally and absolutely without payment* . . . in order to show the Colonists that they were worthy subjects of the Queen. (13 December 1899)

When the joyful news of the relief of Kimberley and Ladysmith was flashed across the wire, the Indians vied with the Europeans in their *patriotic zeal* to celebrate the occasion . . . (16 June 1900)

This meeting of the Indian subjects of Her Majesty the Queen-Empress . . . records with *gratification* the fact that it is *the hero of Kandahar,* and *sometime Commander-in-Chief of the Forces in India* [Lord Roberts], who is leading the British Forces in South Africa from victory to victory. (n.d.)

You have shown *your patriotism* and brought *honour to yourself* and *your country* by joining the Indian Ambulance Corps as a leader and have thereby rendered service both to your own self and *your motherland.* It will, therefore, behove you to look upon that as a reward in itself. (20 April 1900)[78]

These excerpts show how the colonial subject constitutes himself in a loyalist discourse. To turn first to its structural aspect, notice that Gandhi situates "the English-speaking Indians" for whom he speaks in the D/S relation by affirming their subordination to a named sovereign power as "British subjects," "subjects of the Queen," "subjects of Her Majesty the Queen-Empress." The self-subjection is further defined by an "extreme eagerness to serve" and the offer of "their services without pay, unconditionally"—phrases which are both description and measure of the distance between the dominant and the dominated. And the adjectives qualifying those services as "humble" and "menial" are also an index of the loyalist's intention to identify himself with the inferior term in D/S.

As the colonizer and the colonized are thus assigned their respective places in D/S, the discourse proceeds to valorize the terms of the loyalist's subordination, which are specified now as humble,

menial, unconditionally rendered services. These are conceptualized as a duty which derives its value from being performed at two
levels. It is, at one level, "duty for their sovereign." As such, it is a
privilege—a figure of reward bestowed by patron on client. But, at
the same time and at another level, it is duty done for the "motherland," hence an act of patriotism. The effect of this identification of
empire and motherland is to develop a tension within the concept
of duty. For it emphasizes, on the one hand, the filial attachment
of the colonized subject to the colonizing sovereign, "Her Majesty
the Queen-Empress," the mother whose image occurs so often in
so many infantile varieties of Indian politics of the period. It is
thanks to such attachment that the servant, in a state of extreme
alienation, can regard the master's success as his own, celebrate the
"joyful news" of the relief of Kimberley and Ladysmith, and derive
vicarious "gratification" from the South African triumphs of those
very imperial forces which kept him in bondage in South Asia.

Yet, on the other hand, patriotism also implies a sense of belonging to one's *own* country, and as soon as the colonized arrives at a
recognition of the colony as "motherland"—a political domain unmediated by alien power—he may be said to be pulling away from
servility, however feebly, towards an assertion of independence.
That new orientation is hardly perceptible at first. If there is any
movement in it, that is still altogether negative, in the form of a
mere slowing down, but by no means a cutting out, of the engine
of subservience. In that relative stillness, the sense of duty, with all
its externality reduced to nothing by the contrary pulls of subordination and self-determination, looks inward, so that patriotism, as
a service rendered "to your own self," acquires a reflexive value
and becomes "a reward in itself." This inwardness, which could
have been so easily absorbed into religiosity as a typically
Gandhian sort of "spiritualized politics," is forced by the contradictions of imperialism itself to launch on the historic trajectory of
citizenship. Its first tentative and diffident steps in that direction
are also recorded in the demonstrative aspects of this otherwise
grossly loyalist discourse.

For loyalism is not content simply with situating itself in the
structure of D/S and providing an ideological justification for C*.
It is demonstrative by its very nature: it speaks up because it wants
to be noticed. The "motive" which inspired the Indians to offer

their service was an endeavor, writes Gandhi, "to *prove*" their readiness to go to the front and "to *show* the Colonists that they were worthy subjects of the Queen." In other words, the so-called "earnest" of loyalty was meant as a display to secure the white settlers' and the imperial government's recognition of the sincerity and usefulness of Indian collaboration. There was nothing venal about it: the services were offered without any pecuniary expectation and indeed without any condition at all. Although this particular stipulation was eventually turned down by the authorities who insisted on the Indian stretcher-bearers accepting a weekly wage of 20 shillings—15 shillings less than what was paid to the whites for the same job—it does not take anything away from the honorable character of Gandhi's original proposal.[79] Indeed, he went on emphasizing the purely voluntary and disinterested nature of the offer. For the colonized, recognition of their services by the imperial overlords on any terms at all would have been "a privilege," that is, an honor done by the master to his servant by acknowledging the latter's servitude.

But there was an element in Gandhi's proposal which clearly exceeded—and in view of his transparent sincerity, seems to have deviated from—the morality of unqualified subordination. It is true that he asked for no material rewards as the price of collaboration. Yet he had obviously a reward in mind. The Indians, he said, had decided to bury their differences and unite in serving the empire at this crisis "because they were British subjects, and as such demanded rights." What rights? A colonial subject is not a citizen, hence has no rights. The notion of duty as a correlate of right derives from a code that does not recognize the relation between the ruler and the ruled as one between master and servant—that is, a code according to which all who owe allegiance to the state are equal in the eye of the law. Such a code is quite out of place in a colonial state whose legitimacy is based ultimately on the right of conquest and which, unlike the state mentioned by Smiles, has no "duty to perform to the citizen."

In mentioning Indians' rights in the same breath as their duties, Gandhi was therefore switching codes, and going, almost in spite of himself, against the grain of his own well-rehearsed and still undented faith in the legal and moral validity of British paramountcy. In that indecisive switch one can already see the symptoms of a liberal-nationalist dilemma which was to give Indian politics so much of its tone and character. For even when, after Jalianwala-bagh, Gandhi himself had moved from loyalism to opposition in his attitude to British rule, the idiom of Obedience continued to inspire, in varying degrees, the so-called moderate—an euphemism for conservative—trends in Indian liberal politics. More importantly, the same idiom made its influence felt even within that variety of liberal-nationalism where the notion of the colonized subject's right was, for most of the time, so busy chasing its own tail—the notion of his duty to the colonial master—that the cautious anti-imperialism of the elite never managed fully to emerge from the maze of bargaining and pressure-politics to assert, without equivocation, the subject's right to rebel. Hence, the legalism, constitutionalism and the many shades of compromise between collaboration and dissent which were so characteristic of elite nationalism.

If the politics of collaboration was informed by the Humean idiom of Obedience—however uneasy that obedience might have been under the hushed, almost hopeless, urge for enfranchisement among the colonized—it drew its sustenance, at the same time, from a very different tradition—the Indian tradition of Bhakti. All the collaborationist moments of subordination in our thinking and practice during the colonial period were linked by Bhakti to an inert mass of feudal culture which had been generating loyalism and depositing it in every kind of power relation for centuries before the British conquest.[80] The Bhagavad-Gītā served as the ur-text for that ideology, and religion helped to justify and propagate it by an array of cults, precepts, institutions, and codes. That is why the essentials of Indian politics can never be grasped without an understanding of religion.

How Bhakti promotes collaboration is easily demonstrated by a reference to its principal modalities, known as *rasas* (a term in which metaphysics blends with aesthetics), namely, *dāsya, śānta, sakhya, vātsalya,* and *śṛṅgāra.* Of these, dāsya, literally the quality of being a servant, slave, or bondsman, is by far the most important. As a rasa it implies that the devotee regards himself as his deity's servant, and "this feeling of servitude *(dāsyammanyatvam)* is said to underlie and uplift all devotional practices."[81] These devotional practices, as laid down in the shastric injunctions of Vaishnavism, include rituals of overt servility like attending to the deity's feet *(padaseva)*, drinking the water used to wash his feet *(caraṇāmṛta-pāna)*, and "prostration at full length like a log of wood" *(daḍavat-praṇāma)*,[82] the deity being represented of course by an image or a human surrogate such as a guru, priest, or cultic officiant. And, at a philosophical level, devotion stands for ātmanivedana or "complete surrender of self which consists of the feeling that one's body, mind, the senses and soul are all intended for the Bhagavat."[83] Dāsya, this sentiment of total servility to the deity, represents the essential characteristic *(swarūpa-lakṣaṇa)* of Bhakti for many of its adherents, especially those who subscribe to the cult of Rāma.[84] Tulsi Das, from whose work they have drawn sustenance for nearly five centuries, idealizes the services rendered to Rāma by an untouchable (Guha), a woman (Śabarī), and an ape (Hanumān) as the highest spiritual achievement, as witness the many verses bearing on this theme in *The Petition to Ram*.[85] "The ocean of existence"; he writes in the celebrated *Rāmcharitmānas*, "cannot be crossed over without the emotion of the servant for the master."[86]

Even among cults in which dāsya is less emphasized, it dominates over the other rasas as the ruling principle of Bhakti. Of these, śānta, the pacific mode, which stands for an intellectual attitude and hence sometimes called *jñāna-bhakti*, "is regarded as the lowest in the scale of primary Rasas," according to Sushil Kumar De.[87] But the remaining and more substantial modes have all an element of willing servitude—*dāsyammanyatvam*, the internalization of dāsya on the devotee's part—presupposed in them. Thus vātsalya, the filial mode, implies that the devotee acknowledges his subordination to the deity to be of the same order as a child's to its parent. And sakhya, the mode of friendship, also derives from the disparity of status between subaltern and superordinate: conceptualized in terms of Krishna's relation with his adolescent companions during his days as a cowherd in Vrindavan, it is, as in that cycle of legends, a relation among equals of whom Krishna was *primus inter pares*.

Even in śṛṅgāra, the erotic mode, there is no notion of equality between devotee and deity. The function of this rasa is primarily to spiritualize and aestheticize male dominance of gender relations. In the numerous legends about Krishna's sexual adventures among the milkmaids *(gopis)* of Vraj, the initiative is always his to seduce, dally with, and desert his female partners. It is a relationship of love that is an authentic instance of the primacy assumed by the male in the sexual politics of a patriarchal society. This implies, among other things, the passivity of the female. Bhakti actually prescribes such passivity by depicting the gopīs as women who have no sexual passion *(prākṛta-kāma)* of their own, but are merely conducive to Krishna's pleasure: "In all these ecstatic sports the Gopīs never had the slightest desire for their own pleasure, but all their efforts were directed towards effecting the supreme pleasure of the Bhagavat."[88]

The sexual instrumentality of women is then spiritualized by the śṛṅgāra mode (also known as *madhura-bhāva*) into an ideal of love that transcends all that is of the body and of the world. In this transcendental eroticism, says De, "the supersensuous Madhura-bhāva of the Gopīs is different from the sensuous Kāma in the fact that the significance of the former consists entirely in contributing to the pleasure of its divine object, while the latter, as a mundane feeling, aims primarily at one's own pleasure."[89] The only female among Krishna's companions to show any signs of such "mundane feeling," that is, Kubjā, who wanted to relate to him as an active partner, is roundly denounced, "for her desire for sport was entirely for her own sensual pleasure, while that of the Gopīs was exclusively intended for Kṛṣṇa."[90]

In conformity to this mode, says Allchin, "the soul of the devotee becomes a gopī in its relationship to Kṛṣṇa, and this calls for the envisaging of a change of sex in male devotees, who in this sentiment [i.e. rasa] become as it were the female consort of the God."[91] If the male devotee could be transformed, out of Bhakti, into a gopī for the benefit of Krishna's dalliance — and there are sects who cultivate this particular rasa more than the others[92] — why, one wonders, does the god himself, with all his love of play, never undergo a similar transformation for the benefit of his male devotees? The answer must be that even mythopoeia is subject to the morality of male dominance, and since a devotee is a subordinate by definition, even an erotic construction of his relation to the deity is necessarily postulated on the superordinate status of the latter.

Bhakti, in other words, is an ideology of subordination *par excellence.* All the inferior terms in any relationship of power structured

as D/S within the Indian tradition, can be derived from it. This
emerges with striking clarity from the rationalization of rasa theory
by Jiva Goswami, the great theologian of Vaishnavism. He re-
grouped the five primary modalities, and their many variations into
three, namely, "Āśraya-bhakti, Dāsya-bhakti, and Praśraya-
bhakti, in which Kṛṣṇa appears respectively as the Pālaka (Protector), Prabhu (Master) and Lālaka (Superior Relative), and his
devotee respectively as Pālya (Subject), Dāsa (Servant) and Lālya
(Inferior Relative)."[93] There is nothing in the nature of authority
in precolonial India which is not comprehensively covered by these
three dyads — Pālaka/Pālya, Prabhu/Dāsa, and Lālaka/Lālya.

Bhakti may thus be said to have continued the political theories
enunciated and elaborated over the centuries by the Dharmaśāstras
and adapted them to the conditions of later feudalism. However, it
did not derive subordination from *daṇḍanīti* — the principle of the
big stick — which, in the Dharmaśāstras, had made subalternity
predicated on fear generated by the alliance between Kshatriya's
brawn and Brahman's brain. On the contrary, those of its cults
which were addressed to the religiosity of the lower strata of Hindu
society, had it as their function to try and endear the dominant to
the subordinate and assuage the rigor of dāsya thereby.

It was these that spiritualized the effort, fatigue, and frustration
involved in the labor and services offered by peasants, craftsmen,
and subaltern specialists to local elites, in the unacknowledged and
unremunerated labor of women in domestic chores, in the work
done by *kamin* for *jajman*, in the use-values produced by tenants as
gifts and *nazrana* for landlords, and so on. In all such instances
Bhakti conferred on the superordinate the sanctity of a deity or his
surrogate, and translated dominance into the benign function of a
pālaka, prabhu, or lālaka (depending on the nature of the social
relation and services involved) to whom the subordinate related as
a devotee. Correspondingly, the latter's submission, which rested
in the last resort on the sanction of force, was made to appear as
self-induced and voluntary — that is, as collaboration in short.

But that classical idiom of Indian politics was not made into an
ingredient of C* under the raj merely by the force of traditional
religiosity among the subaltern masses unaffected by Western-
style education and liberal culture. Bhakti required a nineteenth-
century Jiva Goswami to adapt it to the requirements of colonial

rule, and Bankimchandra Chattopadhyay was the most eminent of all those intellectuals who came forward to step into that role. The tenth chapter of his celebrated treatise on religion, *Dharmatattva*, is a monument to his theoretical contribution in this respect.[94] Here, he starts off with a reference to the five-rasa formula, but moves on from theology to sociology to characterize Bhakti as a principle of worldly authority: "Whoever is superior to us and benefits us by his superiority, is an object of Bhakti. The social uses of Bhakti are (1) that the inferior will never act as a follower of the superior unless there is Bhakti; (2) that unless the inferior follows the superior, there cannot be any unity *(aikya)* or cohesion *(bandhan)* in society, nor can it achieve any Improvement *(unnati)*."

The contradictions involved in this attempt to match the feudal concept of Bhakti to the bourgeois notion of Improvement are more instructive for us than its inadequacy as a sociological theory. For they are an authentic measure, apart from being an exemplar, of the difficulties of Indian liberalism to cope with the question of authority at a time when the codes which had hitherto been used to signal the latter were being inexorably modified. That modification meant, for Bankimchandra, a radical decline in Bhakti under the impact of colonialism: "Look at the evils and disorders caused by the loss of Bhakti in our country. Hindus were never wanting in Bhakti. It has always been one of the principal elements of the Hindu religion and Hindu shastras. But now Bhakti has completely disappeared from the community of those who are educated or only half-educated. They have failed to grasp the true significance of the western doctrine of egalitarianism *(samyabad)* and perverted it to mean that people are equal everywhere in every sense and nobody owes Bhakti to anyone else." The consequence, according to him, has been to turn family life into a hell, create discord in politics, make education harmful, perpetuate stagnation and disorder in society and fill the individual's soul with impurity and conceit.

The remedy for these evils lay, of course, in the revitalization of Bhakti. But no sooner does the author set out to prescribe how than it becomes obvious that his formula deviates significantly from those time-honored codes whose decline he laments so much. Thus he adheres closely to orthodox Hindu tradition in nominating those who are, in his opinion, deserving of Bhakti within an extended family, but does so with a difference in one important respect. While Bhakti, in that tradition, is due from wife to husband and not the other way round, Bankimchandra makes it reciprocal. "The husband is in every respect superior to the wife and hence the object of her Bhakti," he says; "but according to the Hindu religion, Bhakti is due from husband to wife as well, because it is laid down in that religion that she should be regarded as the very embodiment of the goddess Lakshmi herself (lakshmirupa). However, on this particular subject, the tenets of the religion of Comte seem to be clearer and more worthy of respect than those of the religion of the Hindus."

By a second modification he makes Bhakti conditional on *guna*, in the sense of virtue or spiritual quality, rather than on *jati*, that is birth into any particular *varna* or caste. A Brahman wanting in the guna which is truly characteristic of his status merits no Bhakti, he writes, whereas "we should address our Bhakti to a Shudra who has a Brahman's guna, that is, who is religious, learned, free of worldly desire *(nishkam)* and educates others [by example]." In other words, "A religious person, even if born of a lower caste, deserves Bhakti," according to him.

Furthermore, he makes a distinction between Bhakti for a royal person and that addressed to royalty as an institution. "Think of a country without a king—that is, a republic, and you will understand that *rajbhakti* is not addressed to any particular person. No member of the Congress of the United States or of the British Parliament may be an object of Bhakti, but Congress and Parliament are certainly so. In the same sense, Charles Stuart or Louis Capet might not have been deserving of Bhakti on the part of the inhabitants of those respective countries." Quite clearly there is a deflection here from the classical meaning of rajbhakti: the word "raja" stands here for "state" rather than "king" as in the Dharmaśāstras.

Finally, Bankimchandra specifies *samaj* or society itself as an object of Bhakti, because, according to him, "All the virtues of man are invested in the society which is our educator, law-giver, provider and protector in one—our sovereign, our teacher." There is nothing like this, of course, in the Hindu tradition, and in making samaj hypostatize thus for Krishna or any other godhead, the nineteenth-century theoretician turns sharply away from the theology of Jiva Goswami towards that of Auguste Comte. As he himself puts it, "It is on the basis of an expansion of this thesis that Auguste Comte has recommended the worship of the Goddess of Humanity. No need therefore to elaborate further on this subject."

But, for all its sophistication, this "modernized" Bhakti was still unable to overcome the older tradition. This was so not only because Western-style education and liberal values were so alien to the subaltern masses that they could hardly be expected to take much notice of such positivist-liberal modifications of their cherished beliefs. The reason, more importantly, was that these modifications did not go far enough to question the premises of traditional Bhakti. On the contrary, Bankimchandra's theory proceeded from those very premises. Thus, the family which he wanted to stop from degenerating into a hell, was still the old extended structure, complete indeed with guru and *purohit* (priest), where the order of dominance was much the same as prescribed in the classical Hindu code—parents' over children, guru's over *sishya*, priest's over jajman, the elder's over the younger, and so on—indeed in all familial relationships other than those of husband and wife, where Bhakti was to be reciprocal.

And even there, reciprocity was derived not from any assumption of equality between spouses. On the contrary, the husband was said to be superior to his wife "in every respect" and as such, a proper object of her Bhakti. By contrast, her own claim to Bhakti was not based on any actual societal authority, but on a mythic modeling of her image after the deity Lakshmi. This carries so little conviction that the author himself had to lean on the authority of Comte rather than the Hindu shastras to justify his notion of reciprocity.

Even more relevant for our discussion is the fact that this idea, which dignifies his theory of religion to some extent, is altogether ignored in the discursive practice of his novels. There, as in *Debi Chaudhurani* (by no means the only instance), the godliness of the husband is displayed in all its feudal sanctity: "The Hindu law-givers knew the right answer . . . The husband provides the first step for access to God. That is why to a Hindu woman her husband is her god. In this respect, all other societies are inferior to Hindu society," and "Bhakti for the husband is the first stage of Bhakti for God."[95]

Again, it is the weight of tradition which undermined Bankim-chandra's thesis about guna rather than jati as the principal deter-minant of Bhakti. Whatever promise there was in this of a dynamic social mobility breaking down the barrier of caste and birth came to nothing, if only because the necessity of the caste system and the Brahman's spiritual superiority within it was presumed in the argument. It was only by emulating the Brahman that the Sudra could become an object of Bhakti. In other words, Bhakti could do little to abolish the social distance between the high-born and the low-born, although some of the former's spiritual qualities might, under certain conditions, be acquired by the latter without, how-ever, effecting any change of place.

Finally, the constitutionalization of rajbhakti in this thesis is shown up as yet another shallow intellectualist construct in the light of what it has to say about the function and authority of the raja. Even assuming that raja here means *rashtra* (state), the polity that is depicted is indistinguishable from ancient Indian kingship in all essential respects. In the words of the author,

> The king stands at the head of the society just as the master stands at the head of his household and the parents [of their family]. Society owes its protection to his [king's] spiritual quali-ties, his powers to punish and his provisions *(tanbar palane)*. Just as the father is the object of his child's Bhakti, so is the king the object of Bhakti on the part of his *projas* . . . Therefore, you must regard the king with Bhakti as the father of the society. Cultivate rajbhakti by such initiatives, festivals and other beneficial meas-ures as have been witnessed recently in honour of Lord Ripon. Serve the king in war. Rajbhakti is commended over and over again in the religion of the Hindus . . . There is no rajbhakti left in England any longer. It is still intact in Germany or Italy, where the kingdom (state) continues to improve.

The emphasis put here on the patriarchal character of the monar-chy or (to interpret it more generously) the state dissolves all constitutionalist and republican sentiments into a plea for submis-sion to absolutism. Which shows how in spite of its attempt to forge an idiom to reconcile Western positivism, egalitarianism, and humanism with the tradition of Bhakti, Indian liberalism reverts, at the end of the exercise, to a concept of collaboration framed primarily in terms of subordination characteristic of a precapitalist culture. That concept was to inform not only the naive faith of the peasant soliciting protection from "Mother Victoria;" it was also to figure in the abject loyalism of the panegyric, "Loyalty Lotus," written for a visiting member of the British royal family by Bankimchandra's friend and eminent intellectual, Dinabandhu Mitra.[96]

Rightful Dissent and Dharmic Protest

Resistance (R) comes last. It comes after all the other elements of Dominance (D) and Subordination (S) because there can be no operation of D/S beyond it. For within any particular cycle of the historical reproduction of D/S, R works together with C* (Collaboration) either as an overtly articulate moment of contradiction or as a zero sign shadowing its Other until it finally overcomes the latter, destroys S thereby and with it, all of that phase of D/S itself. The elimination of C* by R thus signals the end of one round of struggle and the beginning of another. That point was of course never reached in Indian politics under the raj, so that S continued to be characterized, throughout the period, by the mutuality of its constituent elements. What made such mutuality possible was that each of the elements understood the other's language, for its idioms, like those of the other, were drawn from the same traditions — British and Indian.

The British idiom of R was what may be called Rightful Dissent. It informed a wide variety of protest in forms unknown to our politics of the precolonial period. Some of its examples would be found in the assemblies, marches, lobbies, and other large gatherings sponsored by mass organizations under leaderships elected according to parliamentary or quasi-parliamentary democratic procedures. The association of the laboring populations of town and country in collective bodies like trade unions and *kisan sabhas*, strikes and other struggles for the satisfaction of demands for wages, employment, better living conditions, and civil liberties, and the mobilization of the subaltern in the institutionalized sectors of nationalist politics by the Congress and other parties, were also instances of this idiom at work.

There was an awareness, in this idiom, of the legal and constitutional limits imposed by the colonial authorities on its articulation; and it contained itself most of the time within those limits, acquiring thus a peaceable aspect which was systematically misrepresented, abused and exploited both by the foreign and indigenous elites—misrepresented by the British rulers as evidence of an ingrained "national" cowardice; abused by the Congress high command in order to stop popular militancy from "going too far" in the nationalist movement, and by the leadership of parties on the left to stop class struggle from boiling over into armed conflict (as, for instance, by Communist leaders during the Tebhaga struggles); exploited ideologically by Gandhism in its insistence on doctrinaire nonviolence, and organizationally by the Congress party everywhere to keep the masses under its control. Yet protest of this kind did not always keep to the path of peaceful expression, as witness the violence of revolutionary terrorism and, on a larger scale, that of the numerous mass struggles against imperialism and indigenous oppressors.

This idiom owes nothing to any Indian tradition. In its concept it derives directly from that important current of English liberalism which, in the eighteenth and nineteenth centuries, relied on the example of the Revolution of 1688 and what Halévy called its "theoretical equivalent," that is, the idea of natural rights based on an original contract as propounded by John Locke. According to the latter, "all men in the state of nature are free and equal, and if the right of liberty of any one man, a right which belongs to all equally, be violated, then, in the state of nature, every individual has the right to punish." It is in order to prevent this right from being abused by war that people alienated it in favor of a contract and formed a civil society based on the law of majorities and the governors' responsibility to the governed. "If, therefore, the governors violate the contract, the governed must have recourse to insurrection, to 'resistance'." The Revolution of 1688 was justified by the fact that James II "had violated the condition of the pact which bound him to his subjects." Indeed, that revolution made the English government "the one legitimate government in the whole of Europe, the one government which is based on a contract whose date can be historically fixed, and which by its very existence makes sacred the 'right of resistance.'"[97]

Much of the democratic movement in England in the late eighteenth and nineteenth centuries, involving such momentous issues as those of civil liberty and parliamentary reform, was inspired by these ideas. Since the conquest and consolidation of the Indian empire were contemporary to these ideas, some of these filtered through the media and institutions of an English-style education and the political culture of the raj to the Indian elite, the principal beneficiaries of that education and culture. The result was a curious paradox. While the colonial regime first took it upon itself to inculcate the notion of rights and liberties upon its subjects and then deny these in full or in part in the principles and practice of governance, the disenfranchised subjects went on pressing the rulers to match their administration to their own ideals. Ironically, therefore, a large part of the politics of protest under the raj, especially when initiated by the educated middle-class leaderships, turned on a certain concern about the "un-British" character of British rule—a theme made famous by successive generations of Indian liberals from Naoroji to Gandhi. They had taken the "sacred" English idiom of Rightful Dissent too seriously for the regime's comfort.

But Rightful Dissent was not all that was there to R. There was also a purely Indian idiom at work in it. Since this was not informed by the concept of right but of Dharma, we shall call it "Dharmic Protest." It was manifested in some of the most dramatic forms of popular protest throughout the colonial period—in peasant uprisings variously called *hool, dhing, bidroha, hangama, fituri,* and so on; in *hizrat* or mass desertion by peasants or other laboring people (such as miners during the Santal Hool of 1855 and Assam tea plantation workers during the Non-cooperation Movement, to cite two out of many instances); in *dharna* or protest by sitting down in the offender's presence, pledging not to move until the redress of grievance; in *hartal* or the general suspension of public activity; in *dharmaghat* or withdrawal of labor; in *jat mara,* or measures to destroy the offender's caste by refusal to render such specialist services as are required to insure him and his kin ritually against pollution; in *danga* or sectarian, ethnic, caste, and class violence involving large bodies of the subaltern population, and so on.

All these have Indian names (with many equivalents in other languages of the subcontinent than those I have used), and they all

derive from a precolonial tradition. But it is not their older standing which alone distinguishes them from dissent framed in the
English idiom. What sets them apart from that idiom is the absence
of any notion of right. They do not derive from what were regarded
as "self-evident truths" in the American Declaration of Rights,
namely, "that all men are created equal, that they are endowed by
their Creator with certain inalienable rights; that among these are
life, liberty and the pursuit of happiness; that to secure these rights
governments are instituted among men, deriving their just powers
from the consent of the governed."[98] Quite clearly all men are not
created equal in a society ordered in a hierarchy of castes. Far from
being endowed with "certain inalienable rights," they are endowed,
by virtue of their birth into one caste or another, with inflexible
duties prescribed by the shastras and by custom. Life, liberty, and
pursuit of happiness are not theirs by right but accrue to them,
when they do, by the benevolence of governments. The latter are
instituted among men by God and derive their powers not "from
the consent of the governed" but from the sanction of Daṇḍa, son
of God.

What, then, does such protest derive from, if not from a sense of
right? It derives from the righteousness of the defense of Dharma,
or to emphasize more precisely the negative aspect of resistance,
from the morality of struggle against adharma. Now, the ruler's
Dharma, rajdharma, insists that the king must protect his subjects.[99] This is so basic that the primeval King Pṛthu, who incar-
nated Viṣṇu himself and served as a model for all subsequent rulers
on earth, is depicted in the Mahābhārata as "the one who protects
the earth and her inhabitants."[100] Indeed, the king's failure to live
up to his protective role amounts to the most serious violation of
Dharma, and leads to the destruction both of himself and his
subjects.[101] The latter are therefore advised—in the Śāntiparva
(57.43–44) of the Mahābhārata—to abandon him "like a leaky
boat on the sea." But the Anuśāsanaparva (6.132–133) goes even
further and calls for regicide as the subjects' duty to redress adharma arising from the king's failure to protect them. Thus,

> The subjects should arm themselves for killing that king who
> does not protect them [who simply plunders their riches, who
> confounds all distinctions, who is incapable of taking their lead,

who is without mercy, and who is considered as the most sinful
of kings.]

That king who tells his people that he is their protector but who
does not or is unable to protect them, should be killed by his
subjects in a body like a dog that is affected with the rabies and
has become mad.

There is nothing in this prescription for violence against rulers
by the ruled that is postulated on the rights of the subjects. In a
polity devoid of any notion of citizenship, they have no rights but
only duties. The duty enjoined upon them is merely to undo the
adharma involved in a lapse of rājadharma, so that the transcendental constitution of Dharma, in which the king serves as an
executive, can be affirmed again. Translated into the politics of
resistance under the raj this implied an effort to correct what
appeared to Indians as a deviation from the ideals of government
inspired by Dharma. The values informing such resistance were
therefore charged with religiosity: *vicāra* which suggested a sort of
providential justice that had nothing to do with the Englishman's
rule of law; and *nyāya* which meant broadly a legitimacy conforming to the ethics of Dharma, far removed from secular political
morality in any modern sense.

Dharmic Protest remained, therefore, one of the most incalculable factors of politics under colonial rule. The notions of authority,
obligation, right and wrong implied in it referred to the traditions
of a precolonial past which the rulers never managed fully to
explore, and to those primordial aspects of community and religion
which they neither understood nor sympathized with. This is demonstrated, among other things, in the consistency with which the
official mind persisted throughout the entire period in misreading
and misinterpreting the elementary aspects of peasant insurgency
in which dharmic protest was more amply and more explicitly
manifested than in any other form.

What made this idiom of R so difficult to comprehend and
control was its plasticity and volatility. Its plasticity tempted the
liberal elite to try and assimilate it to their political philosophies, as
did Bankimchandra to his Anusilandharma when he sought to
marry the Western concept of right to the Hindu idea of a spiritu-

ally legitimized dissent, and Gandhi to his theory of satyagraha where (as in his writings between the Rowlatt Satyagraha and the end of the first Non-cooperation Movement) the Western liberal notions of liberty and citizenship were grafted on the Hindu ideology of Dharma, identified as "satya." In the event, Bankimchandra's theory lost its attraction for the elite to whom it was addressed. Gandhi's less intellectualist construct proved to be more successful precisely because of its eclecticism and its inconsistency. Yet neither the one nor the other really came to terms with subaltern resistance in its dharmic idiom. The volatility of such resistance was something which no liberal-Hindu or liberal-nationalist formula could fully comprehend or cope with. Bankimchandra took fright at the Pabna *projabidroha* (tenants' revolt) of 1873. Gandhi did so at every protest, however dharmic, that involved violence: he had obviously not reckoned with the fact that the authority of the Anuśāsanaparva was still strong among the masses—stronger, on some occasions, than the authority of satyagraha theory itself.

III. Dominance without Hegemony: The Colonialist Moment

Overdeterminations

It should be clear from what has been said so far that D/S is a relation constituted by elements which derive their idioms from two very different paradigms of political culture (Figure 2)—one of which is contemporary, liberal, and British, and the other precolonial, precapitalist and Indian. To put it schematically, one could say that the relation between D and S, that is, between (C, P) and (C*, R), is a relation between two matrices, namely {Order, Improvement, Obedience, Rightful Dissent} and {Daṇḍa, Dharma, Bhakti, Dharmic Protest}.

The ordering of these idioms for discursive purposes is of course not quite the same thing as it is in the actual practice of politics. There, each particular instance acquires its specificity from the braiding, collapsing, echoing, and blending of these idioms in such a way as to baffle all description of this process merely as an

Figure 2. Paradigmatic Derivation of Political Idioms

Constituent Elements	Paradigms	
	Contemporary; Liberal; British	Precolonial, Precapitalist; Indian
C	Order	Daṇḍa
P	Improvement	Dharma
C°	Obedience	Bhakti
R	Rightful Dissent	Dharmic Protest

interaction between a dynamic modernity and an inert tradition, or as the mechanical stapling of a progressive Western liberalism to an unchanging Eastern feudal culture. The shallowness of the first of these metaphors has been exposed well enough to require no further discussion. Its popularity has declined with the end of the developmental illusions generated by post-war capitalism to "modernize" an archaic Third World. But the power of the other metaphor is still intact and calls for some comment.

I think that we should be extremely careful to avoid, in our own work, the mechanicist implications of that metaphor. We can do so only by emphasizing that the interplay of the paradigmatic derivatives of D and S in the politics of the colonial period is in no sense a matter of simple aggregation, but that, on the contrary, those derivatives, functioning as they do as reagents, fashion each of the constituent elements into an original compound, a new entity. Consequently, as a new and original entity, none of the elements is a replica of its corresponding idiom in either of the paradigms. Thus, C as an element of D/S is not identical with the notion of Order in the lexicon of eighteenth- and nineteenth-century British politics nor with the notion of Daṇḍa in that of classical Hindu polity, although its formation owes much to both. Again, P, with all that it owes to the interaction of Improvement and Dharma in its making, is characterized by attributes only some of which it shares with those idioms, while the rest are uniquely its own. And so on for each element.

In other words, what makes the relation of D and S specific and adequate to the conditions of colonialism is an ensemble of overdetermining effects constituted by what Lacan, in his interpretation of that key Freudian concept,[102] calls "a double meaning," with each political instance standing at the same time for "a conflict long dead" and "a present conflict"—that is, for that process of condensation and displacement by which the ideological moments of social contradictions in precolonial India and modern England were fused with those of the living contradictions of colonial rule to structure the relation D/S.

In this sense, there is nothing in our political culture of the colonial era that is not an outcome of this process of overdetermination. That outcome, in its phenomenal form, is a tissue of paradoxes. Whatever is indigenous in that culture is mostly borrowed from the past, whatever is foreign is mostly contemporary. The element of the past, though moribund, is not defunct; the contemporary element, so vigorous in its native metropolitan soil, finds it difficult to strike roots as a graft and remains shallow and restricted in its penetration of the new site. The originality of Indian politics of the period lies precisely in such paradoxes, which pervade the entire spectrum of power relations.

These are displayed, on the side of the colonizers, in the spectacle of a Mother of Parliament presiding happily over a state without citizenship; in a vision of Improvement on capitalist lines degenerating in practice into a neo-feudal organization of property; in a liberal education designed deliberately to perpetuate the subjects' loyalty to an autocratic regime; and other such attitudes and policies which, taken together, gave British colonialism in India its character.

On the side of the indigenous elite, we have an emergent capitalist class keen on masking its role as buyer and user of labor power by pretensions of trusteeship with regard to the labor force; a political leadership of the bourgeoisie resolute in its defence of landlordism; an intelligentsia devoted to social reform in public life and feudal values in private; liberal minds insisting on the "rationality" of *sanatan* Hinduism; critics of the raj concerned to restrict criticism to administrative matters alone and avow their loyalty towards the colonial state itself with the utmost enthusiasm; a nationalist imagination dreaming up the nation-state of the future as a Hindu Samrajya or a Ramrajya, and so on.

And one need not probe too far to discern the play of paradoxes on the subaltern side as well in a peasant rebel's vision of God as a white man who writes like a court clerk; in lower-caste attempts to move up by emulating the conservatism of the upper castes; in a working-class struggle for better wages carried out as a campaign for Truth; in revolts against pre-capitalist property relations calling out for support from the regime which insists, by law and administrative measures, on perpetuating those very relations; and a myriad of other contradictions of that kind.

Colonialism as the Failure of a Universalist Project

The most important and for us the most instructive of all the paradoxes is the co-existence of two paradigms as the determinant of political culture.Its importance lies not so much in the fact that it is the central paradox which sired all the others, but that it stands for a historical deviation which defines the character of colonialism itself. For the question that calls for an answer is: *Why two paradigms and not just one?* Why did the establishment of British paramountcy in South Asia fail to overcome the resistance of its indigenous culture to the point of being forced into a symbiosis? Why did the universalist drive of the world's most advanced capitalist culture, a phenomenon that corresponded to the universalizing tendency of the most dynamic capital of the time, fail, in the Indian instance, to match the strength and fullness of its political dominion by assimilating, if not abolishing, the precapitalist culture of the subject people? For it is that drive which, as Marx argues in *The German Ideology*, makes the emergence of "ruling ideas" a necessary concomitant of capital's dominance in the mode of production and enable these ruling ideas, in their turn, to invest the bourgeoisie with the historic responsibility to "represent" the rest of society, to speak for the nation, and build its hegemony thereby.

Until the ascendancy of the bourgeoisie no other class had ever been called upon to act in this role, because no pre-capitalist mode of production was characterized by the same universalizing urge. As a result, conquistadors, kings, and barons were content to rule over subjugated populations without even trying to integrate or assimilate them into a hegemonic ruling culture. On the contrary, as the eighteenth-century *philosophes* went on insisting (Voltaire, for example, in his essay, *Fragments sur l'Inde* and his play *L'Orphelin de la Chine*), some of these conquerors had been eager to accommodate the culture of their subjects and even acculturate themselves. The despotic state was, in this sense, the reverse of the bourgeois state. The despot, wrote Montesquieu, governed by fear—a measure of his distance from the objects of governance.[103] That distance was mediated by no "education" at all,[104] by no persuasion involving any exchange at the level of culture: all that despotism required was total subordination and all that changed hands was tribute. It did not have a ruling culture, although there was a ruler's culture operating side by side with that of the ruled in a state of mutual indifference, if not mutual acceptance in all cases.

One can, therefore, understand the tolerance, even a certain admiration, for Indian culture on the part of the first colonizers who, in the epoch of Warren Hastings and the Fort William College, were still imbued with the spirit of conquest and mercantilist adventure. But how is it that even after British capital, powered by industrialism, had come of age and the culture corresponding to it had created a homogeneous space for itself by overcoming the resistance of all that was parochial and particularistic in metropolitan politics—how is it that even at its hour of triumph the universalist tendency was resigned to live at peace with the heterogeneity and particularity of the indigenous political culture of an Asian colony? How come that in India universalism failed to generate a hegemonic ruling culture like what it had done at home?

The answer is, simply, that colonialism could continue as a relation of power in the subcontinent only on the condition that the colonizing bourgeoisie should fail to live up to its own universalist project. The nature of the state it had created by the sword made this historically necessary. The colonial state in India did not originate from the activity of Indian society itself. No moment of that society's internal dynamics was involved in the imposition of the alien authority structure which provided the process of state formation both with its primary impulse and the means of its actualization. In other words, the alienation which, in the career of a noncolonial state, comes after its emergence from civil society and is expressed in its separation from that society in order to stand above it, was already there—a foreign intrusion into the indigenous society—at the very inception of the British-Indian colonial state. The latter was thus doubly alienated—in becoming as well as in being.

As an absolute externality, the colonial state was structured like a despotism, with no mediating depths, no space provided for transactions between the will of the rulers and that of the ruled, in short, a polity where, as Montesquieu wrote of its ancient and medieval precursor, "I'l n'y a point de tempérament, de modifications, d'accommodements, de termes, d'équivalents, de pourparlers, de remontrances; rien d'égal ou de meilleur, à proposer; l'homme est une créature qui obéit a une créature qui veut."[105]("No tempering, modification, accommodation, terms, alternatives, negotiations, remonstrances, nothing as good or better can be proposed. Man is a creature that obeys a creature that wants.") That *immediacy* returned long after its time to inform a historic décalage—the insertion of the most dynamic power of the contemporary world into the power relations of a world still living in the past. As an anachronism, this was in agreement with the paradox of an advanced bourgeois culture regressing from its universalist drive to a compromise with precapitalist particularism under colonial conditions of its own creation. An "unconscious tool of history" had obviously lost its edge and was consigned by history to the company of other blunt instruments in its bottom drawer.

That immediacy proved to be an essential factor both in the constitution of dominance and in the construction of the political domain. Its effect on the organic composition of D was to undermine the magnitude of P in relation to that of C within the moment of colonialism. In other words, D as a term of the central relation of power in the subcontinent meant Dominance without hegemony.[106] The Prince who had heeded the Centaur's advice some four centuries ago and taught himself "how to make a nice use of the beast and the man" in politics,[107] appears to have lost his touch over time, and the exercise of authority in realms far from metropolitan Europe came to rely on fear rather than consent.

The primacy of C in the organic composition of D made Order a more decisive idiom than Improvement in the authority of the colonialist elite. The efforts of the "improvers" amongst them, such as Cornwallis and Bentinck, had failed to develop a strategy of persuasion effective enough to overcome the sense of isolation that haunted the regime, a sense in which the alien character of the state was more amply documented than anything else. This failure is clearly demonstrated by the aggressive, militarist, and autocratic nature of the administration for the greater part of British rule until nearly the end of the nineteenth century, when militarism ended but did so without changing the character of the raj as an autocracy. This was so obvious as to make even a blatant apologist for the empire like Dodwell take notice of "the despotic form of Government maintained by the English in India" and speak of his compatriots in the subcontinent as "English despots."[108] Nevertheless, this guru of colonialist historiography was still true to himself as he wrote, at the same time, of "the rule of law, which the English Government had succeeded in establishing," a "rule of law . . . replacing the rule of force as the basis of the state" in the post-Mutiny period.[109]

But what rule of law? What rule of law where the law did not even remotely issue from the will of the people; where Indians, denied the right to vote for most of the duration of British rule, were allowed, during its last thirty years, only a restricted franchise which took decades of struggle and incalculable amounts of physical and spiritual pain to increase, between the Act of 1919 and the Act of 1935, from (an inflated estimate of) three percent of the adult population to fourteen percent? What rule of law where the "law," during the first hundred years of the raj (out of a total of one hundred and ninety), was merely a body of executive orders, decrees, regulations; where, during the next three quarters of a century, all legislative institutions at the central and provincial levels of government were composed either entirely of officials and official nominees or the latter supplemented, for a relatively short period at the height of British constitutionalist magnanimity, by a handful of Indians elected on the basis of restricted franchise? What rule of law where even the devolution of power, promoted by the Act of 1935 to its highest permissible degree, left all strategic decisions for the governance of the country as a whole to a central executive made up of a Viceroy nominated by Whitehall, his own nominees recruited from the colonial bureaucracy and a hand-picked minority of pliant Indians and Europeans? What rule of law where the execution of the laws, made for the people but not by them, was all too often characterized by double standards—one, until the end of the nineteenth century, for the whites and the other for the natives, and during the remainder of British rule, one for the administrative elite, British and Indian, and the other for the rest of the population?

Questions such as these lead to yet another question which is no less important: how come that a knowledgeable historian like Dodwell and indeed many other knowledgeable British intellectuals, bureaucrats, and politicians could go on talking about a rule of law in colonial India when the facts of colonialist practice did nothing to support such assertion? The answer, I think, lies in the pervasive power of the ideology of law in English political thought. It derives from the somewhat older standing of the British legal system and its proven superiority to all other historically evolved systems of the same order up to the age of capital. "Rule of law" is the name given by the common sense of politics to that ideology. As an amalgam of the institutional and conceptual aspects of that system, it has come to acquire the prestige of a code mediating all perceptions of civil conflict. Consequently, there is nothing in the configuration of power that is not referred to and expressed by this code. It stands thus for that universalist urge of bourgeois culture which has realized itself so much and so well in the theory and practice of law under metropolitan conditions as to acquire the aura of "a cultural achievement of universal significance" in the eyes not only of English liberals and colonialists like Dodwell, but also, alas, of English radicals like E. P. Thompson from whom those words are taken.[110]

It is indeed a tribute to the hallucinatory effects of ideology that a cultural development of the bourgeoisie limited to a particular national experience should be hailed as an "achievement of universal significance" both by the friends of that class and its foes. However, neither the special pleading by Dodwell when he speaks of a rule of law following a rule of force in the post-Mutiny period, nor the ingenuity of Thompson when he tries unsuccessfully to disentangle himself from the metaphysical implications of his statement by allowing for the class manipulation of the rule of law,[111] can take away from the fact that bourgeois culture hits an insuperable limit in colonialism. None of its noble achievements—Liberalism, Democracy, Liberty, Rule of Law, and so on—can survive the inexorable urge of capital to expand and reproduce itself by means of the politics of extra-territorial, colonial dominance. Colonialism stands thus not merely for the historical progeny of industrial and finance capital, but also for its historic Other.

There were some Indian liberals on whom that universalist illusion had little or no effect. They were among the more advanced elements of the intelligentsia. They had acquired, by education, an understanding of the rule of law as an ideal, but knew from their own experience as the colonized that it did not work in colonialist practice. In this knowledge, they differed from the mass of their "uneducated" compatriots who had not yet learnt to evaluate the performance of the Sarkar by that alien norm. But they also differed from their opposite numbers in England. For, unlike them, the Indian liberal was not born to a tradition imbued with the ideology of a rule of law, nor was that a code he used systematically to think and express his notions of power. He was, therefore, quick to notice the distortion of that code in the governance of the raj and interpret it as a telling difference between English doctrine and Anglo-Indian deed. In this clash of perceptions between the liberal as the colonizer and the liberal as the colonized, we have yet another demonstration of the parallax of power: since the dominant's angle of vision must differ from that of the dominated in any observation of the phenomenon D by both, there must always be two rather different images of that phenomenon obtained from such observation.

It is not surprising therefore that Dodwell's view of the rule of law in India should differ radically from the view taken of the raj by two representative Indian liberals. One of them, Rabindranath Tagore, turns to this theme again and again in a series of essays between 1893 and 1903.[112] He writes of the illusions of the first liberals: "We had just graduated and undertaken to translate such foreign phrases as equality, liberty, fraternity, etc., into Bangla. We thought that Europe, with all its physical prowess, acknowledged the weak as its equal in terms of human right. We, the recent graduates, were absolutely overwhelmed and looked upon them as gods whom we could go on worshipping for all time and who would go on helping us for ever with their beneficence."[113] But such sentiments proved wrong. The British were quick to demonstrate that they would not treat Indians as equals after all. Tagore cites instances of racist arrogance on the part of the whites in their social transactions with the natives and of racial discrimination on the part of the regime in the judicial and other areas of public administration.[114] He accuses the English of acting on the basis of a morality "split right in the middle *(ðvikhanðita),*"

> so that they find it very difficult indeed to come to a fair judgement in cases of dispute between their own compatriots and others. For it is not unlikely that an Englishman who would not hesitate to try and reduce the Indian population by punching, kicking or shooting without any provocation at all, would still be considered as innocent as a lamb by his own community. Consequently, he would not be regarded by the English as guilty of murder in quite the same way as would be a native murderer . . . To sentence such a man to death by hanging could therefore be considered by them as legal murder.[115]

And, again,

> It is quite easy for an Englishman to hit an Indian — and that, not merely because he is physically strong . . . This is because, in this case, I am merely an individual, while he, an Englishman, stands for the power of the state. In a court of law, I shall be judged as an ordinary mortal and he as an Englishman. And if I hit an Englishman, the judge would consider it as an attack on the authority of the state, as undermining English prestige. As a result, I cannot be tried for anything as simple as common assault.[116]

As Tagore was about to publish the first of this series of articles "speaking bitterness" in 1893, Gandhi too was on the point of launching on his political career in South Africa. There he was quick to notice — indeed, was forced to notice — how professions of bourgeois democracy were violated in the practice of imperialism. "My public life began in 1893 in South Africa in troubled weather," he recalled at his trial at the end of the Non-cooperation Movement nearly thirty years later. "My first contact with British authority in that country was not of a happy character. I discovered that as a man and an Indian I had no rights. More correctly, I discovered that I had no rights as a man because I was an Indian."[117]

However, unlike Tagore whom the arrogance of the rulers had already transformed from a loyalist liberal into a nationalist critic of the raj, Gandhi was slow to shed his illusions. For the next twenty years or so he would still be ready to grant British imperialism the benefit of doubt and explain away white racism in South Africa as "an excrescence upon a system that was intrinsically and mainly good."[118] But the system finally lost its standing with him after the Jalianwalabagh atrocities and the blatant manner in which these were condoned by the colonial authorities both in India and England. "The Punjab crime was white-washed and most culprits went not only unpunished, but remained in service and some continued to draw pensions from the Indian revenue, and in some cases were even rewarded."[119] So Gandhi who had already described the Rowlatt Act as "a law designed to rob the people of all real freedom," went on to denounce "the law itself in this country" as "used to serve the foreign exploiter" and as "prostituted consciously or unconsciously for the benefit of the exploiter."[120]

So much for Dodwell's "rule of law" in colonial India! So much for its standing as "a cultural achievement of universal significance"! Quite clearly its "universality" was not obvious even to such liberals among the subjugated people, who, by their own admission, had started off with a good deal of faith in it. Gandhi spoke of the conceit and self-deception of the colonialists and their native collaborators in this respect thus:

> The greatest misfortune is that Englishmen and their Indian associates in the administration of the country do not know that they are engaged in the crime [of using the law for the purposes of colonial exploitation] I have attempted to describe. I am satisfied that many English and Indian officials honestly believe that they are administering one of the best systems devised in the world and that India is making steady though slow progress. They do not know that a subtle but effective system of terrorism and an organized display of force on the one hand, and the deprivation of all powers of retaliation or self-defence on the other, have emasculated the people and induced in them the habit of simulation. This awful habit has added to the ignorance and the self-deception of the administrators.[121]

Tagore's critique went even further. He attributed the defects of the system not so much to "the ignorance and the self-deception of the administrators" as to the limitations of English bourgeois culture itself. If the "Anglo-Indians" (a nineteenth-century term for the British living and working in India) ignored in their conduct all those liberal norms and democratic ideals they cherished in their metropolitan culture, said Tagore, it was because they had systematized the sense of Western superiority with regard to the peoples of the East into a political philosophy based on the theories of Herbert Spencer and others. According to those theories, the laws of evolution required an adjustment of political and moral principles to the level of any given civilization, so that the application of the more advanced Western principles to the relatively backward and very different non-Western societies could be harmful to their wellbeing and bring discredit upon the civilizing agents themselves. "The point I want to make," wrote Tagore, "is that an idea is fast gaining ground in India as well as in England itself that European principles are meant for Europe alone. Indians are so very different that the principles of civilization are not fully suitable for their needs." Thus, even the most eminent of Indian liberals—one who believed in the universality of culture more than many of his contemporaries—was not deceived by the universalist claim of English liberalism. On the contrary, he identified it as a cultural dialect's pretension to the status of a universal language.

What such pretension meant, in colonialist practice, was that it put an assumption of European superiority at the very core of the governance of India. It meant distancing the governors from the governed and generating among the former a fear of isolation of which Cornwallis and Bentinck had warned, and which their successors now sought to overcome by a display of force. British rule, wrote Tagore in despair, seemed not to recognize that it was good "both for the realm and the rulers that the administration should be as free of conflict and antagonism as possible." He referred to Kipling's imagery of India as a zoo where the natives had to be kept under control by the whip combined with "a promise of bones for food and even a little affection that was owing to pets." But it would be disastrous to introduce "such things as ethics, friendship, civilization, and so on into this treatment, for that might threaten the life of the keeper himself." Colonial rule, he concluded, was "a blend of cruelty and haughty assertion of force."

According to this perception, Dodwell's rule of law had evidently not arrived even thirty years after the Mutiny. Nor was it yet in sight thirty years later, when, as noticed above, Gandhi thought it fit to describe the regime as an "effective system of terrorism and an organized display of force." Thus, in the estimate of even the most "reasonable" Indians, colonialism amounted to a dominance without hegemony — that is, to D with its organic composition seriously undermined by the dilution of the element P. Nothing could testify more to the failure of metropolitan bourgeois culture to inform the structure of authority in Britain's subcontinental empire fully by its own content.

The Fabrication of a Spurious Hegemony

One of the consequences of that failure has been to inhibit the homogenization of the domain of politics. For, under conditions of dominance without hegemony, the life of civil society can never be fully absorbed into the activity of the state. That is why pre-capitalist politics, in which dominance neither solicits nor acquires hegemony, are usually characterized by the coexistence of several cultures of which the culture of the ruling group is only one, even if the strongest, among others. Thus, as Kosambi tells us, during the long era of Indian feudalism cultural modes peculiar to it had to learn to live with those of the historically precedent but still active hunting and foodgathering social formations. What is equally important is that this compromise was rationalized by the dominant culture in such a way as to give it the appearance of a universal, eternal, or some other supra-historical phenomenon or entity. The triumphant Brahmanical culture of later feudalism would therefore inscribe the pastoral, Vedic *yajña* into the Dharmaśāstras as a timeless tradition, adopt a myriad of primitive local deities and refashion them into images of a supra-local Hindu pantheon, and everywhere "the Brahmin would write *purāṇas* to make aboriginal rites respectable."[122]

Even the bourgeoisie, in the course of its striving for dominance in Western Europe, would make a virtue of accommodating its rivals by ideological ploys of the same kind: "for instance, in an age and in a country where royal power, aristocracy and bourgeoisie are contending for domination and where, therefore, domination is shared, the doctrine of powers proves to be the dominant idea and is expressed as an 'eternal law'."[123] In those words the authors of *The German Ideology* noticed how an ascending but still immature bourgeoisie had tried, a hundred years ago, to make its failure to achieve paramountcy appear as a constitutional principle valid for all time. From our own position in the last decade of the twentieth century, it is possible now to look back on the same bourgeoisie which, having come of age, had established its hegemonic dominance in metropolitan Europe and expanded into a colonial empire only to realize that its rule over its Asian subjects must rely, alas, more on force than consent. Consequently, in its attempt to disguise its failure to make dominance informed by hegemony in its colonial project it had recourse again to that well-tried universalist trick.

But there was a difference this time. Unlike in the earlier phase, universalism was no longer a signal of real advance, but merely a gesture in the direction of a past triumph. It was a nostalgia that fed on the historic achievement of the bourgeoisie in its youth when by acting for its particular interest it could still be regarded as acting for the general interest, and when the nation-state, put to use as an instrument of the will of its own class, could still appear as if it was an embodiment of people's will as a whole. In other words, the heady sense of dominance blessed with hegemony lingered on for a while even after the moment of glory had passed and was transformed, by reflection, into a universal and almost transcendental attribute of bourgeois power valid for all time and place. From that abstraction it was but one short step to conceptualizing its last historic "achievement," that is, colonialism, too, as hegemonic.

It was historiography which, more than any other bourgeois knowledge, contributed to the fabrication of this spurious hegemony. "It is the state which first supplies a content," said Hegel, "which not only lends itself to the prose of history but actually helps to produce it."[124] The truth of this observation is fully borne out by the complicity between the formation of a colonial state in India and the production of colonialist histories of the raj. These histories fall roughly into two classes of writing. The first corresponds to the initial, mercantilist phase of British power in the subcontinent. Phrased in the idiom of coercion, it emphasizes the moment of conquest rather than order. Alexander Dow, "Lieutenant-Colonel in the Company's Service," testified truly to the inspiration derived from the sword by the pen in this particular genre as he dedicated one of its most representative specimens, *The History of Hindostan,* to the King of England, thus: "The success of your Majesty's *arms* has laid open the East to the *researches* of the curious."[125]

The works of many other writers of the period—Verelst, Bolts, Scrafton and Grant—to name some of the better known amongst them—are witness to this explicit collaboration between arms and researches. They refute, in anticipation, the attempt that was to be made later on by many a pundit to represent British historiography as a curricular effort to educate Indians in liberal values. For the aim of mercantilist historiography was simply to educate the East India Company. By investigating the relation between government and landed property in the precolonial period it wanted to equip the Company with a knowledge that would help it to extract the highest possible amount of revenue from the conquered territories and use it to finance its seaborne trade.

Most of these writers were quite candid about their political motivation, as witness the administrative prescriptions which figured so prominently in every exercise of this kind. The concentration, in such writing, on the coercive element of dominance also makes for an objectivity rarely found in the colonialist discourse of later generations. Unaffected yet by the idiom of Improvement, hence unconcerned to promote any affection among the conquerors for the conquered, it maintains a considerable distance from the latter. In that perspective the physical features of the land acquired by the sword show up as clearly as do the details of the cultural landscape such as the religions, customs, manners, and so on of the people subjugated by the sword. In both cases it is a matter of observing a set of objects. In all of this genre, therefore, anthropology exudes a self-confidence which parallels and complements that of politics. It is the confidence of the colonizer in his dual role of conquistador and scholar.

Colonialist historiography outgrew such mercantilist concern by the end of the eighteenth century and acquired, within the next two decades, a new look conforming to the requirements of British capital in the age of industrialism and those of metropolitan politics in the "Age of Improvement." This orientation was pioneered, appropriately enough, by the Utilitarian philosopher, James Mill, whose *History of British India*, published in 1818, earned for him celebrity as "the first historian of India."[126] As a measure of contemporary opinion, that sobriquet meant a radical devaluation of the genre produced by the Company's servants before his time. What is more significant is that it indexed a nineteenth-century European prejudice according to which precolonial India was said to have no history, and therefore "the first historian of India" had to be English.

That prejudice is expressed in its most systematic and sophisticated form in the philosophy of Mill's German contemporary, Hegel. History, "real history" as the latter put it, presupposed the existence of the state.[127] For "a commonwealth in the process of coalescing and raising itself up to the position of a state requires formal commandments and laws," and "thereby creates a record of its own development . . . on which Mnemosyne, for the benefit of the perennial aim which underlies the present form and constitution of the state, is impelled to confer a lasting memory." But in India society was "petrified into natural determinations—i.e. the caste system." As "an order based firmly and permanently on nature," it lacked an "ultimate end in the shape of progress and development." An organism endowed with "no intelligent recollection, no object worthy of Mnemosyne," it drifted without "a fixed purpose . . . worthy of history."[128]

No state, no history. The congruence of these two negatives mediated, for Hegel, the contradiction between nature and culture, between Chronos and Zeus:

A nation is only world-historical in so far as its fundamental element and basic aim have embodied a universal principle; only then is its spirit capable of producing an ethical and political organisation . . . In this way, the Greeks speak of the rule of Chronos or Time, who devours his own children (i.e. the deeds he has himself produced); . . . Only Zeus, the political god . . . was able to check the power of time; he did so by creating a conscious ethical institution, i.e. by producing the state.[129]

Zeus stood, of course, for the bourgeoisie itself, and Hegel's theory of the state celebrated its historic conceit in an appropriately mythic form at a time when it was still playing "political god" to Europe, demolishing the remnants of an old absolutist order and replacing it by new republics. But the development of that class was far from uniform, and consequently, republicanism was for the project of the younger continental bourgeoisie what the civilizing mission was for the colonial project of its older and expansionist opposite number in England. The "fundamental element and basic aim" of both the projects "embodied a universal principle" which, taken out of its metaphysical wrapping, could clearly be recognized as none other than the universalizing tendency of capital we have met before.

Hegel's political enthusiasm thus found its foil in the arrogance with which Mill denounced a substantial part of India's precolonial past as barbaric in his *History*. However, even as Hegel argued that India had no history due to stagnation in its social development, he could still write admiringly about "this country, so rich in spiritual achievements of a truly profound quality."[130] But to James Mill it was all a matter of arrested mental development. "It is allowed on all hands that no historical composition existed in the literature of the Hindus," he observed; "they had not reached that point of intellectual maturity, at which a value of the record of the past for the guidance of the future begins to be understood."[131]

Mill's anti-Indian prejudices in the *History of British India* have been noticed and criticized. But all that has been written to refute his errors of fact and failures of judgment leaves one vital question still without answer: What is there in the logic of that work which *requires* the insertion of the denunciatory chapters on Hinduism? There is hardly anything in the narrative that calls for such digression. The work starts with an account of the initial efforts made by the English to sail to the East in order to acquire a commercial base for themselves in that region. However, instead of continuing until the battle of Plassey, the author stops abruptly at 1711 with the foundation of the East India Company, and devotes all of Books II and III to a retrospective survey of ancient and medieval India.

His own justification of this procedure, as given at the end of Book I, derived apparently from the need he thought the readers had for some background information before proceeding to the principal theme of the work, that is, the establishment of British rule in the subcontinent.[132] To that end, the preamble to the work had already announced his intention "to exhibit as accurate a view as possible of the character, the history, the manners, religion, arts, literature, and laws of the extraordinary people with whom this intercourse had thus begun; as well as of the physical circumstances, the climate, the soil, and productions, of the country in which they were placed."[133] Yet as his biographer, Alexander Bain, has pointed out, "This last part . . . has no chapter expressly allotted to it, and is hardly perceptible anywhere."[134] Instead, what we are offered is a dissertation on ancient Hindu culture taking up all of Book II, followed by a historical account beginning with the Ghaznavids and ending with the Mughals in Book III. There is nothing in the subsequent parts of the work which cannot be understood without the help of this introjection. On the contrary, these two Books may be said to be positively unhelpful in one important respect: however interesting in themselves, they break up the narrative and thus undermine the reader's concentration on the developing theme of Britain's relations with India since the sixteenth century with which the *History* begins.

What purpose, then, was served by this massive digression? It served the avowedly didactic purpose announced by Mill at the outset. *"The subject forms an entire, and highly interesting, portion of the British History,"* he wrote,

> and it is hardly possible that the matter should have been brought together, for the first time, without being instructive . . . If the success corresponded with the wishes of the author, he would throw light upon a state of society, curious, and commonly misunderstood; upon the history of society, which in the compass of his work presents itself in almost all its stages and all its shapes; upon the principles of legislation, in which he has so many important experiments to describe; and upon the interests of his country, of which, to a great degree, his countrymen have remained in ignorance . . . [135]

Nothing like this could have been written by a mercantilist historian. The perspective had shifted: it was no longer that of a conquistador, but of a legislator. The author had set out to give India a government administered according to the principles of utility.

He spoke therefore in the idiom of Improvement rather than of Order. And he was very much the child of his age to seek a site for his reforms in the Orient, and stood, in this regard, in a direct line of succession to Pattullo, who, in the 1770s, had dreamt up a Physiocratic utopia in his plan for the *amelioration* of the newly conquered territories of Bengal.

The change in the source of inspiration from the French *philosophes* to a very English "philosophical radicalism" had apparently done nothing to change the visionary's need for a *tabula rasa* on which to inscribe his "principles of legislation." Yet, in the second decade of the nineteenth century, he could no longer hope to proceed, like his precursor of fifty years ago, on the innocent assumption that Indian reform was simply a matter of filling an Eastern void by "important experiments" of Western invention. It was imperative, therefore, for Utilitarian discourse to create a void, since none was given. Accordingly, the author's textual strategy required that the ancient indigenous culture of the colonized should be demolished on intellectual and moral grounds, so that he could then go on to posit his own system into that vacancy.

This demolition was an act of spiritual violence. It amounted to robbing the subject people of their past which was one of the principal means of their self-identification. It also prepared the ground for a substitution: the *bad* Hindu history could now be replaced by a *good* history in the making under colonial auspices. To this end, the record of the intervening period of about five hundred years was mobilized in such a way as to make of the Islamic component of Indian culture an accomplice of colonialism. All of Book III of Mill's *History* was devoted to this tactic. It served, in the first place, to demonstrate the absolute inferiority of Hindus to Muslims in all respects. (This was the function of Chapter 5 of Book III of the *History*.) The contrast was obviously intended to justify the reduction of Hindu culture to nullity, as already done in the previous parts of the work. But it was also meant to support the author's design to "throw light . . . upon the history of society. . . in almost all its stages . . ."

The Muslims who came to India initially as invaders from Western Asia, he wrote, "had in fact attained a stage of civilization higher than that of the Hindus."[136] One had, therefore, to ask "Whether by a government, moulded and conducted agreeably to the properties of Persian civilization, instead of a government moulded and conducted agreeably to the properties of Hindu civilization, the Hindu population of India lost or gained."[137] The answer was, of course, "that human nature in India gained, and gained very considerably, by passing from a Hindu to a Mohammedan government."[138] It followed, therefore, that human nature would gain still further if the country were to be ruled by conquerors even more civilized than the Muslims. The British were such conquerors. For the Muslim, however superior to the Hindu, was still far below the British in the scale of civilization. "He [the Mohammedan] more nearly resembles our own half-civilized ancestors," wrote Mill in an outburst of praise.[139] For a measure of his faith in the benefits of British rule for India, one has simply to read "Europe" for "West Asia," "Christian" for "Mohammedan," "British civilization" for "Persian civilization," and "the raj" for "Mohammedan government" in the observations discussed above.

Thus the substitution of Indian culture by colonialism was completed in two successive movements—the abolition of the historic culture of the Hindus followed by the supersession of that of the Muslims. Taken together, these two movements amounted to a deletion of the entire precolonial past of our people who were then compensated for that loss by the gift of a new history—a foreshortened history with the colonial state as its subject. Henceforth, the history of the subcontinent, like its map, would be painted red, with all of its past since the battle of Plassey assigned to the rubric, "History of British India." Henceforth, too, British annexation of South Asian territory would have its spiritual complement in a British appropriation of the colonized people's past, allowing all of colonialist historiography to be guided by Mill's assertion: *"The subject forms an entire, and highly interesting, portion of the British History."*[140]

But as Mill himself had insisted throughout his work, India was utterly different from Britain in every respect; in religion, manners, civilization, language—indeed, in every qualitative detail. How, then, could one of two such dissimilar entities be said to form a portion of the other? Only in terms of the lineage of power, that is, in terms of the status, function, and activity of the colonial state as an offspring of the metropolitan state and a vehicle of its will.

Hereafter, the discourse of history would be obsessively concerned with "the character and tendency of that species of relation to one another in which the mother country and her eastern dependencies [were] placed,"[141] and consequently, it would represent the life of the colonized as no more than a moment in the career of the metropolitan state.

Note, however, that this state was supposed to rule not (as the mercantilists would have it) by the sword, but by civilization — not by force but by consent. But since the regime, as an autocracy, had little use for consent, both of the measures of persuasion legislated by Mill, namely, culture and government, were conspicuous by their failure to strike roots to any significant depth among the disinherited and disenfranchised population. Liberal culture hardly managed to penetrate beyond the upper crust of Indian society, while the ideal of liberal government persisted only as an idle and empty cant until the end of the raj. This contradiction between Utilitarian principle and "Anglo-Indian" performance, so symptomatic of the metropolitan bourgeoisie's failure to inform dominance by hegemony in its Indian empire, rankles in colonialist historiography as an ineradicable sign of bad faith: ever since the publication of the *History of British India*, James Mill & Sons have been pretending to write the history of India while writing, in fact, the history of Britain in its South Asian career.

The Bad Faith of Historiography

There are two idioms in which this bad faith is typically expressed. Both derive from the political philosophy of Improvement. One of these is cultural, and its function is to document and display the record of colonial rule as a civilizing force. The raj, it argues, introjected liberal Western values and helped thereby to promote social reform, combat superstition and generally raise the level of the indigenous culture.

This claim, which was once the staple of school textbooks throughout the subcontinent, understates the failure of liberalism to overcome the resistance of entrenched feudal customs and belief systems, and the compromises imposed by these on official and nonofficial elitist attempts at social reform. Above all, it amounts to a rather partial view of history insofar as it ignores the urge for reform in a large area of Indian society where many autonomous movements of the subaltern, unaffected by Western influence, were pitted against caste, class, ethnic, and (to a lesser extent) sexual dominance.

In any case, the theme of civilizing mission began to lose its credibility as colonialism had its record assessed by an increasingly critical subject population. To the latter, the benefits of officially sponsored social reform seemed to have been cancelled out by the aggravation of what was believed to be officially engineered caste and communal conflict designed to keep the natives divided in order to perpetuate foreign rule. This skepticism, combined with a nationalist pride that refused to take Western superiority in culture for granted, forced historiography to shift its emphasis from reform to education as the main component of Britain's spiritual gift to India.

Education had always ranked high on the agenda of colonialism. In the eighteenth century, Philip Francis had thought of it as a program of instruction in English to induce Indians "to qualify themselves for employment,"[142] that is, to act as cogs in the wheel of the colonial administration. Macaulay, in the next century, prescribed it as a nutrient for native minds that had subsisted far too long on a poor diet of indigenous superstitions. But as opposition to the raj grew more and more widespread during its last fifty years and politics came to be of cardinal importance in modern Indian culture, the emphasis on bureaucratic and intellectual uses of education was replaced, in colonialist historiography, by its valorization as an instrument of political training. Thus Dodwell, writing in 1936, could describe Western education as what had inducted the Indian to "new political conceptions," to political institutions "such as he had never known save in embryonic forms long forgotten," to "a conception of law totally unfamiliar," to "the rule of law . . . a stern reality instead of an ideal, [under which] every subject was entitled (according to many political authors) to political rights." And, above all, nationalism "was born and nurtured," according to him, "under the stimulus of western education."[143]

Years later, in the postcolonial era, education and politics were to be connected in much the same manner by colonialist historiography speaking in the voice of a Cambridge scholar, Anil Seal. The "general problem" addressed in his monograph on the emergence of Indian nationalism was, he said, "how modern politics in India began," and he then went on to state his thesis: "Education was one of the chief *determinants* of these politics, and their *genesis* is clearly linked with those Indians who had been schooled by western methods."[144] Mill's idea of reducing Indian history to a "portion of the British History" was realized thus in the reduction of Indian politics to Western-style education.

The absurdity of such a reduction is obvious. If it were true, there would be nothing left to Indian politics except the sum of the political activities of "graduates and professional men in the presidencies." Even Seal, who had once presented that thesis with much verve, came to see its deficiencies, recanted, and replaced it by another, but alas equally elitist, interpretation. The "genesis" and "determinants" of politics were no longer sought in education; in the new version, these were situated in government—the second idiom, also derived from Mill, in which the bad faith of colonialist historiography was henceforth to express itself. "It is our hypothesis," wrote Seal, "that the structure of imperial government can provide a clue to the way Indian politics developed."[145]

What is meant by "the structure of imperial government" here is the complex of organizations, activities, and discourses made up of a chain of command extending from Whitehall down to the lowest reaches of British authority in the subcontinent, the bureaucracy with its rules, orders, and schedules, all levels of officially sponsored institutions from the central to the local, as well as the laws and executive decisions made by them and practical measures used to implement these. Taken together, they stand for the ensemble called colonial administration.

The mode of historiography which is primarily concerned to deal with it is administrative history. One of its exemplars, a collection of essays on South India, has been described by David Washbrook (who has worked out the implications of this "hypothesis" more fully than any other scholar) as an "attempt to outline the principal administrative institutions of southern India and to show how they influenced the development of political organisations."[146] This, with the name of the region taken out, would apply to the genre as a whole. But what is truly astonishing about this exercise is its author's claim to novelty. According to him, "a gap has emerged between administrative and political historians"—a gap which, presumably, it has been to the credit of Cambridge historiography to locate and bridge. And to leave the reader in no doubt about the measure of this achievement, it is said that "in its early stages of development, modern political history has not needed to consider administration."[147] In other words, thanks to the intervention of this particular group of scholars, historiography has at last come of age!

The truth, contrary to this claim, is that administrative history had developed as a genre of historiography almost from the beginning of colonial rule, and it has never been anything but an integral part of political history. It was in the very nature of the colonial state that the theme of administration should figure prominently in its earliest accounts. As an autocracy which had originated in conquest and ruled over an alien population almost entirely by the sword for the first fifty years, the early colonial state had no means other than its administrative apparatus by which to record, measure, and assess its own articulation. Imposed externally on the subcontinental population, that is, not having arisen out of a churning of the indigenous society itself, it was completely divorced from the political life of its subjects. Those linkages with the native elite, which the Cambridge scholars have been so concerned to describe, were yet to be formed. In that phase of self-absorption, colonialism was trapped in a reflexivity thanks to which all its political stimulus was addressed singularly to its own administration (understood, in this context, as the sum of all transactions between the developing organs of the state) and matched by a direct and unmediated response from the latter. Consequently, at this initial stage, there was no political history that did not read like administrative history, and vice versa.

This is a condition of historiography with which all students of early British rule in India are thoroughly familiar. One has simply to turn to William Bolts's *Considerations on Indian Affairs* (London, 1772) or Harry Verelst's *View of the Rise, Progress and Present State of the English Government in Bengal* (London, 1772) to realize how impossible it was to talk about the politics of colonialism without being directly involved in an argument about the administration of the Company's territories. Or take the very different case of James Grant's *An Inquiry into the Nature of Zemindary Tenures in the Landed*

Property of Bengal (London, 1790). Written as a contribution to an ongoing debate about the administration of land revenue, it develops into a treatise on the relation between the state and landed magnates in precolonial times and its implications for the East India Company as a successor regime.

Politics and administration were easily conflated in the historical works of these first colonizers, because the two had not yet come to be differentiated within what was still, by and large, a predatory, tribute-gathering, mercantilist project of primitive accumulation. Even later, as colonialist dominance matured into a vehicle of metropolitan industrial and financial interests, its organic composition, in spite of some variations in the magnitudes of its constituent elements C and P, was not altered radically enough to rend politics and administration apart. In other words, the colonial state being what it was, that is, a dominance without hegemony, had to have its administration firmly stapled to politics, and consequently it was not necessary for historiography to develop any modal distinction between the two in its own discourse. A general recognition of this overlap is amply documented in historical writings of our own time at all levels—from the profound, as in W. K. Firminger's penetrating analysis of the relation between sovereignty and Diwani in his magisterial *Introduction to the Fifth Report* (Calcutta, 1917), to the banal, as in the school manuals of the interwar period where political history was almost invariably written up as the administrative record of viceroys and lieutenant-governors.

Thus the notion of a gap between administrative and political history has little to support it either in the facts of historiography or in any intelligent political theory of colonialism. The novelty of the Cambridge approach does not, therefore, lie in marrying administrative and political history, for these two modes were indissolubly bound in a sort of sanatan Hindu wedlock by the very system to which they referred. It lies in the attempt of the Cambridge scholars to clean up the musty mansion of elitist historiography, reject some of its worn out fittings and furnishings, and put a new gloss over it. The job, I say in genuine admiration, has been brilliantly done. It owes its shine and finish not only to the sophistication of craft, but to the chemistry of the paint. It is the old colonialist argument rejuvenated by a new formula of power.

Politics, in this new Cambridge approach, is not different from the previous, though now disowned, thesis of the same school in one fundamental sense: it is still a matter of imperialist stimulus and native response. However, the stimulus, in this version, does not come in the form of culture or education, but of government. How does governmental stimulus work? In two ways. In the first place, it trains the subjects in the use of the institutions of colonial government, rewarding the learners by material and spiritual resources (ranging from jobs and canal water to knighthoods and liberal values), and generating among them both a competition for the available prizes and a shared sense of collaboration with the raj. Secondly, the stimulus works by encouraging the natives to replicate the institutions of government by setting up institutions of their own (called "associations" by Seal) and develop, in that process, a matching nonofficial arena where all, in turn, will be modeled on the institutional procedure, reward system, and patron-client nexus of the primary, official arena. The sum of the relations, activities, and discourses generated by governmental stimulus in these two ways is what constitutes politics according to the current version of Cambridge historiography.

I appreciate this model for its coherence and its lucidity. It is a vast improvement on both the previous (sabre-rattling and civilizing-mission) models of colonialist historiography, which have been, in one form or another, the dominant influence on teaching and research so far. In spite of the hectoring pedantry and the factious pettiness of some of its practitioners, this historiography, at its best, has much to teach us about colonialism both as a political system and as a persistent intellectual influence in the postcolonial era. But with all my admiration for it as a negative example, I reject this historiography as a symptom of blatant bad faith. It is not what it pretends to be. It is not concerned with the history of India at all. Its aim is to write up Indian history, after Mill, as a "portion of the British History." As such, it constitutes a misappropriation, a violence.

The subject of this neo-colonialist historiography is the empire. Its instrument, the imperial government, alone is endowed with the initiative that defines the structure and movement of politics. The colonized, in this thesis, have no will of their own. They simply slot into a framework made by the rulers for them. The metaphor is

Seal's: "The British built the framework; the Indians fitted into it."[148] In agreement with this view, Indian response to imperial initiative is regarded as entirely imitative. As Gallagher put it, "Government impulse had linked much more closely the local and the provincial arenas of politics; and the general trend among Indian politicians, constitutionalist or not, was to react to this initiative by copying it."[149] The force of this argument is to reduce Indian nationalism to a mere echo of imperialism, according to Seal, or as Gallagher suggested, to its offspring.[150]

The only role that can be assigned to Indians in this utterly replicative, imitative politics is that of collaborator. The words, "collaborator" and "collaboration" occur frequently in these writings.[151] Indeed, this interpretation of Indian history rests entirely on a theory of collaboration. Colonialism is described as "British rule through Indian collaboration"; administration at the local level is said to have been guided by "easy-going collaboration" at a particular stage in the career of the raj; at another stage, we are told of a "new system" of representation "casting wider nets to find collaborators," and so on.[152]

Now, it may not sound particularly revealing to most people that British rule in India had to rely on Indian collaboration. Any regime that is not exclusively based on force must rely to a certain extent on the collaboration of those over whom it rules. The adequacy of a theory of collaboration must therefore be judged by its ability to specify the extent to which collaboration succeeds in mediating the contradiction between the rulers and the ruled. The strategy of the Cambridge approach is to credit that mediation with complete success in this regard and represent the colonized subject's relation to the colonizer as one in which Collaboration (C*) triumphed effectively over Resistance (R). In other words, it is a strategy aimed at characterizing colonialism as a hegemonic dominance.

Two devices have been adopted to this end. The first is to endow collaboration with a set of liberal-bourgeois attributes by making it a matter of competition and representation. Competition is a key concept in this view of Indian history. It is what transforms the relation between rulers and the ruled into a patron-client relationship. It is what constitutes the dynamics of politics, for it is by competing for rewards made available by the raj that the natives learn how to use the institutions of government, politicize themselves, and involve others in such a way as to direct the thrust of the political process from the upper to the lower levels, from provinces to localities. In other words, competition is assigned the role of generalizing the distribution of power. The point is driven home again and again by metaphors of the market place: the object of competition is "opportunity" and "resources"; competitors "haggle" and "bargain"; politics is "transactional politics"; transactions are mediated by "contractors" and "subcontractors," and so on. The vocabulary of political economy is smuggled into a description of politics in such a way as to give the latter a semblance of freedom and openness.

But where, in the politics of the raj, was that freedom, that openness? Resources and opportunities were addressed selectively to a small, a very small minority of the population—the elite, and this was done with deliberation, as a matter of policy. Consequently, most of the land was appropriated by landlords and the upper strata of landowning classes; irrigation benefited primarily the rural rich; education was monopolized by upper castes and upper classes; and jobs circulated among those who had been already nominated for them by their access to education. Seen in this light, the so-called "opportunities" and "resources" look more like privileges and perquisites, and "competition" more like feudal jousting than free bargaining in an open market.

This is not to deny the movement generated by colonialism in Indian politics but to assess this movement for what it really was—that is, a force which, even as it disturbed the traditional power relations to some extent, was still wanting both in the strength and the will to destroy them and ended up by redistributing their moments within the existing parameters. It is difficult, therefore, to justify conceptualizing the politics of collaboration in terms of the transactional ideals of political economy. Yet it is hardly possible to overestimate the importance of this approach as an ideological intervention aimed at construing colonialism into a hegemonic dominance. For the Cambridge effort at squaring this particular circle is symptomatic of the failure of liberalism, hence of neo-colonialist historiography as one of its instruments, to come to terms with the fact that the universalist urge of metropolitan capital meets in colonialism a limit it can never overcome.

The notion of representation, too, is designed to endow the raj with a spurious hegemony. The function of representation, like that of competition, was to promote collaboration. "It brought more Indians into consultation about the management of their affairs; yet it kept them at work inside a framework which safeguarded British interests," writes Seal. A rather narrow system designed for "the recruitment of Indian assistants at the levels where they were needed" and for setting them "to work particularly at the points of execution rather than of command," the organs of local government are rightly described as "modest representative bodies."

Yet the claims made for these "modest representative bodies" are far from modest. It is these, we are told, which "enabled government to associate interests in the localities more widely," making representation "one of the vehicles for driving deeper into local society." Integrated into a system of indirect representation, they also helped the British to add "first a representative, and later an elective, veneer to the superior councils," so that "the spread of representation . . . produced a legislative system which extended from the lowest to the highest level in India." Thus the modest local institutions were said to have constituted a key link in "a chain of command stretching from London to the districts and townships of India . . . so that even the pettiest official intervention in a locality issued from a general authority."[153] In other words, representation, according to this theory, succeeded in mobilizing Indian cooperation and consent on a scale so wide as to put the regime in a nonantagonistic relation with its subjects and thereby make for a hegemonic and unifying dominance.

An achievement of that order would require a very wide representation, one of so vast a magnitude that the collaboration generated by it would be massive enough to cope with the tasks of persuasion and linkage entrusted to it. Yet, as we know, representation in colonial India was a pretty restricted affair. It consisted either of nomination alone, or subsequently of nomination combined with election based on a very limited franchise. In a land of paupers, only a handful of property owners were allowed the right to vote; in a land of illiteracy, only a handful of those lucky enough to have access to higher education. Representation never approximated even remotely to democracy, and there is nothing to suggest otherwise in the Cambridge thesis. On what grounds, then, can it credit the raj with such a broad-based collaboration and so deep a local penetration — in short, with hegemony? Only by wishing away the phenomenon of resistance both as a matter of fact and as a historical necessity.

If collaboration, brought about by competition and representation, may be said to be the first affirmative device by which colonialism is endowed with hegemony in this historiography, a second, negative device it uses for the same purpose is a conjuring trick to make resistance disappear from the political history of India under British rule. In this respect not much seems to have changed in the Cambridge approach since its previous stance, which, taking Seal's 1968 monograph as an exemplar, put popular resistance firmly outside politics. The Indigo Rebellion and the Deccan Riots were dismissed by him as "peasant risings of the traditional type, the reaching for sticks and stones as the only way of protesting against distress. Of specific political content they show little sign." There are some other instances as well which are scoffed at as "scufflings produced by . . . religious and agrarian agitations" and do not qualify as political either because they originated in "simple societies" with "an inborn propensity to revolt," or because they were "grounded on local grievances and local aspirations, and . . . dependent on local leadership" (at that time, five years before the updated thesis, the local was still sub-political!), or because they were, even as all-India movements, "an old-fashioned sort . . . seeking to march backwards with fire and sword to the good old days of Aurangzeb."[154]

Such exclusion would have been quite in order, if the explanatory power claimed for this historiography were less comprehensive. One doesn't have to explore the specificities of such "scufflings" if the politics of union board and chaukidari tax is all that one wants to write about. But the Cambridge scholars are nothing if not ambitious. They have set out to provide an interpretation that would explain all of politics for us, they have a general theory. As Seal modestly states his aim: "In order to provide a more general explanation, we propose an alternative approach."[155]

But what kind of "general explanation" of the history of India under British rule are we offered, when there is no room in that

history for the phenomenon of resistance, which occurs throughout the period in every region of the subcontinent and does so in
many different forms ranging from the most peaceful to the most
violent, involving participation in numbers ranging from a few
individuals to tens of thousands at a time? What kind of "general
explanation" of politics is this alternative approach, which does not
know how to proceed except by denying this massive, recurrent,
and widespread phenomenon of resistance any "specific political
content," when in every instance that resistance is nothing but
political? To be asked to place our trust in so partial a view of
history and politics as a "general explanation" seems to me to be a
kind of academic confidence trick.

Like all confidence tricks, it works by dressing up what it is
required to prove as a premise for the unwary reader to accept
without questioning. The premise, as noticed above, is a notion of
politics defined as Indian collaboration with the raj mediated by
the institutions of government. Once that premise is agreed upon
and nothing is left to politics but collaboration, resistance stands
expurgated as an irrelevance and an aberration without requiring
further argument. But resistance is a stubborn thing and would not
be so easily left out of history. To guard against its intrusion it is
necessary, therefore, to ensure that its symptoms—solidarity and
ideology—however explicit and widespread in history, are not
allowed to spoil the tidiness of historiography.

Two vanishing tricks are adopted to deal with these symptoms
in all recent writings of the genre under discussion. By the first of
these, horizontal solidarity is spirited away from the political processes of the colonial era. Thus "What seems to have decided political choices in the localities was," according to Seal, "the race for
influence, status and resources. In the pursuit of these aims, patrons regimented their clients into factions which jockeyed for
position. Rather than partnerships between fellows, these were
usually associations of bigwigs and followers. In other words they
were vertical alliances, not horizontal alliances."[156]

This is fully consistent with the Cambridge view of politics as a
rat-race between collaborators handpicked by the raj from the elite
strata of the indigenous population. All is therefore a matter of
"bigwigs" mobilizing their "followers" into "factions" in the scramble for "influence, status and resources" put out by the regime as

the prize for collaboration. Hence, there is no solidarity between fellows; there are only vertical alliances. However, if at this point you start wondering about such things as class struggle, caste conflict, communal strife, or adivasi campaigns, described by some benighted leftists as instances of horizontal alliance, Seal, whom we have cited above, is there to rescue you from misconceptions of that order. "Local struggles were seldom marked," he says, "by the alliance of landlord with landlord, peasant with peasant, educated with educated, Muslim with Muslim and Brahmin with Brahmin."[157]

There you are! You must be utterly naive if you thought that there was an alliance of landlords against tenants in Pabna in 1873 or millowners against workers in Ahmedabad in 1918. You delude yourself in discerning any "partnership between fellows" of the same caste in the anti-*bhadralok* campaign among the Namasudras of Barisal during the Swadeshi Movement, of the same tribe in the Munda uprising led by Birsa, of the same class in the general strike of jute-mill workers in 1929 or sharecroppers in the Tebhaga campaigns of the 1940s, of the same religious community on each of the warring sides involved in the Partition Riots of 1947, of the same nation in the great anti-imperialist struggles of 1919–1922, 1930–1932, and 1942–1946. Insofar as these are instances of political mobilization, they are vertical by definition; and insofar as these are instances of horizontal mobilization, they are prepolitical by definition. One is simply not allowed to mix politics and solidarity, for that would put resistance on a par with collaboration in any "general explanation" of Indian history under colonial rule and thus bring down the entire edifice of neocolonialist historiography!

The denial of horizontal alliance complements the other conjuring device by which ideology is made to dissolve as an element of politics. This too is designed to keep resistance out of history. For if there was nothing to politics other than collaboration offered to secure rewards from the raj, it follows that people were urged by interests rather than ideas to respond to the "governmental impulse" on institutional lines. This, according to David Washbrook, was an instance of the "purely political," that is, the "political" which was purged of the dross of "public ideology" and "avowed ends" to derive primarily from "the mechanisms of power and . . . the behavioural conventions which developed around them."[158] It is not that ideology did not exist, but it existed only as an element of culture and not of politics. "It is important to remember that religious, caste and linguistic groupings are not political groupings unless they can be shown to behave as such. They are categories of cultural but not necessarily political activity."[159] This distinction may strike one as rather odd. For it is difficult to think of any historical situation in which politics would not be an element of culture. Moreover, in a precapitalist culture, prior to the emergence of any clear distinction between the sacred and the secular in the affairs of the state, politics, one would have thought, was so thoroughly mingled with religion as to permit of no categorical separation between the two.

Yet, I can see some use for this entirely fallacious distinction in the neocolonialist reading of Indian history. It serves to sever casteism and communalism from the ideological formations of precolonial India and display them as products of what the Cambridge scholars believe to have been entirely an innovation of the raj, namely "politics," or what is the same thing according to them — the native collaborators' pursuit of resources and opportunities within the institutional framework of British rule. This enables Washbrook to speak of the temple politics of South India as "closer to company politics than to those of religious movements"[160] and go on to claim that his study of the non-Brahman movement "reveals three important points which are relevant to all the communal movements of the period."[161]

But it is precisely because there is no acknowledgement of the role of ideology in any of these three points that they lose their relevance for the study of communalism in northern and eastern India during this period. Thus to say that "the language of the movement was closely related to the language of government" would do little to explain the scale and force of the support evoked by that language, unless it were made clear that the idiom of elite communal politics, however related to the official legal-constitutional discourse, had to be translated into a code of traditional politics, much of it religious, in order to mobilize the masses in communal political activity. How this works in the Muslim and Hindu communal politics of Bengal and Uttar Pradesh is amply illustrated in some recent studies by Partha Chatterjee and Gyanendra Pandey.[162]

Again, how relevant would the following judgment be for any understanding of the politics of Hindu-Muslim or inter-caste relations? According to Washbrook,

> ... these movements, whatever their pretensions, did not need to have, and many did not have, a political existence prior to the creation of the publicist and administrative categories which they filled. It is idle for the student of politics, although not perhaps of ideas, to search through the history and meaning of "non-Brahmanism" to discover when in the past or at what level of abstraction in "traditional" thought a notion of the non-Brahman similar to that propagated by the leaders of the non-Brahman movement can be found. The movement emerged when the very novel political processes of early twentieth-century Madras gave it life. What is interesting to political history is not the ideational antecedents of the movement but the contemporary processes.[163]

I am not in a position to assess the validity of these observations for South India, since I have no specialized knowledge of that area. But I believe that they will be of little or no use to students of caste and communal movements elsewhere in the country. To say, for instance, that the twentieth-century conflict between bhadralok and Namasudra, Mahar and Brahman, Rajput and Chamar, Hindu and Muslim derived its politics, in each case, from the administrative categories of colonialism would certainly be true—indeed, it would ring with the hollow truth of a truism—if politics were defined merely by administrative categories, as in the Cambridge approach. Otherwise, how can one possibly maintain that these ancient antagonisms "did not need to have, and many did not have, a political existence prior to the creation of the publicist and administrative categories" of the raj?

For insofar as conflicts like those mentioned above existed in precolonial India as a matter of undeniable fact, and they were conflicts between entities related as dominant and subordinate, their political character was affirmed, in all instances, as an articulation of D/S. In other words, there could be no caste or communal conflict under those conditions that was not necessarily political. The emergence of the colonial state and the substantial effect this had on such conflicts, both in assigning new names and categories to them and in generating new strains in some cases, did not amount to the transformation of an apolitical phenomenon into a political one, but to a significant shift from one kind of politics to another. For us, therefore, communalism stands for an important aspect of the historical movement of D/S which cannot be studied in any meaningful way without relating the contemporary processes to what had gone before in ideation and in social practice.

The exclusion of ideas forms a pair, as we have seen, with the exclusion of solidarity from politics. Predictably, therefore, Washbrook sees nothing but "vertical systems of political connection" in communal movements.[164] In northern and eastern India communalism was a mass phenomenon — truly an idea that had gripped the masses — and no explanation based solely on vertical alliance can illuminate its forms and its passions which were so vigorously displayed outside the narrow precincts of union boards, district boards, and legislative assemblies. Such an explanation would, on the one hand, reduce communalism simply to an effect of collaboration between the ruling elite and the indigenous elite and of competition between groups amongst the latter. On the other hand, it would exclude the masses from politics on the ground that such of their activities in a communal movement as had not been prompted by their social superiors amounted merely to "reaching for sticks and stones," while such of their ideas as had not been put into their heads by the elite were simply expressions of what Seal has called "zealotry." Politics, as designed by neo-colonialist historiography, could thus be kept neatly elitist and collaborationist.

Far from providing a "general explanation" of politics of the colonial period, this approach seems to us to be a monistic, reductionist tactic to impoverish politics by an arbitrary expurgation of its mass content and by narrowing it down merely to an interaction between the colonizers and a very small minority of the Indian population made up of the elite. It is monistic because it is designed to contain all of politics within a single elitist domain; because within that domain all initiative is assimilated to a singular "governmental impulse"; because the only response to that impulse it recognizes is self-interest chasing officially designed rewards; and because the only activity it allows for is the collaboration of subordinate with superordinate at every level. With the subaltern domain surgically removed from its system, all initiative other than what emanates from the colonizers and their collaborators strictly ruled out, and all elements of resistance meticulously expelled from its political processes, colonialism emerges from this historiography as endowed with a hegemony which was denied to it by history. The Cambridge approach achieves this feat by an act of bad faith — by writing up Indian history as a "portion of the British History."

IV. Preamble to an Autocritique

To conclude this discussion on a note about its purpose, it should be made clear that nothing of what has been said above is addressed to the practitioners of colonialist historiography in Britain today. We recognize it for a fact that South Asian history of the period between Plassey and Partition continues to be taught, written, and otherwise propagated there, for the most part, as a "portion of the British History" in accordance with the agenda formulated by James Mill. That, so far as we are concerned, is a cultural problem rooted in British society itself. It is up to that society and its intellectuals to deal with it, if they wish to do so.

For that problem is symptomatic of a distemper created by one nation's oppression of another, the consequences of which for the culture of the oppressor nation it is primarily, though not exclusively, for the latter to worry about. To those who, in our part of the world, are condemned to live with the legacy of that oppression as its victims, it is evident that Britain's paramountcy over its South Asian empire has induced its political and intellectual culture thoroughly to absorb the knowledges, techniques, and attitudes which informed and sustained that paramountcy for two hundred years. The result has been to produce a literature still incarnadine with the glow of imperial "achievements," a language that permits racist insults to pass in everyday use as harmless jokes, a pervasive and often violent discrimination against Asians who live in the pores of British society. It is a culture which has iron deposited in its soul, and not all the vigor of a minority of truly anti-imperialist tendencies has succeeded in dissolving it.

There is a possibility — the future can always be trusted to work miracles — that some day, generations from now, Everyman in Britain will no longer take pride in the colonial record of his ancestors and even begin to develop a little embarrassment about it. But it is a safe guess that for a long time yet, during intervals between one Falklands War and another, he will go on contentedly feeding on tales of the raj to sustain his sense of national grandeur. The only critique which can discourage the historian from abetting such spiritual mastication is conspicuous by its absence from the British intellectual scene, even from its radical wing. It is hard to find as much as a twinge of self-critical recognition there of the need to challenge the Mill-Dodwell tradition of writing on India and join issue with the recycling of imperialist historiography by teaching and research at all the major centers of South Asian studies in the United Kingdom. But if that is how academics and other intellectuals of that country want their work on colonial India to stay, that is their problem.

For our part, we present our views on the structure of dominance in colonial India and historiography's relation to it as a critique of our own approach to the Indian past and our own performance in writing about it. The purpose of this work is, therefore, simply to stimulate a degree of self-criticism within the practice of Indian historiography. What calls for such self-criticism is our complicity with colonialist historiography. There has never been a school or tendency in Indian historiography that did not share the liberal assumptions of British writing on the colonial theme. Since the first quarter of the nineteenth century, every mode of Indian historical discourse has conformed faithfully to the rationalist concepts and the ground rules of narrative and analytic procedure introduced in the subcontinent by official and nonofficial British statements on the South Asian past. Systematized and propagated by school manuals and other instruments of a Western-style education, this knowledge helped to free our sense of the past from Puranic thraldom, but committed it at the same time to that fundamental tenet of liberal thought according to which British rule in India was a truly historical realization of the universalist tendency of capital.

This commitment has frustrated all attempts made so far to develop a view of colonial rule and its ruling culture that could be said to have broken away, in any fundamental sense, from the standpoint of colonialist writing on the structure of power relations under the raj. The theories which inform the conceptualization of the colonial state in such writing are the same as those which inform liberal-nationalist historiography as well. Even the militant-nationalist and left-nationalist objections to British presence in the subcontinent imply no departure from such commitment. For one may conceptualize the South Asian colonial state as a measure of British capital's universalist drive in the era of imperialism and still militate against the British connection. The contradiction between indigenous capital and metropolitan capital does not need an alternative theory of state for its representation in historical discourse.

On the contrary, there is good reason for believing that the inability of radical nationalism to act up to its promise as the harbinger of an autonomous historiography has been due to its failure to back its critique of the raj by a theory which makes colonialism and the colonial state understandable as the barrier at which the universalist urge of capital must necessarily stop. Nor, as a consequence, has it been possible for any tendency within our own intellectual practice to come up with a principled and comprehensive (as against eclectic and fragmentary) critique of the indigenous bourgeoisie's universalist pretensions, which are articulated nowhere more prominently and significantly than in its hegemonic, but spurious, claim to speak for the nation and its use of historiography in support of that claim. In short, the price of blindness about the structure of the colonial regime as a dominance without hegemony has been, for us, a total want of insight into the character of the successor regime too as a dominance without hegemony.

It is out of an awareness of such a lacuna in the study of our colonial past that we have proceeded, in this chapter, to examine the nature of dominance and its discourses. This, we hope, may assist in the self-criticism of our own historiography—the historiography of a colonized people—by situating it outside the concave universe of liberal ideology and enabling it thereby to confront its own practice and its own assumptions by asking: What is colonialism as exemplified by British rule in India? What is there in the power relations of that rule which makes the colonial state in our subcontinent so fundamentally different from its architect, the British metropolitan state? Where lies the originality of Indian culture of the colonial era and why does it defy understanding either as a replication of the liberal-bourgeois culture of nineteenth-century Britain or as the mere survival of an antecedent pre-capitalist culture? And how adequate are our representations of that colonial past to any genuine search for an answer to these questions? It is only by negotiating the complexities of such questions that we may be able to move forward towards an autonomous historiography of colonial India—a historiography which will no longer labor under the tutelage of Mill's paradigm.

Why, it may be asked, should this critique of Indian historiography require a critique of colonialist historiography as its preamble? For two reasons, one of which is a function of affinity and the other of opposition. The affinity is historical as well as conceptual. Taking the early nineteenth-century Bangla writing on British rule as a convenient point of departure for any study of the development of our historiography, one can see how closely it was modeled, in its first specimens, on mercantilist writings by the East India Company's soldiers and administrators, and subsequently, on Mill's *History.* That influence had so thoroughly permeated the indigenous historical imagination by the second half of the century that British and Indian narratives of the history of the raj were soon to acquire a family resemblance in spite of a note of incipient nationalism which occasionally slipped in, as, for instance, in the works of Nilmani Basak and Rajanikanta Gupta.[165] But nationalism, even when it became strong and strident as it did by the 1890s, hardly weakened the bond of this initial affinity. On the contrary, the rationalist, evolutionist, and progressivist ideas which had helped to assimilate colonialist historiography to the post-Enlightenment view of world and time were now ushered into Indian historical thinking and implanted there more firmly than ever before by the force of nationalism itself.[166]

Yet it was that very conceptual affinity which was to instigate an antagonism between these kindred modes. For these concepts had a decisive impact on nationalist thought in one of its characteristic drives—namely, its insistence on reclaiming the Indian past. Historiography was one of the two principal instruments—the other being literature—which would henceforth be put to increasingly vigorous use for such reclamation. In other words, historiography would proceed from now on to construct the Indian past as a national past that had been violated and appropriated by colonialist discourse. The indigenous historian's mission to recover that past was therefore to acquire the urgency and vigor of a struggle for expropriating the expropriators.[167]

All of Indian historiography in its dominant, that is, liberal-nationalist mode, has been caught up since its inception in the contradictory pulls of such affinity and opposition. It is therefore not possible either to understand its character or to subject it to a proper criticism without situating it first in the relationship that bonds it to colonialism — a dominance without hegemony — and its historiography. A critique of colonialist historiography is, therefore, an essential condition and a necessary point of departure for any critique of Indian historiography itself.

2

Discipline and Mobilize
Hegemony and Elite Control in Nationalist Campaigns

I. Mobilization and Hegemony

Anticipation of Power by Mobilization

Dominance in colonial India was doubly articulated. It stood, on
the one hand, for Britain's power to rule over its South Asian
subjects, and on the other, for the power exercised by the indigenous elite over the subaltern amongst the subject population itself.
The alien moment of colonialist dominance was matched thus by
an indigenous moment within the general configuration of power.[1]
Common to both was a lack—a lack of hegemony. But this lack
worked in fundamentally different ways in the two instances. With
colonialism, dominance affirmed and realized itself entirely in the
authority of the state. All of the institutional and ideological resources of the latter were at its disposal and indeed used by it in its
attempt to acquire hegemony. Even the liberal-imperialist project
of improvement, which sought so assiduously to persuade the
colonized in favor of the raj, was altogether interventionist in
character. There was nothing about it that was not entirely governmental in concept or practice. Indeed, the more the regime solic-
ited the consent of Indians by measures which gave them no real
choice in decisions supposed to have been made for their own
good, the more it alienated itself as an autocracy singularly incapable of relating to the society on which it had imposed itself.

100

By contrast, for the indigenous bourgeoisie under colonial rule, state power and sovereign governmental authority were no more than aspects of an unrealized project, an aspiration yet to be fulfilled, a dream. The striving for hegemony on the part of this bourgeoisie appeared therefore as an anticipation of power rather than its actualization. However, even as an aspirant, it had to express its hegemonic urge in the form of universality. For, it has been observed, "each new class which puts itself in the place of one ruling before it is compelled, merely in order to carry through its aim, to present its interest as the common interest of all the members of society, that is, expressed in ideal form: it has to give its ideas the form of universality, and present them as the only rational, universally valid ones."[2] But since, in the case under consideration, the new class happened to be a bourgeoisie reared by colonialism, and the rule of the class it hoped to replace was seen as the subjugation of one nation by another, the universality of its aspiration had to express itself inevitably as a nationalism. Inevitably, because the very first language in which the dominated learn to speak of power is that of the dominant. In other words, thanks to the historical conditions of its formation, the Indian bourgeoisie could strive towards its hegemonic aim only by constituting "all the members of society" into a nation and their "common interest" into the "ideal form" of a nationalism.

Now, for any class "to present its interest as the common interest of all the members of society" means, simply, to represent them. But how was such representation to be achieved in a polity which had so completely perverted that process as to degrade it into overt collaboration? For "representation," so called during the greater part of the long history of the raj, amounted to little more than a selective recruitment of collaborators by its bureaucracy. Even when it made some allowance, under pressure, for local and regional elections, these were based on far too fragmented and far too limited a franchise to be representative in the sense carried by that phrase in the lexicon of British parliamentary democracy. The only way the indigenous bourgeoisie could hope therefore to compete for hegemony was to mobilize the people in a political space of its own making—that is, to enlist their support for its programs, activate them in its campaigns and generally organize them under its leadership.

It was such mobilization which, according to that leadership, was what situated Indian nationalism in the world, armed it with a practice and married its concept to its historic project—the project of a South Asian nation-state. Mobilization, it would argue, was the most visible and unquestionable evidence of the fact that the masses had transferred their allegiance from the raj to the nationalist leadership and its party—the Indian National Congress. Mobilization, by this interpretation, was another name for popular consent, for hegemony, for an overwhelming vote of the disenfranchised against an autocracy which had reduced them to second-class citizens in their own land—a vote for self-determination.

It is not surprising therefore that nationalist discourse, in all its dominant modes, should speak of mobilization in the idiom of enthusiasm. Crowds turning up in their hundreds of thousands to listen spellbound to the leaders, column after column of men and women parading through festooned streets singing hymns in honor of the motherland and calling on their compatriots to rally to freedom's flag, people coming forward to donate their properties, their savings, and all other material resources to fighting funds, and the youth giving up the security of home and employment in order to serve as activists in the cause of liberation—all this is the staple of the story of India's struggle for independence written from a nationalist point of view. Its function has been to depict mobilization as that integrated will which had presumably overcome the divisive effects of caste, class, gender, and regional interests in its drive to forge the unity of the nation.

There is an element of poetic justice in this rhetoric. For the valorization of enthusiasm is nationalism's answer to the emphasis on collaboration in colonialist writings on South Asian politics.[3] It explodes the ma-baap myth of a filial attachment on the part of Indians to their rulers. It helps to neutralize the lie that speaks of the promotion of collaborative structures as constitutional reform—a semantic sleight used to dignify measures for imperial control over the subcontinent by a spurious parallelism with the radical constitutional initiatives of nineteenth-century European revolutions.

However, this corrective, so eminently justified on moral grounds, is not without its problems. It tilts too far to the other side by attributing mobilization to the dynamics of enthusiasm alone. Its consequence for historiography is a rewriting which is both elitist and abstract. It is elitist insofar as it feeds on that messianic tendency of nationalist discourse according to which mobilization was the handiwork of prophets, patriarchs, and other inspirational leaders alone and the mobilized were no more than an inert mass shaped by a superior will. It is abstract, too, because it empties mobilization of that very real tension between force and consent from which Indian nationalism acquired its form and substance.

Working for dominance itself and motivated to endow it with hegemony, this historiography makes the contest for the latter too easy as the project of a desire for power, too smooth as a resolution of complex social and political rivalries. For, if hegemony as we understand it is a condition of dominance in which the moment of persuasion outweighs that of coercion,[4] it is self-evident that in striving towards it the leading bloc within Indian nationalism must have met with the resistance of a political culture in which force had been privileged over consent by virtue of an age-old and nearly sacrosanct tradition. To try and document that resistance is to take the first steps—however tentatively, as in the present exercise—towards a study of nationalist mobilization as the history of a struggle for hegemony. We do so by considering some of the disciplinary aspects of the Swadeshi Movement of 1903–1908 and the Non-co-operation Movement of 1920–1922—the first two campaigns of this century in each of which an elite leadership sought to enlist the masses in its opposition to the raj.

The question of hegemony was at the core of both these campaigns. Both were precipitated by official measures which left nothing unsaid about the alien and unrepresentative character of the regime. In both instances the nationalist leadership came forward to speak for the people by mobilizing them in opposition to the government. This was true even for the first of these two movements, which was based on a mobilization much smaller in scale than that for the other and led by politicians far less mature than those who headed the upsurge of the next decade. For with all the differences which were there between the principal tendencies within Swadeshi,[5] all those nuances which made Boycott vary in interpretation and practice from school to school, all that set

Atmashakti (self-reliance) apart from Passive Resistance as a doctrine—all that notwithstanding, nationalists were agreed, in general, about the need to withdraw cooperation from the raj in order
to demonstrate that it did not rule by consent.

Bal Gangadhar Tilak spoke for that common outlook when he
said:

> The whole Government is carried on with our assistance and
> then [the rulers] try to keep us in ignorance of our power of
> co-operation . . . We shall not give them assistance to collect
> revenue and keep peace. We shall not assist them in fighting
> beyond the frontiers or outside India with Indian blood and
> money. We shall not assist them in carrying on the administra-
> tion of justice. We shall have our own courts, and when the time
> comes we shall not pay taxes. Can you do that by your united
> efforts? If you can, you are free from tomorrow.[6]

By mobilizing for a nationalist campaign more or less in line with
such objectives, the Swadeshi leadership tried not only to show up
the colonial state as a dominance that had failed to acquire hegemony. It also gave notice of its own hegemonic ambitions at the same
time.

A Fight for Prestige

Both of these strategic aims were to be affirmed once again and
even more explicitly by the mobilization of 1920–1922 under
Gandhi's leadership. The point he was never tired of reiterating
throughout the Non-cooperation Movement of those years was
that it was a fight for prestige. By refusing to cooperate with the
raj, Indians could, in his opinion, expose the hollowness of its claim
to govern by persuasion and destroy any credit it derived from that
claim. At the same time, by refusing to collaborate with an unjust
and oppressive—the epithet he preferred was "satanic"—regime,
his compatriots might recover some of the self-respect and moral
purity they had lost by allowing themselves to be subjected to
foreign rule. Either way, Non-cooperation was, for him, a struggle
for hegemony, a struggle to prove that coercion exceeded persuasion in the organic composition of Britain's power over India, and

conversely, that the nationalist leadership derived its authority entirely from popular consent.

A controversy over the visit of a member of the British royal family during the campaign illustrates how the contest for hegemony was dramatized by both the contending parties — nationalists and colonialists — as a fight for prestige. The visit, insisted the Government, was to be a purely nonpolitical gesture on the part of the Prince of Wales to keep royalty in touch with its Asian subjects. Gandhi opposed the proposal as soon as he came to know of it and campaigned vigorously against it for about fifteen months until November 1921, when it materialized.

He justified his opposition as a "clear duty of educating [the public] to a truer perception of the meaning of the proposed Royal visit." Truer, because it would refute the not-so-true claim made by the administration about the visit being above politics. "If the Prince is not coming for political reasons," he asked, "why is he coming at all?" The answer, so far as he was concerned, was obvious. Contrary to what they said in public, "the ministers want[ed] to make political capital out of the proposed visit," use it "to demonstrate to the world that under their benign administration the whole of India [was] happy and contented," that "the unrest among the people [was] to be taken as peace," and that "all this talk of their having been hurt [by official violence in Punjab and imperial policy towards the Khilafat was] the work of a few disgruntled men." In short, he concluded, "The Prince is coming here to uphold the prestige of the present Government."[7]

With the "meaning" of the visit established thus as politics calculated "to demonstrate the might and glory of the Empire,"[8] Gandhi called for counter-demonstrations. It was to take the form of a *hartal* throughout the land to coincide with the prince's arrival on 17 November 1921, followed, during the rest of his tour, by local boycotts of all ceremonies, receptions, and other activities organized to celebrate it. Accused by the Secretary of State for India of encouraging disloyalty by such means, he made no secret as to whom he owed his loyalty in the first place. "This is a sign of changed time," he wrote. "Not only do I not see any disloyalty in refusing to welcome the Prince, but I consider it disloyalty towards the people to act otherwise in this difficult predicament."[9] Quite clearly, the time for divided loyalties had come. Faced with a

choice, the nationalist leadership opposed the old loyalism of collaborators by a new loyalty—loyalty to the people, and in doing so
signaled for their support in the ensuing contest for prestige.

Since loyalties were sharply divided and the ground of collaboration was cracking under the impact of an upsurge against
the raj, it was inevitable that something so deeply symbolic of
imperial authority as the presence of a royal personage in the
midst of his subjects should inspire mutually hostile interpretations. It is hardly surprising, therefore, that accounts of the tour
written from imperialist and nationalist standpoints should come
up with radically different views about the event and what it
meant. A comparison of two authorized versions, one of which
was produced by L. F. Rushbrook Williams for the Government
of India and the other by the Civil Disobedience Enquiry Committee [CDEC] for the Indian National Congress, makes this
clear.[10]

The tour, according to Williams, was "a remarkable success"
achieved "despite the whole force of non-co-operation." By contrast, in CDEC's view, it was "the *Hartals* [which] were an unqualified success" in spite of the draconic measures (such as,
"wholesale and indiscriminate arrests and prosecutions under the
Criminal Law Amendment Act, and sections 107, 108 of the Code
of Criminal Procedure and sections 124-A and 153-A of the Indian
Penal Code") used "to secure a quiet atmosphere during the visit
of H[is] R[oyal] H[ighness]." People responded to it, in town and
country, either by abstaining *en masse* from all official functions to
welcome him or by turning up in strength to greet him with defiant
cries shouted in honor of Gandhi. "That splendid thing—the *Hartal*," remarked CDEC in mocking allusion to its description as a
"despicable thing" by a senior bureaucrat, "followed H.R.H. wherever he went."

These estimates about the scale of mobilization for and against
the royal tour were matched by equally contradictory evaluations
of its significance as well. Its value, for Williams, consisted of the
"additional encouragement" it gave to "many substantial elements
of society . . . in their loyalty," which he was quick to identify as
"the deepest feelings of real India." By the same token he saw, in
the so-called "success" of the visit, evidence of "the powerlessness
of the non-co-operators effectively to mar any item of His Royal

Highness' programme" and the disappointment of "those who believed that the non-co-operators spoke for India."

Who spoke for "real" India? CDEC's answer to that question
drew upon the same experience, but put a completely different
political construction on it. The success of what it called "the
memorable All-India *Hartal*" stood for it as "a remarkable manifestation of the determined will of the nation to condemn the exploitation of the Royal Family for political ends." And with that will
distinguished clearly from loyalism, the Enquiry Committee
turned to the crucial question of speaking for the nation—the
question of representation. Joining issue with the Viceroy, who
had said that the protest against the tour "did not represent the real
view of the Indian people" and was brought about only by nationalist "coercion and intimidation," it argued:

> Can it be that despite the strenuous efforts of the representatives
> in India of the "most determined" and "hard fibred people in the
> world" the whole country from end to end throbbed with one
> impulse as a result of the coercion and intimidation employed by
> the handful of those, who, in the words of [the Viceroy] Lord
> Reading, "did not represent the real view of the Indian people,"
> and most of whom were secured behind prison walls? If so, the
> sooner the most determined people in the world withdraw their
> present representatives and entrust their good name to the safe
> keeping of the handful, the better it would be for the future
> happiness and progress of both.

It is not possible to emphasize too much the significance of this
polemic as a rejection of any unitary notion of representation. The
latter occurs in this text under the sign of a splintered hegemony.
"You can't *rule* India as a colonial power and *represent* it at the same
time," it seems to be saying in riposte to the representative of
imperial Britain. "Pack up your bureaucracy and go. For it represents nobody here amongst the colonized people who have constituted themselves as a nation. Their real representatives are the
nationalist leaders and activists whom you have gagged and put
behind the bars. Let them take over."

Thus the question of hegemony shaped up as an issue of central
importance in the politics of Swadeshi and Non-cooperation. How
did their respective leaderships deal with that question? By what

organizational means and ideological tenets did they bring about mobilization in order to make strategic use of it in the battle for hegemony? A historic rupture in the first of these movements offers us a point of entry into the problematic framed by these questions.

II. Swadeshi Mobilization

Poor Nikhilesh

One of the principal leaders of the Swadeshi Movement during its initial phase was the great Indian poet Rabindranath Tagore. In 1906 he led a much publicized demonstration through the streets of Calcutta, singing nationalist hymns and distributing *rakhi* among the crowd. The rakhi, a gaily colored twine used as a wristband in some Hindu communities and lineage groups to celebrate the solidarity of their members, was adopted, for this occasion, as a symbol of unity — unity of the two fragments of Bengal forced apart by the alien rulers, unity of Bengal as a whole and the rest of India — in short, the unity of the nation against the raj, the wicked instrument of division and subjugation. The anti-partition march, which dramatized that will to unity, had a big impact on the agitation. So had Tagore's poems and songs written to celebrate the glory and sanctity of the motherland, and his elegant prose which expounded his thoughts on colonialism and nationalism in a number of political essays. One of these essays, "Swadeshi Samaj," contained the vision of a self-governing and self-reliant nation and formed the core of a patriotic curriculum at all those young people's associations *(samiti)* from which the movement recruited its most dedicated activists. By 1907 Swadeshi enthusiasm had found in him its poet, its philosopher, and its political leader — a Platonic combination par excellence.

When, therefore, within a year or so Rabindranath started back-pedaling and eventually withdrew from politics altogether, he aroused a great deal of hostility. His withdrawal was variously interpreted as capricious (for poets could be notoriously fickle in their attitude to affairs of the world), as irresponsible (for, being rich, he couldn't care less for his people), and as cowardly (because he was against the politics of violence). Sensitive to such criticism, he tried to explain his position in a series of five articles written at the time. And then, in 1916, eight years after the event and five after Bengal had been departitioned, he resumed the debate, making it clear that so far as he was concerned the argument was far from closed. Only, the intervening years had enabled him to cast it imaginatively in the form of a novel called *Gharey Bairey*.[11]

Nikhilesh, the hero of this novel, is an enlightened landlord who, unlike some others of his class, does not oppress his tenant cultivators. He is also a patriot and an idealist, and has been trying for many years even before the advent of Swadeshi to set up Swadeshi-style enterprises, all of which turned out to be much too uneconomical and prone to bankruptcy. Nikhilesh is thus a paragon of virtue — a compound of patriotism, idealism, intellectualism, and unworldliness highly regarded by middle-class Bengalis nurtured on a diet of romantic literature.

Appropriately, our hero has a young, beautiful, and adoring wife, and all goes well until about the middle of Chapter One, when the villain, Sandip, his best friend, arrives on the scene. He resolutely sets about working towards his dual objective — of breaking up Nikhilesh's marriage by trying to seduce his wife, and ruining his estate by turning it into a sort of base area for the Swadeshi campaign. His activists are let loose all over the place, promoting Swadeshi by a technique that includes blackmail, deceit, bullying, assault, and plain robbery. The poorer of the Hindu peasants feel harassed. The Muslims are particularly outraged by the blatant display of Hindu chauvinism on the part of the nationalists. Eventually, Nikhilesh, after he is himself relieved of a great deal of cash by his wife acting under her lover's influence, decides to call it a day, throws Sandip and his gang out of his estate, and prepares to retire to Calcutta himself. But events move far too quickly for him. An anti-Hindu jacquerie, instigated by roving *moulavies*, flares up among his Muslim tenants. He, goes out, unarmed, to pacify them and is gravely wounded. The novel ends with his repentant wife anxiously overhearing a conversation between the estate manager and the family doctor about a body with a battered head.

That head wound was a metaphor for the author's own battered reputation of 1908. For the fate of Nikhilesh reflected his own predicament of the Swadeshi days, when, like his noble but thoroughly misunderstood hero, he too had courted unpopularity by refusing to conform. What concerned both was the individual's freedom to choose his own way of serving the cause of social and political emancipation. If, therefore, patriotism were allowed to base itself on fear and coercion rather than persuasion, that would be altogether self-defeating for the national cause.

Caste Sanctions

Coercion had already established itself as a means of mobilization for Swadeshi quite early in the campaign. A dossier compiled in 1909 by the Director of Criminal Intelligence cites several hundred cases,[12] some of them going back to 1905. These were of two kinds. First, there was a massive indulgence in physical coercion aimed at the destruction of imported goods as well as intimidation and assault of those who bought, sold, or otherwise patronized such imports or cooperated with the administration as active opponents of the movement. It goes without saying that no mobilization based on such violence could have any claim to popular consent. We shall therefore move on to consider the implications of the other, less obvious if no less sinister, kind of coercion—social coercion—which directly addressed the mind and destroyed persuasion at its source. Reported in large numbers both by the police and the contemporary press, coercion such as this came in the form of caste sanctions which meant, in effect, withdrawal of ritual services, refusal of inter-dining, boycott of wedding receptions and funeral ceremonies, and other pressures amounting to partial or total ostracism of those considered guilty of deviation from Swadeshi norms.

Social coercion was, for Tagore, at least as obnoxious as physical coercion. To him as to many other liberals Swadeshi, with its emphasis on self-help, self-cultivation, and self-improvement, was less of a struggle for power than a social reform movement of exceptionally lofty character. Its purpose was to unite all in an endeavor to liberate society from thraldom precisely to those conservative and obscurantist institutions, values, and customs which authorized caste sanction. The latter, he said in an outspoken essay, was as "conducive to the perpetuation of spiritual servitude" as the propagation of Swadeshi by the threat of arson or assault.[13]

The use of caste sanction is indeed basic to Hindu orthodoxy. It constitutes the most explicit and immediate application of what is regarded by some as a governing principle of the caste system, namely the opposition between purity and pollution. If therefore it transpires, as it does from the evidence, that mobilization for the Swadeshi Movement relied on caste sanction to no mean extent, it should help us to grasp the character of Indian nationalism itself as a tissue of contradictions with its emancipatory and unifying urge resisted and modified significantly by the disciplinary and divisive forces of social conservatism.

The incidence of sanction as documented in the intelligence reports mentioned above is quite striking in its geographical distribution. It shows that most of the cases were reported from small, sleepy villages located far in the outback. That is quite clearly an index of the grassroots character of the movement, the religiosity of which was perhaps in no small measure a function of its rusticity. Taken together with the fact that sanctions were more numerous in the politically more active districts (generally speaking, the eastern districts of Bengal as compared to the western ones), this would appear to suggest a fairly high correlation between nationalism and casteism.

The implication is even more disturbing when one takes into account the fact that the available statistics are far from complete and grossly underestimate the phenomenon. For the total number of sanctions must have been far in excess of the number reported. Being subjected to caste discipline was a stigma that put a Hindu to shame. Attached to an individual or a family, it had a tendency to outlive formal absolution. One would rather not report such a thing to the law, for to do so would be to let the local grapevine magnify the offense many times its original size. And, more often than not, the sanction would be such as to make it impossible for any court to take cognizance of it in legal terms. As an ill-humored note scribbled by a Home Department official on the memorandum mentioned above reads: "Cases of social boycott did not come before the courts."[14] We are not surprised.

The quality of evidence is, however, extremely rich and can be used to throw much light on the nature of the offenses which called for caste sanction. These fall into three classes, each of which may be said to correspond to a category of offense punishable according to the canon of sanatan Hinduism. The first of these includes what would be subsumed, under that tradition, within the broad category of *patakas* (sins) arising from the violation of dharma (as by a breach of rules forbidding incest or theft or slaughter of cows) and *acara* (by the transgression, for instance, of such duties as those related to the daily routine of bath, meditation, and worship, or to ritually prescribed services, and so on).

Under the Swadeshi conditions, too, violations of dharma and acara were regarded as equally culpable. Only, these terms had now acquired an entirely new range of connotations. These were political connotations according to which loyalty to the motherland qualified as an instance of dharma, while certain demonstrative aspects of nationalist behavior assumed the sanctity of acara. Caste sanction was therefore imposed on those who were considered guilty of violating the new dharma of patriotism because they continued to work for the alien regime as police officials, prosecuting lawyers, crown witnesses, and in other equally despicable roles, or had failed as landlords in their duty to ban the sale of foreign goods within their estates, as grocers—to stop retailing Liverpool salt, and so forth. Among the victims, too, were those who could be said to have transgressed the new acara by refusing to go through the ritual of oath-taking in support of Swadeshi or wear rakhi on the wrist as a token of solidarity with the campaign.

A second class of offenses were those which resulted from impurities acquired from contact with unclean objects. Taken strictly according to the traditional Hindu norm of purity, the number of such objects could be legion. These could range all the way from human excreta or spittle to shorn hair to food cooked by a person lower than ego in the caste hierarchy, or a glass of alcoholic drink, or even a garment left unwashed after being worn overnight. The list could vary considerably from area to area, and the local lists could be quite different from, though not necessarily shorter than, those given in the Dharmaśāstras.

The ancient law-givers often operated by what was known as *tādrūpya*—the rule of resemblance—in order to extend the scope of sin and impurity to allow, in effect, a modification of established blacklists by the addition of some new items and omission of some of the older ones. A highly creative exercise in tādrūpya did indeed occur during the Swadeshi Movement when foreign manufactures of all kinds, including those from Germany and Austria, were put on a par with British imports and regarded as impure by analogy. These included umbrellas, glass bangles and chimneys for paraffin lanterns, chinaware, canvas and patent-leather shoes, colored prints, cigarettes, sugar, salt, and cotton textiles.

The last three items had the stigma doubly rubbed into them: they were impure not merely because of their alien origin but also because the salt and the sugar were believed to have been adulterated with ground cow-bone powder, while the Manchester textiles were said to have been made out of yarn processed with the fat and blood of the same sacred species. These substances were regarded as a most serious source of pollution, for they presupposed the slaughter of cows—a grave sin for a Hindu to commit or condone. Thus the Swadeshi idea of impurity associated with what was foreign *(bilati)* was reinforced by a traditional notion of impurity associated with what was sacrilegious. The ambivalence these objects acquired as being offensive in terms of politics as well as of religion corresponded to the dual manner of the pollution they caused: physically, as unclean things which contaminated those who ate, wore, touched, or otherwise came into direct contact with them; and politically, as imported goods which it was unpatriotic and against the economic doctrine of Swadeshi to buy, sell, or consume.

A third class of anti-Swadeshi offenses included those which were regarded as transitive, like the traditional caste offenses, and called for sanction against the offender even at several removes away from the source of pollution. Pollution by *saṃsarga*, that is contact or association (for instance, with such unclean objects as those mentioned above), is elaborately prescribed by most of the Dharmaśāstras, although the texts often differ in their classification of such contacts. Some would organize them into nine categories, others into three, and so on. Where they all seem to agree is to ascribe a high degree of transitivity to such contamination. As the *Parāśara-Mādhavīya*, a fourteenth-century text, put it rather graphically: "Sins spread like drops of oil on water" *(saṃkrāmanti hi pāpāni tailavindurivāmbhasi)*.

Transitivity of this order was not altogether unknown under the Swadeshi conditions. It is indeed on record that individuals who refused to withdraw their ritual services from people excommunicated for anti-national activities were themselves excommunicated.[15] The offenders, in most of these cases, were Brahmans. Authorized by tradition to officiate at Hindu religious ceremonies, they polluted themselves by acting as priests for those who traded in foreign goods and had thus been contaminated by the impurity of their merchandise. The relative infrequency of this particular kind of offense was a sign, no doubt, of the regime of castes losing some of its ancient vitality. Yet it is an interesting reflection on the calibre and quality of this phase of nationalism that it could find any use at all for such a measure of caste discipline.

Social Boycott

The manner in which offenders of all three categories were disciplined shows how deeply casteism had penetrated Swadeshi mobilization. The name by which that discipline came to be known was "social boycott." It linked itself by this name to the central strategy of the campaign, that is, the boycott of foreign goods, and sought its justification in the authority of a nationalism poised to challenge the hegemonic pretensions of the raj. At the same time, by a play on the word *samaj,* Bangla for "society," the designation made that discipline into a concern of the micro-society of jati or caste which, in most of its numerous denominations, had a samaj or caste council to deal with those of its members who violated its code. Heedless of what a maturing nationhood could do, in theory, to undermine primordial caste formations, social boycott set out to serve the interests of the big society that was the nation by insisting on procedures used by the little society of castes to resist innovation and change. A look at the measures by which social boycott was imposed should make this clear.

Under the sanatan conditions, each of these measures would stand for an authoritative form of penalty imposed by a Brahman or a king or a caste council against anyone violating dharma or acara or the rules of purity in one form or another. A common form of punishment, not altogether unknown in the West, was to shave the hair off an offender's head. Unlike in the West, however, depilation, according to the Hindu tradition, was not merely punitive but also expiative. An element of ritual expiation was quite pronounced in both the cases we have on record. In one, the offender was a shopkeeper excommunicated for selling goods of foreign make. On pleading for redress, he was ordered by his caste association to pay a fine of two hundred rupees, shave his head, and vow never to deal again in such merchandise.[16]

The other instance involved a trader who had sold a piece of English textile for about half the price of an indigenous fabric of the same quality. When a group of schoolboys raided his shop in protest against underselling bilati products against those which had originated in national enterprise, he happened inadvertently to strike a Brahman youth with a shoe in the ensuing melee. The local Swadeshi leaders retaliated by ostracizing him and setting up a picket to stop all transactions at his shop. At a meeting held soon afterwards he was made to apologize to those boys, donate a part of his stock of imported cotton goods for burning in public, and have his head shaved as punishment for beating up a Brahman.[17]

In the first of these cases, the authority of a caste association made the readmission of one of its members conditional on shaving his head—a punitive ritual meant to redeem the offender from pollution incurred by sinning. In the other case, the prescription might have been lifted out of the ancient law books. For causing hurt to a Brahman—and that too by an instrument as mean and impure as a shoe made of leather—was considered a *mahāpātaka* (grave sin) for a member of any other caste. Tonsure was a vital part of the expiation required to absolve a person of sins of this order. It is indeed a measure of our advance into modernity that the offending shopkeeper was allowed to get away with an apology, a fine, and a thoroughly clean shave, and was not in fact forced to offer a cow or its price in gold to everyone of an assembly of ten thousand Brahmans as the strictly shastric condition of his return to a state of purity.

Some of the instances of social boycott had to do with commensality. Cooked food was a potent carrier of pollution. For a member of any caste, therefore, inter-dining was permissible only within a prescribed range of the hierarchical relationship. The contact established through a meal between host, guest, cook, and dispenser of food had to be such as to guarantee freedom from impurity for all concerned. An invitation to dinner was therefore a highly sensitive and responsible act. It was a device for the host to claim legitimacy for whatever ritual he had undertaken to perform; it was also the guest's privilege and obligation to confer or withhold such legitimacy by accepting or refusing the invitation. A funeral cere-mony and a wedding would both require legitimation by commen-sality: in the first case, to indicate social recognition of the fact that a state of ritual impurity had indeed been terminated, and in the second, to put the seal of social approval on the most recent cou-pling forged within a caste network.

Such approval had sometimes to be dearly bought by opponents of the Swadeshi cause. This is illustrated by the case of the police officer whose "Hindu brethren" would not dine at his house and thereby authorize his daughter's wedding until he made a gift of a thousand rupees to compensate some local activists for the fines the courts had imposed on them.[18] Again, a boycott of funeral ceremonies was, in all the reported instances, directed at patrons of imported goods. Brahmans and other guests refused to attend some of these ceremonies held by villagers who had been found guilty of buying Manchester cloth and fined by a nonofficial board of arbitration. In at least one of these cases the pressure worked: the offender paid up and the ceremony was allowed to proceed.[19] But in another, some Brahmans took exception to guests who had turned up in clothes made of bilati cotton. The upholders of Swadeshi stopped the ceremonial meal by spitting on the food cooked for the occasion and defiling it, for spittle is a notorious agent of pollution.[20] The link between commensality and Swadeshi was made quite explicit on yet another occasion by the refusal of patriotic villagers in a part of Dhaka district to attend a wedding banquet where a number of police officials had been invited as well. One could not dine with traitors, they said. The banquet had to be called off.[21]

Liberal Politics, Traditional Bans

The largest single class of specified sanctions constituted the denial of the services of five professional groups. In view of the popularity of this measure it would not be too wild a guess, perhaps, to suggest that most of the unspecified sanctions in the official dossier were also of the same kind. These were reported from every-where — from Calcutta, from the mofussil towns, and from villages in most of the districts. Sanctioning authorities of all denominations—professional groups and local elite, caste associations and nationalist organizations—appear to have reached out for this particular form of social boycott more often than any other as if by some tacit agreement.

No less curious is the fact, which may not be left without comment, that this pernicious and illiberal measure was advocated openly and repeatedly by many of the principal leaders of the movement, including Surendra Nath Banerji, Aswinikumar Datta, and Aurobindo Ghosh,[22] all of whom had been schooled in liberal thought as a part of their upbringing. That they should not only condone but actively promote this kind of social sanction makes one wonder whether Indian liberalism, thanks to the rather peculiar condition of its development within colonial power relations, did not indeed belong to an ideological and cultural category altogether distinct from its Western prototype.

The services denied included those of the priest, the barber, and the washerman. These were regarded as amongst the most indispensable of purifying agencies in Hindu society. From the moment a child was conceived to the moment the last guest departed from a funerary feast, there was no ritual occasion of any importance that would not be mediated by members of one or more of these communities. Their combined operations alone could guarantee the removal of impurities which, within the caste system, accreted all the time and required, therefore, the services of these specialist groups to function, in effect, as a set of well coordinated, automatic wipers. Hence, to deny such services was to trap a Hindu irretrievably in a state of impurity. And since status within the caste hierarchy related critically to the degree of one's freedom from ritual uncleanliness, the imposition of this discipline could condemn its victim to total excommunication. No wonder that those who wanted Swadeshi to win out in a short and swift campaign settled on this device as their most favored weapon.

The list is dominated by priests. They were responsible for imposing more than a third of all social boycott: sanction in eighteen out of the fifty reported cases listed in Table 1 was executed by sacerdotal means. This is significant and requires an explanation in terms of two factors, neither of which can be considered at great length within the scope of this chapter. First, this is an

indication of what I believe to be the resurgence of priestcraft
(pourohitya) that had been gathering strength throughout the second half of the nineteenth century—a phenomenon which, if properly investigated and substantiated by research, may dim the
luminosity of the so-called Bengal Renaissance to a considerable
extent. Secondly, it is also a measure of the Brahman's pre-emi-
nence in Hindu revivalism so conspicuous in Bengal during the
fifty years before the First World War. In all contributions to this
ideology, whether from Bankimchandra Chattopadhyay,
Dwarakanath Vidyabhusan, or Rabindranath Tagore—to mention
three shades respectively of right, center, and left liberalism—the
image of the Brahman was promoted as that of the mentor and
warden of Hindu society.

The importance acquired by this caste at local levels of the
campaign was very remarkable indeed. Not the most literate
amongst the bhadralok elite, whose politicization in this period was
supposed to have resulted directly from Western-style education,
nor by any means the most numerous amongst the militants involved actively in nationalist activities, the Brahmans still shared
the movement's leadership on a par with the other two groups at
the top of the Hindu social hierarchy in Bengal, namely Kayasthas
and Baidyas. For what they lacked in other respects was made up
by the ritual authority they alone could exercise to confer purity
on those who had polluted themselves by some breach of the
Swadeshi code. In the prevailing political climate, therefore, the
use of such authority to withhold priestly services from doubters
and defectors proved as effective as any other based on education
and activism. There were, of course, other communities such as
those of tradesmen and agriculturists, who too tried to act as
cohesive political groups with regard to Swadeshi. But they did so
in order to defend themselves against the pressures exerted by an
increasingly assertive nationalist culture. The Brahmans, on the
contrary, acted as a caste that put the pressure on.

Doctors and lawyers too emulated the traditional service castes
by refusing to work for patients and clients opposed to Swadeshi.[23]
Strictly speaking, this was not an instance of caste sanction in the
sense discussed so far. For these modern professional groups,
made up of members of many different communities and trained
for the most part in liberal vocational institutions (that is, barring

those who still practiced medicine according to the Ayurvedic tradition), had no ritual function whatsoever. The pressure they brought to bear upon those regarded as unpatriotic could do nothing, therefore, to condemn the latter to a state of impurity. However, with the political ethos soaked so thoroughly in Hinduism and the discrimination between purity and pollution established as a defining principle of nationalist conduct, a traditional disciplinary idiom had no difficulty in translating even some of the liberal professions identified with modernity and secularism for its own use.

The translation was helped by many factors. First, the elite groups which usually acted as the highest tribune for all decisions concerned with caste discipline were identified in the popular mind precisely with those who dominated the medical and legal professions as well. In other words, the sanctioning authority was perceived to be the same in both cases and that, in the given context, made the sanctions look rather similar. This was particularly true of the lawyers. In the politically more active districts they often operated as a well-knit nationalist force, with the local Bar Association assuming some of the functions of caste councils and advising priests, barbers, and washermen not to serve those considered guilty of deviation from the Swadeshi code.

Secondly, the hardship caused by the withdrawal of professional services matched caste sanction in severity, and there was not much point for the victims to distinguish between their separate effects. Any denial of the little that was available as medical care was therefore a source of considerable anxiety to communities, which were as short of drugs and doctors as they were chronically and pervasively racked by disease. A boycott by lawyers too could seriously hurt. The scale and complexity of the judicial system introduced by the raj had created a massive demand for their knowledge of the law and its institutional procedures. Consequently, it was very much in their power to harass a person by denying him counsel, and worse, by involving him in the most inextricable of legal tangles.

In practice, however, none of these bans ever worked by itself. On the contrary, it was customary for a nationalist rally to call upon all the five professions—that is, priests, barbers, washermen, doctors, and lawyers—to boycott the opponents of Swadeshi in a

Table 1. Cases of Actual or Threatened Withdrawal of Services by Professional and Ritual Agencies from Clients Opposed to Swadeshi[a]

District	Lawyer	Doctor	Brahman	Washerman	Barber	TOTAL
Backergunge	2	0	0	0	0	2
Bankura	1	0	1	0	1	3
Bogra	0	0	1	0	0	1
Burdwan	1	1	1	0	0	3
Calcutta	1	1	2	2	2	8
Chittagong	0	0	1	0	0	1
Dacca	1	0	2	2	2	7
Dinajpur	2	1	0	0	0	3
Hoogly	0	0	2	0	0	2
Howrah	0	0	0	1	1	2
Khulna	1	0	1	0	0	2
Midnapore	1	1	1	0	0	3
Mymensingh	0	0	1	1	0	2
Nadia	1	1	2	0	0	4
Noakhali	0	0	1	0	0	1
Pabna	1	0	2	0	0	3
Rajshahi	1	0	0	0	0	1
Sylhet	0	0	0	1	1	2
TOTAL	13	5	18	7	7	50

[a]For the most part, social boycott managed to evade the law and no more than the tip of an iceberg has been made visible for us by our source, the Home Department compilation. Even there, out of the total number of reported instances, only 50 from 18 districts specify the professional and/or ritual agencies withdrawn to enforce boycott.

given area, so that the sanctions imposed according to this advice would all be seen as parts of a single patriotic measure to mobilize an entire local society dependent on such services.

Swadeshi by Coercion or Consent?

It was thus that the ancient and conservative ideology of caste came to be grafted on a developing nationalism supposed to be modern and progressive in concept. The paradox prompted Rabindranath Tagore to interrogate the very character of Swadeshi mobilization and ask how far it was based on popular consent at all. In an article published in 1908, when the campaign was still full of vigor, he denounced its reliance on coercion and the alienating impact this

had on the masses it claimed to enthuse and activate.[24] His objection
to the use of force and plea for persuasion read, in part, as a defense
of the humanist and religious ideals—*manushyatva* and dharma—he
cherished so much.[25] But this assimilation of hegemony to morality,
which anticipated some aspects of Gandhian thought by a decade,
did little to hide the central political concern of his argument about
the movement's adequacy to its project of legitimizing itself by
popular consent.

Rabindranath focused on this question without allowing any
legalistic distinctions between physical and mental coercion to
influence his notion of violence, which included, for him, the use
of force in any form whatsoever. It made little difference whether
a boycott of imports was brought about by threats against person
and property or by caste sanction.[26] On this he was presumably
less inclined to compromise than even the Calcutta police chief,
according to whom it was simply a case of "inducement . . . by
argument and not by force" for Swadeshi propaganda to warn a
"purchaser or would-be purchaser" that by patronizing foreign
goods he would "drink the blood of his father or mother and would
practically kill a lac of Brahmins."[27] These were acts of mahāpātaka, the gravest order of sinning, which the shastras punished,
if not by death, by total excommunication from society, condemn-
ing the sinner to a living death. That was the ultimate form of
violence which could be perpetrated against a human being. From
Rabindranath's point of view, therefore, to pronounce a purchaser
of *bideshi* or foreign goods as guilty of mahāpātaka was to subject
him to the most inhuman use of force.

The pervasive use of social boycott and other forms of coercion
was therefore regarded by him as evidence of the Swadeshi activists' failure to persuade people to rally to their cause. "We have not
been patient enough to work our way gradually towards winning
popular consent," he wrote.[28] That, according to him, defeated the
very aim of the movement, which was to unite all Indians in a
grand patriotic mobilization. As he observed without any attempt
to conceal his bitterness: "To enforce unity on a person by twisting
his neck can hardly be called an act of union; nor, by the same
token, can the use of threat or journalistic slander to stop any
public airing of disagreement be regarded as working for national
unification."[29]

Going by this verdict, mobilization for the first nationalist campaign of this century proved to be of little help to the hegemonic aspirations of its leadership. The verdict was all the more telling for being pronounced by one who had done more than any other of its leaders to generate the enthusiasm of its initial phase. It did not go unchallenged, of course. But even the most closely argued rejoinder, like that of Aurobindo Ghosh,[30] was less than adequate as an answer to Rabindranath's critique. Concerned mainly to shift the ground of the debate to one about the justification of violence in tactical, moral, and theological terms, Aurobindo and other opponents of Tagore failed to address the question at issue, namely, the balance of force and consent in nationalist practice. But the question would not go away. Only it had to wait for the next wave of anti-imperialist struggle and a historic change of leadership to re-inscribe itself in political discourse.

III. Mobilization for Non-cooperation

Social Boycott in Non-cooperation

Between the end of the Swadeshi Movement of 1903–1908 and the great upsurge of the post-World War I years Indian nationalism came of age, and it was the sign of a growing maturity that mobilization for its next mass campaign in 1920–1922 was no longer critically dependent on caste sanctions. But since the culture which informed such sanctions was the clay that nationalism itself was made of, social boycott continued inevitably to feature as a tactic at the local level. It became important enough to call for Gandhi's intervention again and again—about ten times, on a rough count—between March 1920 and February 1922.[31] And, as with many other questions in which morality tangled with politics during this campaign, he improvised a policy by adjusting his stand on first principles to the quickening pace of events.

"Non-co-operation does not apply to services under private individuals," he wrote in March 1920; "I cannot approve of the threat of ostracism against those who do not adopt the remedy of non-co-operation." But this categorical objection was to be modified, within weeks, by an appraisal of the force of circumstance. Indeed, he conceded that "the possibility of non-violent social ostracism under certain extreme conditions" could not be altogether ruled out.[32]

He recalled how "in South Africa in the initial stages of the passive resistance campaign those who had fallen away were ostracized." In India, where "social boycott [was] an age-old institution" and "coeval with caste," it derived much of its force from the tradition of consensual politics in small, "self-contained" rural societies. But such near unanimity, when "occasions of recalcitrancy were rare," no longer obtained. Quite to the contrary, "opinion is divided, as it is today, on the merits of non-co-operation." He would therefore do nothing to give up his opposition to social boycott.

However, he was realistic enough to concede that "ostracism to a certain extent [was] impossible to avoid" and sought to control the damage this could do to the current campaign by insisting on a distinction between "social boycott" and "political boycott." Urged for guidance by a Congress leader of Sind where "several Hindu non-co-operators" had discussed social boycott but felt they could not approve of it, Gandhi advised by telegram: "Will certainly dissuade people against *social as distinguished from political boycott.* Hold latter absolutely necessary."

The distinction, elaborated over the next six months in a number of articles in English and Gujarati,[33] amounted to an opposition between political boycott and social boycott formulated as one between civility and incivility, between love and hate, between a tactic of dissociating voluntarily from persons subjected to boycott and that of imposing punitive sanctions on them. Thus: "Boycott is of two kinds, civil and uncivil. The former has its roots in love, the latter in hatred. In fact, hatred is another name for uncivil boycott . . . The underlying idea in civil boycott is that of refraining from accepting any services from or having any social association with the person concerned. The idea behind the other form is to inflict punishment and pain."[34]

All sanctions which led, in current practice, to the denial of medical care, of access to wells and ponds, and of customary services such as those of the village barber and washerman—the much dreaded, because ritually polluting, *naudhobi bandh*—were classified by Gandhi as social boycott. Sanctions of this kind outraged him. The refusal of a local doctor to attend to an opponent of Non-cooperation who had fallen ill was denounced by him as "inhumanity tantamount in the moral code to an attempt to murder." To debar anyone from the use of public wells was, he said, "a species of barbarism." Generally speaking, he regarded all acts of social boycott as "unpardonable violence" which, "if persisted in," was "bound to destroy the [Non-cooperation] movement."[35]

In sharp contrast to such measures adopted to punish the opponents of Non-cooperation, the aim of political boycott was, for nationalists, to court self-deprivation. Concretely, "it means refusing to accept water or food at such [a boycotted] person's place and entering into no marriage connection with his family." In doing so, wrote Gandhi, "We do not want to punish [the person concerned]; we want, rather, to express our own grief by refusing to associate with him."[36]

However, as the history of Non-cooperation was soon to testify, the rules of discrimination so ingeniously laid down by Gandhi did not altogether stop "civil" boycott from slipping into the "uncivil." The thin line of morality separating the two "ideas" was smudged again and again in practice as non-cooperators, bent on "refraining from accepting any services from or having any social association with" their opponents, were induced by tradition and local pressure to resort precisely to those punitive acts which were so abhorred by their leader.

Such failure on his followers' part to measure up to the prescribed standards of morality had perhaps not a little to do with a logical flaw in the distinction made by Gandhi to stop such slippages from occurring. "The alternative to social boycott," he had insisted, was "certainly not social intercourse." For "a man who defies strong, clear public opinion on vital matters is not entitled to social amenities and privileges." He had then gone on to distinguish these "social amenities and privileges" from "social service," the denial of which constituted social boycott in his opinion.[37] But judging by what those amenities and privileges were according to Gandhi himself, it is not difficult to understand why any concerted effort at dissuading people from their use could easily degenerate into social boycott under the given conditions.

Instances of "social amenities and privileges" specified by him included a person's right to seek the appropriate "marriage connections" for his family, host "social functions such as marriage feasts," entertain guests on other occasions involving commensality, confer ceremonial gifts, and so forth.[38] Now, in traditional Hindu society—and the traditions concerned were still very strong in the 1920s—a wedding feast and a ceremonial gift were obligations rather than "amenities and privileges" for the host and the donor. A marriage had to rely on commensality for its validation, a funeral ceremony on gifts made to Brahmans. Contrary to what Gandhi suggested, there was little that could be said to be "optional" about these. The codes governing such social conduct were binding almost to the point of inviolability. For host and guest, donor and donee were ritual partners meant to help each other play their roles on such occasions by their reciprocal functions.

Nothing could therefore be more punishing for the host than to be boycotted by those he had invited to his feast, or for a donor than to have his *dakṣiṇā* (ceremonial gift) turned down by Brahmans. Want of reciprocity would, in both cases, so gravely impair the ritual legitimacy of wedding and funeral as to call for caste sanctions—that is, precisely those punitive measures which constituted social boycott. If withdrawal from relationships based on intermarriage, inter-dining, and exchange of gifts was political boycott, it is difficult to see how, with the cultural imperatives of the time being what they were, it could have been any less coercive than social boycott.

No wonder then that in spite of Gandhi's concern to keep social boycott out of Non-cooperation, it continued to defy his exorcising authority throughout the campaign. It was reported (occasionally with some exaggeration,[39] which did little to reduce its significance as a tradition militating against Gandhian doctrine) from Hyderabad in Sind and from Amraoti and Jhansi in Central India, from Calcutta and Delhi, from Sultanpur, Pratapgarh and Jhajjar in UP, from the Mahatma's own stamping-ground in the Patidar country of his native Gujarat, and even from the model district of Bardoli chosen by him to set an example of nonviolent Non-cooperation for all others to emulate.[40]

Indeed, he was honest enough to acknowledge its persistence and went so far as to ascribe the violence of demonstrations against the royal visit in Bombay to a certain "subtle coercion" which had never ceased to trail his campaign. In an article published within a week of those riots in November 1921, he spoke of them in a metaphor of morbidity, which for all of its obvious symptoms had not been properly attended to and turned malignant. "There was social persecution, there was coercion," he wrote. "I must confess that I did not always condemn it as strongly as I might have . . . We soon mended our ways, we became more tolerant, but the subtle coercion was there. I passed it by as I thought it would die a natural death. I saw in Bombay that it had not. It assumed a virulent form on the 17th [of November]."[41]

An admission such as this was of course a measure of Non-cooperation's failure to reach the high moral ground its leader had marked out for it. However, judged by any standard other than that of his perfectionist ideal of spiritualized politics, the historical achievement of the campaign far outweighed the flaw, which amounted only to a marginal use of social boycott in its mobilization. How marginal can be readily grasped from the fact that the incidence of social boycott had been much higher in the Swadeshi Movement, even though it fell far short of Non-cooperation both in its territorial scope and mass support. But more than any quantitative consideration, it was the attitude of their respective leaderships to this sanction which made for a difference in the quality of the two campaigns.

Social boycott was condoned and indeed quite actively promoted by most of the Swadeshi leaders (with the possible exception of Rabindranath Tagore),[42] whereas it persisted in Non-cooperation, not by virtue of any encouragement from Gandhi, but in spite of unrelenting opposition on his part. The significance of this contrast cannot be emphasized too much. For it was the measure of a new self-confidence which the nationalist leadership of the previous decade had conspicuously lacked. A look at the ground of Gandhi's objection to social boycott should make this clear.

Gandhi's Opposition to Social Boycott

The reason Gandhi gave for his disapproval of this form of sanction played, as always, on two registers at the same time—the moral and the political. The channel noise which this generated so often could be misleading: an audience predisposed to look for the spiritual alone in all he said could miss the politics of his message.

But that is easily recovered by any close reading, say, of passages like the following, where he answers the charge that opponents of the campaign were subjected to ritual pollution by having the services of sweepers (known as the Bhangi in some parts) withdrawn from them.

> How can we dissuade *Bhangis* and others from serving our brethren who, holding views different from ours, enter Councils? We wish to win over everybody through love . . . we do not want to force anybody to be on our side but want to propagate our views by awakening people's reason and pleading with them. Non-co-operation springs not from hatred but from love, not from weakness but from strength, not from falsehood but from truth, not from blind faith but from faith based on knowledge, from enlightened judgement and from reason; it does not spring from adharma but from dharma, from faith in oneself.[43]

The mixture of politics and ethics in this passage leaves much of the running to be done no doubt by the latter, which is phrased here in terms of polarities such as love and hate, falsehood and truth, adharma and dharma, and so on—all very evocative of *Hind Swaraj*. Yet this does not prevent a secular political intention from shining through. *Against* the use of force *for* an appeal to reason, *against* blind faith *for* enlightened judgment, it is a statement that means to affirm the primacy of persuasion in nationalist strategy.

The theme of persuasion runs through all of Gandhi's writings on social boycott. Painfully aware of the fact that Non-cooperation with all its apparent success had still to overcome a large body of dissent, he cautioned his followers against any temptation to act from a position of strength and cut corners by the use of force. "The rule of majority, when it becomes coercive, is as intolerable as that of a bureaucratic minority," he wrote. "We must patiently try to bring round the minority to our view by gentle persuasion and argument."[44] The point was to engage in "a programme of propaganda" in order to "try patiently to convert our opponents," concede to them "the freedom we claim for ourselves" and "evolve a spirit of democracy" thereby.[45] The campaign and all its reformist initiatives such as those against the sale and consumption of alcohol had to rely exclusively on "public opinion."[46] For it was only by persuading the public to side with the nationalist cause that "the battle of non-co-operation" could be won.

That, as we have already discussed, was a battle for prestige. The alien government was eager to acquire prestige by recruiting collaborators, parading them as truly representative Indians, and flaunting their support as evidence of a rule based on consent. Since it was the law courts and legislative councils which provided collaboration with its armature, a total boycott of these institutions was regarded by Gandhi as the most effective means of undermining the prestige of the raj. Non-cooperation had, in his view, "greatly demolished the prestige of law courts and to that extent of the Government."[47] The same, he believed, would be the fate of the loyalist councillors too, if their constituents made no "use of the services of those whom they [had] declined to regard as their representatives" and decided, in a gesture of political boycott, "to refrain from giving these [so-called] representatives any prestige by attending their political functions or parties."[48]

Non-cooperation was designed thus as a counter-hegemonic strategy by its leadership. Its aim was, on the one hand, to mobilize the masses in order to destroy the structures of collaboration by which colonialism had hoped to endow its dominance with hegemony. On the other hand, it was essential for that mobilization to be based on persuasion in order to entitle the nationalist elite to speak for all of Indian society. The instrument which was to promote that counter-hegemonic strategy on behalf of the leading bloc was the Indian National Congress. Its function, defined in Gramscian terms, was to serve as the organ by which the bourgeoisie would want to exercise its "leadership before winning governmental power."[49]

Cast in that role, the Congress was made to stand forth as a supra-class representative of the nation. Its leaders were ever so keen to paint it in the image of an organization subsuming all other organizations, parties and interest groups — "the only truly national political organization in the country," as Gandhi put it.[50] Nehru too was equally emphatic about the all-embracing character of his party. "The Congress," he declared, "claims to speak for *India as a whole* . . . That is to say what it demands is not for any particular group or community but for *the nation as a whole*."[51] Since the nation was imagined thus as an integer and the Congress as "the only truly national political organization," its primacy was established by definition, for the whole is greater than any of its parts. Consequently, its claim to speak for the nation carried with it a concomitant claim of superiority to all other organizations in every respect.

It was, according to its leaders, the biggest and the best. "The Congress," said Nehru, "is by far the biggest mass organization in the country . . . far and away the most powerful and the most widespread organization in India . . . Other organizations are not even bad seconds."[52] It was also the most effective—"the only organization that appeals to the nation . . . the one organization which . . . can without doubt secure freedom for the nation," wrote Gandhi in 1929.[53] "No other body besides the Congress can solve the Indian question and take us towards the goal," echoed Nehru. It was obviously not enough for him that the Congress was "the dominant organization in the country." Its "predominance" had to be projected on a world scale as well: "There is hardly any national body in the world to match the Congress."[54]

Corresponding to such dominance, Nehru's own role as a spokesman of that party would sometimes be gilded by a touch of reflected glory: "When I speak, I do not speak as an individual but I speak with the authority of the hundreds of millions of India."[55] And he would expatiate on the strength of his party with a solemnity bordering on megalomania thus:

> The growing strength of the Congress organisation has resulted in a change in its tone, language and method of expression . . . It is not the way of the Congress at present to shout mere slogans. Rather it has assumed the position of any government of a free country in the diplomatic language in which it conceals its intention . . . If the government of one country wants to declare war against that of another then the former would only announce that the latter was unfriendly.[56]

It is difficult not to be tickled by the self-importance indexed by *bhasans* like this. Yet there is no doubt that even such grandiloquence, taken together with Gandhi's quiet assertiveness, succeeded between them in sketching the crude outline of a hegemonic project. For, by their claim about Congress power, these leaders were staking out a claim for power on behalf of the indigenous bourgeoisie. That they did so in the name of the nation was evidence of their effort to present the interest of that class as the common interest of all members of the society.

In the classic instance of the rise of the bourgeoisie to power in Western Europe, this "illusion of the *common* interests" worked rather well at first, for, as Marx has observed, "in the beginning this illusion is true."[57] Up to a point, India proved to be no exception either to this historic paradox of an illusion acquiring the semblance of truth. For it is an undeniable fact that the Indian National Congress was far ahead of all other organizations in its mass appeal and its ability to mobilize people from all social strata in the name of nationalism. However, the recursive affirmation of primacy by its leaders, indeed the need they had to flaunt it so obsessively, was also symptomatic of a lacuna: the illusion was working, but not quite so well as could be wished.

This is why Gandhi, even as he announced the recruitment of nearly half a million members to his party in the autumn of 1929, was not satisfied that this quantitative growth could, by itself, be regarded as a sufficient measure of the nation's allegiance to the Congress. The other organizations were still competing with it effectively enough to make its influence fall short of hegemony, which was conceived by him as a "consummation" of the union of the Congress and all the other political bodies. This worried him:

> Indeed there should be no competition between the Congress and the other organizations. If we would be true to ourselves, the Congress would be admitted by all to be the only national organization to which the members of the other organizations, whilst retaining their own, would deem it a pride to belong. For this consummation Congressmen should show striking results in constructive effort and broadest toleration towards those holding opposite views, so long as they do not come in conflict with the avowed object of the national organization.[58]

That "consummation" never materialized. Even a decade later, the Congress party had not achieved its goal of being acknowledged as "the only national organization to which the members of the other organizations . . . would deem it a pride to belong." On the contrary, its claim to speak for all was being contested more and more vigorously along both the major axes—that is, the communal and class axes—of Indian politics.

Hegemonic Claims Contested

Ever since the end of the Non-cooperation Movement, communalism had been gaining momentum both as a mass political phenomenon and as an aspect of elite politicking. The last twenty years of colonial rule were racked by wave after wave of Hindu-Muslim conflict. Instigated and promoted by sectarian organizations of both the denominations, and expressed in its most acute form as communal violence, it was clear enough evidence of the fact that the Congress was no longer unmatched either in its appeal to the masses or in its power to rally them. It is an irony of Indian history that the political mobilization which signalled the end of the raj—that is, the partition riots of 1946–47—turned out to be the most decisive test of Congress's claim to undivided popular allegiance and a test the Congress failed to pass.

Corresponding to such an increase in the mass and force of sectarian strife, there was also the growth of communalism as a constitutionalist activity which, with a little help from the administration and its Indian collaborators, split the arena of politics into rival segments from top to bottom, so that at each level the unitary notion of nationalism upheld by the Congress had to confront and eventually compromise with the dualist two-nation concept propagated by Muhammad Ali Jinnah and the Muslim League.

The outcome of all this was that even Jawaharlal Nehru, whose aversion to separatism was often indistinguishable from a wishful thinking which denied the existence of any communal problem except as a peripheral nuisance created by British intrigue, had ultimately to come to terms with the fact that the Indian National Congress alone did not represent the whole of India. Even before the Pakistan Resolution was formally adopted by the League, he had written to Jinnah in terms which amounted to a renunciation of Congress's claim to be the sole representative of the nation. While maintaining that his party, unlike the League and the Hindu Mahasabha, was open to all, irrespective of the religion they professed, he admitted that "the Congress does not represent everybody in India . . . In the ultimate analysis it represents its members and sympathisers."[59] The image of the Congress as "the only national organization" was discarded thus in favor of a recognition of what it really was—that is, a nationalist party among others, even if the largest of them. In a perverse sort of way, old man Gandhi was proved right again: a purely quantitative increase had not been enough to endow the Congress with that hegemony which alone would have enabled it to speak for the nation as a whole.

The claim to hegemony ran into difficulties on the class axis as well. Although there was no other organization that could rival the Congress in the extent of its influence over peasants and workers, that influence was still not good enough for its leaders. Both Gandhi and Nehru are on record as having found fault again and again with the quality of popular response evoked by their campaigns. The reproach addressed to the masses on such occasions has often been interpreted by historians and hagiographers alike as some kind of a counsel for spiritual perfection. But a more sensible, if less pious, reading would perhaps be that such admonition was an index of despair. It was an admission on the part of the elite that the allegiance of the masses was eluding its grasp, and so was the hegemony it coveted so much. For the realization of that hegemony depended largely on the support of the two most important constituents of the subaltern population—that is, the peasantry and the working class. Yet by the time they were called upon to mobilize in the campaigns initiated by the nationalist leadership at the end of the First World War, both these groups had already developed class aims which it was not possible for the bourgeoisie to accommodate in any program sponsored exclusively under its own auspices.

It could not be trusted to defend the interests of the peasantry. Fostered by colonialism and dependent on the latter for its very survival during its formative phase, it had learnt to live at peace with those pre-capitalist modes of production and culture which made the perpetuation of British rule possible. As such it was unable to break away from its symbiosis with landlordism and complicity with many forms of feudal oppression, including the appropriation of the peasant's surplus by means of quasi-feudal tenancies. Consequently, with all its concern to involve the peasantry in nationalist politics, it could not bring itself to include the struggle against rents in its programs. Indeed, it was on the ques-

tion of withholding rents from landlords that the bourgeoisie de-
marcated itself sharply on class lines from the mass of tenant-cul-
tivators. The peasantry, for its part, defied the bourgeois and
landlord elements within the Congress leadership on this particular issue whenever local conditions and alternative local leaderships permitted it to do so.

The relation of the bourgeoisie to the working class took much
the same course as the development of nationalism during the
interwar years coincided with that of trade unionism and socialism.
The impact of a war economy followed by that of the Depression
combined with the influence of the October Revolution and the
spread of socialist ideas to imbue the more politically conscious
sections of the workers with a militancy which the Indian industrialists were quick to identify as a threat to their class interests, and
the raj as a threat to law and order. As a result, the attempts made
by the organized sections of workers to find a role for themselves
within the anti-imperialist struggle created problems which the
nationalist elite could not resolve or even face with equanimity.

The war crisis had accentuated the contradictions of the Indian
colonial society in such a way as to transform the working class
into an increasingly self-conscious entity which, far from being
assimilated to a bourgeois hegemony, began to range itself in opposition to the latter both in political practice and in theory. In
practice, parties, groups and alignments identified with the working class intruded more and more vigorously into a political arena
that had been the exclusive preserve of the elite until then. In
theory, the conceptualization of Indian nationalism as the struggle
of an undifferentiated patriotic mass against foreign rule came
under the challenge of an alternative view according to which the
conflict between exploiter and exploited, and between oppressor
and oppressed within the indigenous society, was an integral part
of the nation's struggle for self-determination.

Much of the specificity of Indian politics of this period derives
precisely from the failure of nationalism to assimilate the class
interests of peasants and workers effectively into a bourgeois hegemony. Nothing testifies more clearly to the predicament of a
bourgeoisie nurtured under colonial conditions and its difference
from its opposite numbers in Western Europe. There the bourgeoi-

sie came forward, as Marx and Engels have observed, "not as a class but as the representative of the whole society, as the whole mass of society confronting the one ruling class," and did so "because initially its interest [was] as yet mostly connected with the common interest of all other non-ruling classes, because under the pressure of the hitherto existing conditions its interest [had] not yet been able to develop as the particular interest of a particular class."[60] In other words, it was initially as an acknowledgment of the connection between its own interests and those of all the other nonruling classes that the bourgeoisie had led the struggle against feudalism and established its hegemony over the peasantry, whereas in India the influence it gained over the rural population in the 1920s and 1930s did not develop into a full-fledged hegemony because of its reluctance to break with landlordism.

Again, in Western Europe, the conditions prevailing under the *ancien régime* did not allow the interests of the bourgeoisie to be reduced at once to "the particular interest of a particular class." The immaturity of the working class, which at this stage corresponded to the immaturity of the bourgeoisie itself, helped to keep their relationship nonantagonistic for some time and enabled the latter initially to speak for a proletariat that had not yet become a class-for-itself. By contrast, the contrived character of industrialization under the raj and the autocratic nature of the regime had, from the very beginning, left no choice for the Indian bourgeoisie to develop its interest as anything other than the particular interest of a particular class. Trapped in conditions which did little to encourage any organic growth and expansion, it hardened quickly into a parasitic and precocious outcrop on the surface of the colonial society and defined itself sharply by its antagonism with its Other—the working class, an antagonism which, from the very beginning, it sought to resolve by discipline rather than persuasion.

Thus, while the bourgeoisie in the West could speak for all of society in a recognizably hegemonic voice, even as it was striving for power or had just won it, in India there was always yet another voice, a subaltern voice, that spoke for a large part of society which it was not for the bourgeoisie to represent. The voice, unheeded for a long time by those who lived within the walled city of institutional politics and academic scholarship, rang out of the depths of a parallel and autonomous domain which was only partially penetrated by elite nationalism. This was an unrepresented, unassimilated, subaltern domain where nationalism, like many other phenomena in the social and spiritual life of our people, worked according to a chemistry of power rather different from that which obtained in the elite domain. That is why the elite nationalism of the Congress leadership and that party's official platform could never be adequately representative of Indian politics of the colonial period.

IV. Gandhian Discipline

Discipline versus Persuasion

Gandhi in his quiet way and Nehru with his boasts were both keenly aware of and sensitive to their party's inadequacy. And both registered that awareness in their nervous reiteration of the need for discipline, which figures as an obsessive theme in so much of what they had to say about the activity of the masses in the nationalist upsurge. One can hardly make any sense of such obsession except as an attempt to compensate by discipline for what the bourgeoisie had failed to gain by persuasion — except, that is, as an attempt to settle for dominance without hegemony.

Discipline had not been unknown to nationalism even before Gandhi. For many of the militant nationalist groups and parties which believed in the use of force against colonialism and worked in secret were highly disciplined. The intelligence reports in the Home (Political) Series of the National Archives of India testify amply to the role of discipline, indeed to its cultic function, in the organization of revolutionary terrorism during the first two decades of this century. But militant nationalism of this particular kind was not a mass political phenomenon. On the contrary, it relied for its striking power on conspiratorial methods and armed intervention by individual activists or tightly welded commandos — in short, on the exclusion of the masses.

That kind of discipline was of course very different from what Gandhi wanted to introduce into the principles and programs of the Congress after its transformation into a mass party under his leadership. The conspiratorial, underground organizations used discipline as an armor to protect themselves from their enemy — the colonial state with its secret police, agent-provocateurs, and other agencies of coercion against which they were constantly on guard. But discipline, for Gandhi, was a weapon for fighting the enemy within. That enemy, designated with some condescension as "enthusiasm" by his most trusted lieutenant, Nehru,[61] was nothing other than the initiative of the masses unbridled by elite control.

Such initiative had been a distinctive feature of the subaltern domain of politics even before the emergence of the Congress as the largest nationalist party. Expressed in its most dramatic and comprehensive form in peasant insurgency, it was the source of much that was creative about the mobilization of the rural poor on such occasions. It was thanks to such initiative that individuals with no previous record of militancy would suddenly come forward as leaders of local action, bandits turn into rebels, a second wave develop within an ongoing struggle sharpening its contradictions, and communal labor like hunting or fishing assume the modality of corporate violence against sarkar, sahukar, and zamindar.

What worried the Congress high command most about initiatives of this kind was their refusal to be left out of nationalist politics — indeed, about their articulation precisely at those points where the elite and subaltern domains intersected and the controlled rhythm of a campaign would suddenly be disturbed by the irruption of an Aika movement, an exodus of Assam coolies, an uprising at Chauri Chaura, or by any of those numerous transgressions which stepped beyond the limits of passive disobedience. Such transgressions were, for Gandhi, a positive evidence of the lack of "sacrifice, discipline and self-control" among the masses — the three qualities without which there could be no "deliverance and no hope." And, of these three, discipline was the most essential, for without it, he believed, even sacrifice was of no avail.[62]

Discipline became a matter of vital concern for the bourgeois leadership, as with the end of the First World War the masses began to participate in the nationalist movement on a scale larger than ever before. The war crisis had radicalized the subcontinent from end to end and energized most of the body politic except at the very top, where a small minority of landed magnates still retained their faith in the raj. But within the rest of the population scarcities and the rise in prices and taxes, harsh security measures and reduction of civil liberties even below the prewar levels, sympathy for Pan-Islamic and revolutionary-terrorist activities, and widespread resentment against the use of force for recruitment to the army had all added up to a critique of colonial rule in which even the usually silent voice of the peasantry made itself heard.

Indeed, it is the participation of peasant masses that made all the difference in size and tone between Non-cooperation and the anti-Partition agitation of the previous decade. Some of the urban, middle-class pageantry of Swadeshi times lingered on to some extent as a mark of continuity. The posses of well-behaved saffron-robed volunteers, dawn squads of pleaders and pensioners sounding reveille to the tune of *samkirtan* in small mofussil towns, schoolboys marching behind local *dadas* shouting "Bande-mataram," ceremonials of welcome and farewell for garlanded leaders under festooned archways—all were still there.

But they came increasingly to feature in the company of a new type of demonstrators whose presence in the nationalist crowd had never been particularly conspicuous so far. It was the peasantry and the urban poor who represented this type—uncouth, unruly, unheeding to all advice not to insist on a visiting leader's *darsan* or touch his feet, not to drown his voice by what Gandhi called "unmusical noises" as he spoke at meetings,[63] not to stop the itinerant celebrities at unscheduled wayside gatherings as they traveled by car from town to town, and not to disturb their sleep on a hard day's night by assembling at railway stations, banging on the doors of locked compartments and refusing to disperse without being treated to a speech or two. And thus, as the Congress turned, for the first time, to the masses for support in a nation-wide struggle and the latter responded in earnest, there was inevitably a clash between two styles of mobilization.

The irritation caused by such discordance was frequently reported by Gandhi in the columns of his journal, *Young India,* as he toured the provinces during the Non-cooperation campaign. Here is how he described his experience at a railway station in southern India in August 1920:

We were travelling to Madras by the night train leaving Bangalore . . . We needed [a] night's rest but there was none to be had. At almost every station of importance, large crowds had gathered to greet us. About midnight we reached Jalarpet junction . . . Maulana Shaukat Ali requested the crowd to disperse. But the more he argued, the more they shouted "Maulana Shaukat Ali ki jai," evidently thinking that the Maulana could not mean what he said. They had come from twenty miles' distance, they were waiting there for hours, they must have their satisfaction. The Maulana gave up the struggle, he pretended to sleep. The adorers thereupon mounted the footboards to have a peep at the Maulana. As the light in our compartment was put out they brought in lanterns. At last I thought I would try. I rose, went to the door. It was a signal for a great shout of joy. The noise tore me to pieces. I was so tired. All my appeals proved fruitless in the end. They would stop for a while to renew the noise again. I shut the windows. But the crowd was not to be baffled. They tried to open the windows from outside. They must see us both. And so the tussle went on till my son took it up. He harangued them, appealed to them for the sake of the other passengers. He produced some effect and there was a little less noise. Peeping however went on to the last minute. It was all well-meant, it was all an exhibition of boundless love, yet how cruel, how unreasonable! It was a mob without a mind.[64]

But complaints and admonitions seemed to be of no avail. A night's journey by train from Kasganj to Kanpur and another from Lahore to Bhiwani were both made equally uncomfortable by similar demonstrations. And it was not only the want of much-needed sleep and rest ("I was resting, did they want me to die a premature death?") that upset the Mahatma. The crowds spoiled his days as well.

He wrote with annoyance bordering on anger about "an unmanageable crowd on the Kanpur platform, yelling the national cries, pressing towards my compartment," about the "painful" experience of having his feet touched as a mark of reverence ("an uncontrollable performance causing much waste of time"), about their insistence on having his darsan ("they had come many miles to have darsan and darsan they must have"), about the victory cry (jai) as an "unmusical," "piercing and heart-rending" noise, about the disorderly conduct of those who gathered at his meetings ("I shiver in fear when setting out for meetings") barring his way to the speaker's platform ("I often very nearly lost my balance through the jostling"; "My feet got crushed as I was passing through the mass of people and I was irritated by the slogan-shouting"), and so on.

Such boisterous, unruly behavior was not limited to any particular region or community either. The chaos and confusion Gandhi witnessed at Jalarpet in the south pursued him everywhere—at Karachi in Sind, at Bhiwani in Punjab, at Calcutta in Bengal, at Hathras, Kanpur, Kasganj, Lucknow, Tundla in UP. This was indeed an all-India phenomenon, and the name the Mahatma gave to it was "Mobocracy."[65]

Two Disciplines—Elite and Subaltern

"Mobocracy": an ugly word greased with loathing, a sign of craving for control and its frustration, it is lifted directly out of the lexicon of elitist usage as a measure of the distance between those on the side of order and others who are regarded as a threat to it. Gandhi's own frustration was documented in the adjectives he used to describe the crowds: they were "unmanageable," "uncontrollable," "undisciplined." They testified to the fact that India was "passing through the mob-law stage." Even demonstrations organized under the auspices of the Congress itself were "unquestionably mob-demonstrations." And he referred to them with barely concealed disgust as he wrote, "During the memorable tour of the Khilafat mission through the Punjab, Sind and Madras, I have had a surfeit of such demonstrations."

He did not doubt for a moment the "perfect good humour" of the crowds on such occasions, nor, indeed, the fact that "it was all well-meant, it was all an exhibition of boundless love" on their part. But that did not make it any the less reprehensible, for "all the same this is mobocracy." It was his mission therefore, he said, "to introduce the people's law instead of mob-law," to "evolve order out of chaos" and "to evolve democracy" out of mobocracy.[66]

[Such demonstrations] cannot . . . procure swaraj [self-rule] for India unless *regulated* and harnessed for national good. The great task before the nation today is to *discipline* its demonstrations if they are to serve any useful purpose.

The nation must be *disciplined* to handle mass movements in a sober and methodical manner.

Workers must either organize these demonstrations in a methodical manner or not have them at all . . . We can do no effective work unless we can pass instructions to the crowd and expect *implicit obedience.*[67]

But how to go about this task of regulating, harnessing, disciplining, and instructing the crowds in order to elicit their obedience? "How to evolve discipline out of this habitual indiscipline?"[68] The question was certainly not asked in the spirit of a sergeant-major. Gandhi would not want to conquer indiscipline by force, but by regulating and harnessing it. This is an important distinction to make between two idioms of dominance.

Unlike the colonial rulers, he did not think of discipline as issuing from the barrel of a gun. But he and the indigenous bourgeoisie for whom he spoke shared with the colonialists an elitist prejudice which was always on its guard against any mobilization of the masses on their own initiative and all too prone to condemn it as indiscipline. In this sense, the voice that asked the question about disciplining the habitually undisciplined, though not quite the same as a sergeant-major's, was still the voice of one who stood outside and above the ranks he wanted to bring to order. That being so, Gandhi's description of his own faith in the masses as "boundless," was less than convincing. He dismissed the views of the critics of Non-cooperation as "nothing less than distrust of the people's ability to control themselves."[69] But his own distrust is inscribed so firmly and so copiously in his writings and speeches that it is hard to imagine anyone scoring better.

To say that is not to deny that Gandhi's distrust of the masses was very different from that of his loyalist opponents—the so-called "liberals" and "moderates." These had no use for the masses at all in their kind of politics, which was primarily an exercise in begging and toadying or in some narrow constitutionalist manoeuvering. By contrast, Gandhi did have a use for the masses. It was of fundamental importance for the philosophy as well as the practice of his politics that the people should be appropriated for and their energies and numbers "harnessed" to a nationalism which would allow the bourgeoisie to speak for its own interests in such a way as to generate the illusion of speaking for all of society. Although he shared the aversion of all elitist politicians for what he called "mob rule" and was quick, like them, to condemn it as "cruel" and "unreasonable,"[70] he distinguished himself clearly from the others by his acumen to discern an inexhaustible fund of energy in the "mobocracy" he hated so much and exploit it in order to power the Congress campaigns. He was not going to throw away this material which he described as "an exhibition of boundless love" and set about regulating and employing it "for the national good."

To regulate what defied control, to discipline the undisciplined, was to subject them to a critique. What was it about the crowds that Gandhi criticized so vehemently, what was it that he found so unreasonable in their behavior? What, in short, did he mean by indiscipline? If all the instances of noise and confusion, of boisterousness at meetings and breaking of ranks during marches, of insistence on darsan and foot-touching, of nocturnal gatherings at railway stations and unscheduled wayside assemblies during the day—if all these were added up for an answer to that question, the indiscipline he complained of would seem to amount to a particular style of popular mobilization.

It was a style that agreed fully with conventions well understood by the masses. For them, the "disorder, din, pressing, yelling and shouting,"[71] taken together, constituted an idiom of the discipline they willingly imposed on themselves as they mobilized for corporate labor or communal rejoicing or local conflict, in all of which the modalities of work and festivity combined to give their participation its distinctively popular character. In other words, what the people brought to the nationalist campaigns was a discipline that informed the politics of the subaltern domain—a discipline governed by those rules of association which made them work together in the production of goods and services as well as in the articulation of a shared spiritual culture. As such, this discipline was truly "habitual" with the masses in the sense (given in the *Concise Oxford Dictionary*) of being "customary," "constant and continual." By denouncing such discipline as "habitual indiscipline" Gandhi was simply owning up to his failure to make the traditional forms of mass mobilization compatible with the new forms which were evolving at the time within the nationalist movement.

What was at issue, therefore, was not a conflict between indiscipline and discipline. It was a question of conflict between two different disciplines characteristic of the separate and parallel domains of subaltern and elite politics. What was it that made them

so incompatible in Gandhi's judgement as to call for the substitution of one by the other? How come that with all his taste for
traditionalism in so many other respects, the traditional idiom of
popular mobilization proved so unacceptable to him? The answer
must be sought in his implacable hostility to the *immediacy* which
was the very essence of that idiom. For, the authenticity of such
mobilization, its agreement with its concept, required that it should
turn the will of the Many into an activity of the masses without any
mediation external to the subaltern domain. The autonomy of that
domain as well as the popular initiatives sited there had that immediacy as their *sine qua non*. In short, this constituted the originality
of subaltern mobilization.

It followed, therefore, that such mobilization would resist assimilation to the other domain so long as its immediacy remained intact.
Gandhi was the first political leader of the Indian bourgeoisie to
identify that resistance and attempt to overcome it as a precondition
for harnessing the mass and energy of popular mobilization to his
campaigns. His condemnation of the idiom of such mobilization in
its original form was, therefore, an integral part of his strategy to
replace a discipline specific to the subaltern domain by a discipline
appropriate for the elite domain, and his plan to "evolve order out of
chaos" was a design to impose one kind of order on another. And he
was tuned well enough to the amplitude and temper of mass political
activity during the postwar years to formulate a notion of leadership
which would be adequate for this strategy of undermining the immediacy of subaltern mobilization and dealing with its consequences in such a way as to enable the bourgeoisie to power its drive
to hegemony by the energies of a surging nationalism.

During the initial phase of Non-cooperation, in the autumn of
1920, when he was still somewhat dazed by the impact of the
popular upsurge and frustrated by his inability to control it,
Gandhi could sometimes refer to a demonstration as made up of a
moronic mass: "It was a mob without a mind. There were no
intelligent men of influence among them."[72] But the tone changed
before long and a note of respect crept into it, as he wrote on that
subject again some time later in *Young India* (3 November 1920).

> The fact is that the formation of opinion today is by no means
> confined to the educated classes, but the masses have taken it

upon themselves not only to formulate opinion but to enforce it. It would be a mistake to belittle or ignore this opinion, or to ascribe it to a temporary upheaval . . . The masses are by no means so foolish or unintelligent as we sometimes imagine. They often perceive things with their intuition, which we ourselves fail to see with our intellect. But whilst the masses know what they want, they often do not know how to express their wants and, less often, how to get what they want. Herein comes the use of leadership.[73]

Quite clearly, the role of leadership was no longer premised on any assumption about the mindlessness of the mob. There was already a significant shift away from the crude, if uncharacteristic, arrogance which had made him profess, only about three months earlier, a "boundless faith" in the people and remark at the same time: "nothing is so easy as to train mobs, for the simple reason that they have no mind, no premeditation."[74] The intelligence of the people was henceforth to be taken for granted. But it was an intelligence which operated at a naive intuitive level and had not developed yet into intellect. The task of "the educated classes" was therefore to help that intuition to mature by giving it voice and direction, for the masses did not know how to formulate their wants into demands nor how to go about securing them. "Herein comes the use of leadership" designed explicitly to interpose between the will of the masses and its political articulation.

Gandhi's theory of leadership amounted thus to a formula to dissolve the immediacy of mobilization in the subaltern domain, and open up a space for the nationalist elite to step in with its own will, initiative, and organization in order to pilot the political activity of the masses towards goals set up by the bourgeoisie. Discipline, in the lexicon of Gandhism, was the name of that mediating function.

Crowd Control and Soul Control

This disciplinary leadership operated by two kinds of mediation. Together, they formed a spearhead which had its cutting edges in *crowd control* and *soul control.* It is by wielding this instrument with consummate skill that Gandhi became the most important of bourgeois politicians in the subcontinent to lead the masses and develop the Congress into a popular nationalist party. It was a mighty achievement. What it meant, concretely, for the relation of forces within Indian nationalism was that he "regulated and harnessed" a fund of subaltern energy which had originated in the wartime economic hardship and antigovernmental discontent and had been blowing up the circuits of local elite politics from time to time until the inauguration of Non-cooperation.

Crowd control was the first of the two controls that made up the Gandhian harness. "The nation must be disciplined to handle mass movements in a sober and methodical manner. This means previous training of volunteers and previous discipline of the masses,"[75] wrote Gandhi at the height of Non-cooperation in May 1921. To introduce sobriety and method into a field already activated by the people was thus what the nationalist movement was all about. Regarded from his point of view it was to be a scenario with no room in it for enthusiasm — for any "mobocratic" storming of a Bastille or an insurrection taking on the air of a carnival. On the contrary, he considered training and discipline as the prerequisite of any success the movement could possibly hope for.

In that regime of sobriety and method, volunteers were to play a key role. The Congress volunteers of the early phase of Non-cooperation were still modeled largely on the patriotic *karmi* or *sevak* of the prewar period who had featured invariably as a controller of crowds at Swadeshi meetings and at fairs and festivals. But they were not professional enough for Gandhi. He complained again and again about their failure to enforce order. "The volunteers were in the way," he wrote on one occasion. "Instead of dispersing themselves among the crowd and keeping it back, they clustered together . . . The result was that the pressure was all directed towards where they and we were standing." On his arrival at a railway station his coach would be taken over by the waiting crowd, "volunteers being the greatest sinners." At a meeting, they would shout "all at the same time . . . Ten volunteers have been heard to give the same order at the same time." The problem with volunteers was that they tended to merge in a crowd instead of standing apart and disciplining it: "Volunteers often become demonstrators instead of remaining *people's policemen.*"[76]

A twenty-point instruction published in *Young India* (September

1920) speaks of Gandhi's concern for bringing the masses to order and using volunteers to that end.[77] Although he himself did not regard the advice as comprehensive, it shows in what meticulous detail he had thought out the problem of crowd control at railway stations, in street demonstrations and at meetings: at what points the public should gather, what distances must be maintained between them and the "heroes" (the word is Gandhi's own), and how to deal with noise. He wrote about "national cries," that is, patriotic exclamations made in unison at public gatherings, and reduced them to a set of three to be shouted in a particular sequence. When it came to organizing a conference, he could be unsparing in his attention to the minutiae of what had to be done to provide delegates with food and accommodation, with water for washing and drinking, with pits dug for latrines and notices in many languages to instruct users how to keep them clean. He also had ideas about arrangements for large meetings, the construction of a speaker's platform, its position vis-a-vis the audience, the acoustics of the traditional Indian auditorium *(pandal)*, the advantage or otherwise of seating people on chairs, and so on.

It is in order to operate with such a schema that he wanted to alter the character of the Congress volunteers and turn them into professional "handlers" of the mass movement. Henceforth, there would be nothing amateurish about them. "Much greater discipline, method and knowledge must be exacted from volunteers," he wrote, "and no chance comer should be accepted as a full-fledged volunteer. He only hinders rather than helping. Imagine the consequence of the introduction of one untrained soldier finding his way into an army at war. He can disorganize it in a second."[78]

The rules formulated for making "people's policemen" (a phrase that echoes his reference to the "soldier") out of Congressmen are evidence again of the same insistence on discipline that made Gandhi such a superb organizer for his party. No "raw volunteers" were to be allowed to work at the bigger demonstrations. All volunteers were to be reviewed before a demonstration and issued with special instructions suitable for the occasion. Each of them had to carry a book of general instructions about organizing "national cries," escorting the "heroes" through large gatherings, protecting women, signaling messages, and conducting similar activities at railway stations, public meetings, and street marches.[79]

Eventually, the concern for crowd control, which had been just an irate response to subaltern enthusiasm at first, developed into a basic principle of Congress organization. What had started off as an irruption of the masses into a narrowly conceived movement broadened, with the quickening of the struggle, into a general mobilization against colonialism. The Report on Draft Instructions for Congress Organizations, published soon after the formal inauguration of Non-cooperation, registered that concern by advising provincial, district and town organizations of the party to "form volunteer corps for the purpose of disciplining the people and maintaining order."[80]

Some of Gandhi's own statements made during and immediately after the Khilafat tour of 1920 refer so often to the purely physical hardship caused by crowds that one might be tempted to seek in that alone an explanation of his concern for "disciplining the people and maintaining order." To do so would be to take an utterly superficial view of the matter. For there is nothing in his words and deeds to justify the imputation that comfort had ever been important to him at any point of his political career. On the contrary, a masochistic inclination for discomfort was fairly pronounced in many things he preached and practiced. To understand his obsession for crowd control, one must recognize that it had less to do with the body than with the soul. Indeed it was a foil to his concern for soul control.

The correspondence between these two controls rested on a relation which was fundamental to Gandhian theory—that is, the relation of swaraj to self-discipline or self-control. Used interchangeably in all his numerous statements on the subject, these last two words played on the double register of his spiritualized politics. Both could be understood, in certain contexts, as transparently secular signals enjoining restraint on non-cooperators in their public conduct, especially when confronted by the police and other official agencies.

However, the prefix "self," common to both phrases, is English for *ātma*, which, derived from the Sanskrit *ātman*, means "self" as well as "soul" in many Indian languages, including Gujarati. Because the word is loaded with a wide range of metaphysical and ethical connotations in Hindu thought, its use enabled these expressions quickly to shift their semantic ground and transform tactical advice into moral prescription, so that self-control would be confounded with soul control and enlisted in the battle for swaraj as a spiritual weapon honed by some inner purity. "To be able to win swaraj," wrote Gandhi, "we should become pure, and to be pure is to be self-controlled."[81]

Soul control, that is, self-control conceived as a spiritual discipline, came thus to assume a strategic importance in the campaigns led by Gandhi. He made its implications clear for Non-cooperation by linking it directly to Swadeshi. "This self-control," he wrote, "can only be attained by complete swadeshi," which he specified as "a boycott of foreign cloth and effort put forth to manufacture the required quantity of khadi."[82]

It would appear therefore that swaraj was to be attained by soul control, that is, spiritual self-control, which itself was to be cultivated by swadeshi, which, in its turn, was to be based on the two-pronged program of boycott and khadi. There was nothing in either of these that could not be thought or practiced in entirely secular terms. But propelled by self-control they were both assimilated to the idea of self-purification, regarded by Gandhi as central to his project of giving Non-cooperation the semblance of a religious movement.

Purity had already emerged as an essential attribute of self-control in this movement. Gandhi himself had emphasized this by his dictum: "To be pure is to be self-controlled." In effect, this meant displaying boycott, khadi, and all else that constituted the Non-cooperation program prominently on the menu of a comprehensive morality. Indeed, the Mahatma often gave the impression that, for him, Non-cooperation was nothing "if it [did] not mean downright self-purification."[83] However, pressed at times by the demands of an ongoing mobilization, he felt called upon actually to name those attitudes and activities which he regarded as conducive to self-purification. To cite only two out of many such statements: "We must understand thoroughly what self-purification means. Give up drinking alcohol, smoking ganja, eating opium. Give up visiting prostitutes . . . give up drinking, give up debauchery."[84] Or, elaborating further, with a few more items thrown in, "If it is true that this movement is for self-purification, then, in addition to wearing khadi, you should give up liquor, eschew immorality, learn to be upright, see that you do not lose your head as the people of Male-

gaon did, stop looking upon Bhangis and chamars as untouchables
. . . Do not bring flowers; for swaraj, bring money instead."[85]

As should be obvious from these extracts, the menu of right and
wrong varied in size and its contents adjusted to occasion and
audience. But there was a logic to this shuffle. It was the logic of
two complementary moral drives operating on an awakening mass
consciousness in order to displace the secular-political elements of
its register by spiritual-political ones. Each of the drives was characterized by a certain negativity in its relation to ideas and objects
on which it was predicated. In one, that negativity stood for abstinence; in the other, for purgation. Pressed together into a code,
they constituted self-purification for Gandhi.

Abstinence meant giving up. Give up imported cotton, give up
alcoholic drinks, give up all other intoxicants, give up extra-marital
sex, give up violence, give up obsequiousness, give up untoucha-
bility. Give up, give up, give up . . . That was Gandhi's advice — advice not to indulge in certain pleasures of the body and not to
conform to certain inclinations of the mind, an indefinitely expand-
ing series of negative prescriptions for self-restraint and self-denial
which added up to self-purification. "India is today nothing but a
dead mass . . . Let her become alive by self-purification, i.e., self-
restraint and self-denial," he wrote.[86] Self-purification, construed
thus, became indistinguishable from the spiritual disciplines of
self-control and soul control.

Purgation backed up abstinence in this code to complete the
process of retreat from temptation by the destruction of its object.
Its purpose was to reach the innermost recesses of the soul, identify
the sediments of desire and flush them out. Dramatized in the
bonfires made of imported textiles, some of them lit by Gandhi
himself, this ceremony was popularized and defended by him in a
language that emphasized both its negativity and its sanctity. Negativity, insofar as its function was to expel foreign matter out of a
healthy, indigenous system ("Foreign cloth to India is like foreign
matter to the body") and cleanse it. The cleansing agent could, on
rare occasions, be a chemical, figuratively speaking. ("When soda
is applied to dirty clothes, the dirt is washed away. Self-purification is like this soda.") But, more often than not, it was fire. Used
liberally throughout this campaign — the instances are too numerous in Gandhi's writings to require citation — the metaphor helped

to invest negativity with sanctity. It evoked some of the most potent imageries of fire and heat in the Hindu rituals of sacrifice and penance, such as those of *yajña* ("the sacred task of burning foreign cloth . . . this *yajña*") and *tapas* ("When even one man performs *tapaścaryā*, the atmosphere is cleaned,") and associated this act of boycott and all else involved in swadeshi with the concepts of *prāyaścitta* (ritual expiation) and *ātmaśuddhi* (self-purification).[87]

The rhetoric of burning thus equipped the discourse of spiritualized — and, indeed, to an extent, hinduized — politics with some of its most telling figures of speech. Not only did it enable Gandhi to justify this agitational form as a technique of self-purification ("Why I burn English cloth . . . For self-purification . . ."), but also to extend its symbolic scope to the whole of the Non-cooperation Movement by characterizing it as a struggle for self-purification: "*A ladat atmaśuddhini chhe.*"[88]

It was thus that self-purification with its negative drives came to serve as the key to all the moral controls used by Gandhi to give Non-cooperation the character of "a movement . . . relying upon soul-force."[89] Its implications for mobilization could hardly be exaggerated. Since all aspects of the movement, in precept as well as practice, were subsumed under self-purification, any deviation in thought or deed was necessarily defiling, and every defilement called for a reimposition of soul control. Mobilization which failed to conform strictly to the rules laid down by the leadership could therefore be referred to the central moral code of self-purification. For one had to be "religious and pure of heart," and "no one who [was] wicked and of impure heart [could] succeed in the non-cooperation struggle."[90]

In the case of any serious deviation as, for instance, what had occurred in the Malegaon incident when public protest against a miscarriage of justice turned violent, the corrective would be sought in an "atonement" (prāyaścitta) which meant, in effect, demobilizing the people in order to restore the leadership's control over them. "What atonement shall we make for the Malegaon incident?" Gandhi asked.[91] In answer, he went over a list of typical mass activities which made for mobilization and condemned each as incompatible with Non-cooperation and swaraj. There was to be no assembling in crowds, no rioting, no inflammatory speeches, no meetings and hartals "on every occasion." These by then familiar injunctions were to be matched by prescriptions taken out of the moral menu "to give up harmful addictions, discard any foreign cloth . . . and forthwith start working on the spinning wheel." Measures for crowd control were thus matched by advice for soul control, and together, they were to serve as a "fit atonement for the Malegaon incident" by promoting "greater control over our minds and anger."

When at the peak of mobilization, as in Bombay in November 1921 and at Chauri Chaura in February 1922, militancy exceeded the limits set by the nationalist leadership, Gandhi sought to regain control either by slowing down the pace of mobilization (as after Bombay) or by a command for total demobilization (as after Chauri Chaura). In each case, politics as a collective secular activity was made to yield to spiritualized politics in its ultimate monadic form as the Mahatma, atoning for the violence of the masses, subjected himself to the ritual of a punishing and purifying fast.

A gesture of self-denial, this was perfectly in accord with his doctrine of dual control. But it was also evidence of a historic shortfall made up of the difference between the leadership's desire to mobilize the people by persuasion and its inability to do so. Gandhi, honest and discerning as ever, wrote a lament for that elusive hegemony when, in despair after the Bombay riots, he blamed himself for his loss of control over the masses: "I am more instrumental than any other in bringing into being the spirit of revolt. I find myself not fully capable of controlling and disciplining that spirit. I must do penance for it."[92]

V. Conclusion

We started off by noticing how the theme of mobilization has a tendency to figure in all modes of dominant discourse as the nationalist elite's entitlement to hegemony. What is highlighted in such discourse is that aspect of the phenomenon which speaks only of the enthusiasm of the mobilized. But as should be clear from our survey, there was also another side to it—that is, the rigor and extent of the discipline used to bring it about.

That discipline changed its character over time as nationalism matured both in its ideology and its practice. But insofar as any such discipline was needed at all, it was witness to a tension within nationalism which would be glossed over if the mobilization informed by it were presented simply as an idyllic and untroubled festival of the masses.

We have tried, therefore, to point out how the secular and spiritual controls devised by Gandhi for Non-cooperation had, by and large though not completely,[93] displaced the caste sanctions of the Swadeshi period. Yet, we have argued, such controls were, if anything, symptomatic of a sharpening contradiction between the elite and the subaltern domains of politics and an increasing concern on the part of the leading bloc to resolve it in terms of its own interest construed and idealized as the interest of the nation.

All of which goes to show that coercion set out to compete with persuasion in the nationalist project from the moment its elite leadership began systematically to destroy the immediacy of popular mobilization and invest the energies of mass political movements in its bid for hegemonic dominance. But as witness the disciplinary imperatives of that very project, it was a bumpy road which the elite had to negotiate in its ride to hegemony. It never arrived.

3

An Indian Historiography of India

Hegemonic Implications of a Nineteenth-Century Agenda

I. Calling on Indians to Write Their Own History

Mobilization, we have noticed, was an issue of prestige for Indian nationalism as it matured into a mass political phenomenon during the first half of the twentieth century.[1] Under whose banner would the people rally? Who was to speak for them? A response to such questions was regarded as a critical measure of the support commanded by the Congress party in its claim to hegemony—a claim it pressed vigorously and relentlessly at every forum and by all means of publicity at its disposal not only against the colonial regime but also against all its indigenous rivals such as the Muslim League and some of the left-nationalist and socialist parties.

An outstanding feature of this hegemonic claim was the uses it made of the Indian past. The idioms of such use would differ according to tendencies prevailing within the nationalist ideology at any given time and the inclinations of its principal protagonists. With Rabindranath Tagore, for instance, the emphasis came to rest on an idealized past in which an autonomous and self-reliant civil society lived in peace with itself. With Gandhi, on the other hand, all that was good and great about that past lay in its spiritual achievements and moral superiority; with Nehru—in the secular unity of its politics and the synthesis of its diverse cultures.

152

During the period of high nationalism between the Swadeshi and the Quit India movements variations on these themes and others formed a body of literature which was extensive and distinctive enough to merit recognition broadly as a nationalist historiography. This was nationalism's answer to the hegemonic pretensions of the raj advocated and publicized by the James Mill tradition of colonialist writing on the Indian past. However, like that tradition, which bestowed on our alien rulers a hegemony denied them by history, nationalist discourse too sought to endow India's own ruling elite with an equally unhistorical hegemonic role.

That role, propagated since Independence, by the educational and other agencies of the state, is now an integral part of India's official history. It stands for a syncopated view from which the contradictions involved in the development of an Indian historiography of India have been displaced in favor of a progressive and liberal spirit whose triumph is fully in accord with the telic formation of a modern nation-state.

To leave this view unchallenged would be to undermine the autocritique of Indian history even before it took its first hesitant steps in that direction. For this would oversimplify the process of a colonized people's struggle to reclaim its past and by simplifying disarm criticism itself. We must therefore try and face up to the difficult truth that the question "Who speaks for the Indian people?" was historically predicated on another: *"Who has the right to interpret their past?"*

The voice in which that question was asked first was an educated middle-class voice heard throughout the second half of the nineteenth century urging Indians to write their own history. The words by which that call is most remembered are those of Bankimchandra Chattopadhyay, who wrote in the *Bangadarshan* of 1880: "Bengal must have her own history. Otherwise there is no hope for Bengal. Who is to write it? You have to write it. I have to write it. All of us have to write it. Anyone who is a Bengali has to write it. Come, let us join our efforts in investigating the history of Bengal . . . It is not a task that can be done by any one person alone; it is a task for all of us to do together."[2] Read Bengal and Bengali as notations often used by the author respectively for India and Indians, and you have an agenda here for a truly Indian historiography of India. It was an agenda in the straightforward sense of the phrase as "things to be done," and the strident note of that passage could leave no one in doubt that it was meant for immediate action. Why such urgency? What presuppositions about the past went into the making of this agenda? How was it acted upon? It is our own agenda for a critical historiography and its imperatives that require these questions to be addressed today to that other, ancestral agenda.

There is no way to answer any of these questions without first distinguishing this agenda from its common-sense construction as a simple recall of the past. The importance of that distinction cannot be emphasized enough. For Bankimchandra's appeal to Bengalis to write their own history has often been linked to the nostalgic strain in some of his writings in such a way as to allow memory to usurp the estate of history. The ideological function of this linkage has been to generate an *atideśa* effect by which a knowledge of the Indian past is converted into a category of Indian nationalist thought. The importance of such conversion is known too well to require comment except to point out that there is a fallacy here—a fallacy of confounding necessary and sufficient conditions. For, although the nineteenth-century agenda for an alternative historiography was ineluctably and necessarily charged with a longing for the past, the latter was not all that this agenda had for its content. Indeed, nostalgia, working on its own, does not produce historiography for a nation any more than it produces autobiography for an individual. The domains of Mnemosyne and Clio always intersect, but seldom coincide.

The remembrance of things past in a people's life and the urge for a people's own historiography have, of course, one thing in common. Both are informed by a notion of the Other. What that Other is, may be determined by culture or contingency or both, as it often is the case. Depending on the character of a cultural idiom or the contingency of an event or circumstance otherness may be reckoned in biological, environmental, economic or political terms, or in any combination of these. But whatever the kind of alterity, the presence of the Other at any given time always casts a shadow in the form of another time—in the form of a past.

The notion of the Other as another time need not be registered necessarily in a historiography. Under historical conditions where the flow of goods and services does not correspond to the linearity of secular time, the past is often recuperated not so much as a point on the path of time's arrow but as a moment of cyclical return. Such moments are variously recorded in our culture in chiliastic fear (as in the fear of *pralaya* that punctuates the Mahābhārata, especially on the eve of a heroic death), in millennial hopes (as in Birsa Munda's homilies on Satjug during the *ulgulan*), in Hindu rituals such as the annual worship of the spirits of dead ancestors, and so on. Yet for all their importance, these are no more than lingering traces of that long night of early feudalism during which the weakness or near absence of commodity production arrested the linear movement of time and made it spin around in myths.

However, when seven hundred years after Kalhaṇa and three hundred after Abū-l Faẓl, the agenda for an Indian historiography of India came to be constructed by the late nineteenth century, history had already taken over from Purāṇa as the dominant mode of reckoning the past. This mode would henceforth be the vehicle of that alterity which was so essential for any alternative reading of the Indian past. For, by designating itself as "Indian," that alternative announced its organizing principle as one of distantiation from what was paradigmatically un-Indian, because British and colonialist. Indeed, the sense of the Other which informed the agenda for another historiography was itself planted in a sense the colonized had of the pervasive and powerful presence of colonialism.

To acknowledge such a relationship of alterity was, of course, to recognize colonialism as a condition, indeed an essential condition, for the formulation of that agenda. But this did not make of it a spiritual gift pressed by British liberalism on India for the benefit of the natives. Contrary to such a cargo cult theory of culture, blithely retailed by imperialist writers and their Indian imitators, the production of a colonialist historiography was from the very outset an exercise in dominance and not an act of charity. It is, therefore, not possible to deal with the question of an Indian historiography of India as anything other than a question of power.

II. Historiography and the Formation of a Colonial State

Early Colonial Historiography

How the writing of history was mediated by the exercise of power can be grasped by considering a nodal point in the development of the colonial state. At this point, in 1765, the East India Company's conquest of Bengal acquired legitimacy by a Mughal grant enabling it to collect the land revenues of the eastern provinces and to administer civil justice on behalf of the Nawab. Known technically as the Company's accession to Diwani—a technicality which has, alas, made some scholars insensitive to its significance as the truly inaugural moment of the raj—it brought together in one single instance all the three fundamental aspects of colonialism in our subcontinent, namely, its origin in an act of force, its exploitation of the primary produce of the land as the very basis of a colonial economy, and its need to give force and exploitation the appearance of legality. Much of what was distinctive about British rule in India and set it apart from the Dutch, French, and Portuguese regimes elsewhere in Asia, derived precisely from this characteristic combination of politics, economics and law. And it was this combination again which provided the emerging colonial state with a node for structural developments in its apparatus at both the administrative and the ideological levels.

Developments at the first of these levels required that the Company should set up a bureaucracy adequate to its dual function as merchants and Diwan, which meant, in effect, the collection of land revenues in order to finance its so-called "investments." But India was a country where, for centuries, landed property had been the very foundation of both wealth and prestige, where all aspects of culture, including religion, had land as their common denominator, and the relation between producers, proprietors, and the state had evolved over time into a bewildering variety according to differences in the local structures of dominance and economies. Consequently, fiscal operations here depended for their success on an intimate knowledge of traditions, continuities, and past procedures—a knowledge of history, in sum.

The uses of such knowledge had been impressed upon the Company, albeit somewhat negatively, since the beginning of its involvement in the land question even before 1765, when its administration of some of the Ceded Districts ran into difficulties because of the refusal of the indigenous specialists to help its officials with their expertise. "After an infinite deal of trouble we have at last got a full and particular statement of the resources of this province," wrote an exasperated Harry Verelst and his Council from one such district, namely Chittagong, in 1761: "The villainous intentions of these people that had the management of the revenues here before endeavouring to secrete from us and make as intricate as possible whatever they could, has delayed [the report] thus long."[3]

Complaints of this kind increased many times both in number and bitterness with the Company's graduation to Diwani, if only because the territories it was given to administer were considerably larger in extent, the revenues much greater in volume, and the local variations in such things as tenurial structures, customary dues, and accounting procedures more numerous, hence more intricate. The inability of its servants to cope with such problems was expressed, at every level from the Collector to the Board of Revenue, in a concerted effort to blame their own failure on want of native cooperation. James Grant spoke for all of them when he mentioned what he believed to have been a defalcation of about fifteen million rupees of the Company's revenues every year owing to "the collusive chicanery of native agents, in withholding official intelligence from their new masters, and fraudulently converting the use of such knowledge, to their own private emolument at the public expense."[4]

These words, written in 1786, twenty-one years after accession to Diwani, were quite obviously the symptom of an unresolved tension characteristic of the early, formative phase of the colonial state. The latter had not quite succeeded yet in replacing the old bureaucracy by an entirely new one. A delay of that order, which is merely the effect of a structural *décalage*, is characteristic of all state formation. The site of a new state is always cluttered with the remains of the one that preceded it; and the individuality of each state, as it comes to be formed, derives to no small extent from the quality and degree of resistance put up by the debris through which it has to make its way.

It is significant, therefore, that some of the resistance to the formation of a colonial state in India should have been identified by the first colonialists as a refusal on the part of the natives to share a certain kind of knowledge with them. To notice this is already to take a step towards problematizing the question of colonialist knowledge, to threaten if not subvert the hegemonic assumption about its role as a western wisdom poured into an oriental void, to query whether the native informant represented so often in the archetype of Warren Hastings's pandit had always been a pliant collaborator, and so forth. I cannot, alas, digress into any of these important matters here, and must press on to consider the colonialist response to what was perceived as the reluctance of indigenous specialists to share one particular kind of knowledge — a knowledge of the Indian past.

For a start, let us recall once again Grant's strictures upon the "misconduct of native Hindostanny agents." Complaints on that score had by this time accreted into a widely held official opinion constituting, as he said, a "theme of general declamation."[5] By joining in, he lent to such declamation the weight of his expertise as one who knew more about the subject than most of his contemporaries.[6] "The collusive chicanery of native agents" was manifest, according to him, "in withholding official intelligence from their new masters." Clearly, this was an indictment uttered in a master's voice. It spoke with the authority of the East India Company as the "new masters" and required the natives to make their knowledge readily accessible to the masters so that the latter could convert it into "official intelligence." The alleged "chicanery" consisted, therefore, of two shortcomings on the part of the natives: first, their refusal to part with a knowledge that owed nothing to the alien rule to which they had been recently subjected; and secondly, their resistance to "the use of such knowledge" in the "public" interest — the word "public," the first term of a dichotomy hitherto unknown to Indian polity, being understood in this context as an attribute of the master's domain — the domain of the colonial state.

But what was this knowledge that the servants had and the masters were so eager to acquire? To put it in plain language, it was concerned with information about the volume and value of agricultural produce, the rules for appropriation of the producer's surplus by landlords and the state, the nature of land tenures and proprietary institutions, the technicalities of estate accounts, and above all, the laws and traditions governing the relationship of peasants, landlords, and the state. The skills required to handle one or more aspects of such information on behalf of local societies or governmental agencies had, in precolonial India, frozen, like all other skills, into craft-like structures contained within caste-like institutions. The density of such structures and the complexity of these institutions in any region tended to correspond directly to the stability of landlordism and the depth of dependent tenurial relations there.

Since the Company, as Diwan, happened to launch on its career as revenue collectors in the eastern provinces with their well-established zamindaries and many-tiered system of subinfeudation, it was no wonder that the first British administrators had hit the hard and intractable end of traditional expertise in land management. The want of sympathy between indigenous specialists and local officials was aggravated further at this stage by the rapacity of the farming system, the ruin of many an ancient landed family under the pressure of excessive fiscal demands, the quickening pace of tax collections, and displacements caused by the impact of colonialism on an old rural society slow to respond to change.

The outcome of all this was mutual antagonism and suspicion which vitiated transactions relating to land revenues and made the grudging cooperation elicited from the so-called "intermediate agents" appear as a wicked ruse to deceive the Company's officials. Grant expressed some of these sentiments in his long-winded prose when he set out

to prove that through the medium of natives, hitherto almost exclusively employed in real effective operations of finance, we [i.e. the Company] have been . . . grossly deceived in respect to the nature, form and extent of the annual assessment of Bengal; that such intermediate agents themselves have always been fully or more perfectly informed on these subjects, though they withheld their knowledge from European superintendents; and that when they have been regarded, or officially consulted as oracles to determine the most essential rights of government, they have in most cases, stood in the predicament of judge and party against the sovereign ruler . . . holding in the same hands . . . all the great offices of state, . . . together with the entire volume of authentic documents, accounts or official forms, so indispensably necessary to control their conduct with intelligence, while the ruling administration were still unaided by the lights of free extensive self experience.[7]

It would be some time, of course, before such "self experience" was to accumulate and mature enough to be effectively opposed to native intrigue. Meanwhile, the territories had to be governed and revenues collected in order to pay for trade and war, all of which urged the fledgling raj to try and break out of what it perceived as a circle of deception. The means used for that purpose was history. Some of the very first and most important works on Indian history written from a British standpoint belong to this period of thirty years between Diwani and Permanent Settlement. Quite a few of these ranged widely over time from antiquity to the most recent past; others were content to take a relatively foreshortened view of the past going back no further than the thirteenth century. All were conspicuous by their interest in the historical aspects of the land question—an interest they shared with the Company's administration which provided most of their authors with their livelihood.

Three Types of Narratives

Taken according to the scope and emphasis of their interest in the land question, these historical dissertations could be said to be of three types. The first of these came in the form of comprehensive surveys with the narrative extended over long periods of time and large parts of the subcontinent. Written up as political histories in which the ruling dynasties served for protagonists and their changing circumstances for plot, these narratives sought to explore the relation between power and property in pursuit of an answer to the question: Who owned the land—the king or the landed classes? Alexander Dow's well-known work, *The History of Hindostan*, published in three volumes in 1768–1772, was one of the best examples of this type.[8]

A second type, overlapping the first to some extent and equally comprehensive in its territorial and temporal surveys, differed somewhat in emphasis. The argument about landed property hinged here on the economic aspect of the land question: How much wealth did the land produce and how was it shared between proprietors and the state under the precolonial regimes? A good deal of politics, and that, too, in the form of dynastic histories, entered such narratives of course. But what they were primarily about was political economy—a term which frequently occurs in the works of Grant, one of the best writers of this genre.

The third type differed from the other two in scope. It did not have their subcontinental sweep, but focused on the relationship of power and property at the local level. Written up, in most cases, as official reports and still buried in the archives, narratives of this type are among the first local histories we have of colonial India. These, too, were concerned with the problem of proprietorship and power, but only on the much smaller scale of region and estate. The question which prompted the production of these reports, taken in its most general aspect, ignoring all its numerous variations, was: How much of his share of the produce did the landlord pass on to the state?

These three types of narratives, considered together as a genre, stand for the beginnings of a colonialist historiography of India. Each of these had the material and political interests of the emerging colonial state branded on it as a birthmark. None had anything to do with the promotion of a liberal culture among the subject population. They all owe their origin to the Company's urge to inform itself about the character and value of landed property, so that it could reduce its dependence on wily native intermediaries and use the office of the Diwan to maximize and systematize the collection of revenues. Which makes one wonder why of all possible means it was history that was summoned to rescue the "new masters" from the deceptions supposed to have been perpetrated by their indigenous servants. For if the latter had deceived the British authorities at all, they had done so not by any superior understanding of history but by what the Company's officers themselves had identified as a traditional knowledge which had mastered the highly specialized technique of Indian land management.

Grant himself paid a tribute to the power of that technique as he described what he thought was its abuse by a native specialist, a certain *mutsuddi,* who, he wrote, was "endowed with greater cunning or secrecy [than anyone else] in his profession; [and was] more skilled in the detail of the exchequer dues; the fraudulent emolument of the zemindars and other officers of government; practical arts in composing or deciphering revenue accounts; dividing, sub-dividing, intermixing, annexing, reducing, or entirely concealing portions of rent and territory . . ."[9] Put in such terms, clearly paranoiac terms with the string of gerunds quivering as if on the verge of a hysteric fit, the "practical arts" of accounting are made to look like a particularly sinister sort of black art, as in the passage where Grant refers to the native specialists as "oracles" with obvious contempt. False oracles no doubt. But his contempt for them was not altogether free from a fear of that unknown power of indigenous knowledge which made the European feel insecure so often while abroad in Asia and Africa.

That fear was the unmistakable sign of an ethnological encounter. For the Western observer, whether a traveler, adventurer, scientist, or administrator, regarded the withholding of an indigenous knowledge of any kind invariably as an assertion of ethnic identity, which excluded him, by that very gesture, as an alien. The fear and indeed the sense of humiliation generated by the want of access to what he thought was his by virtue of an undefined racial, cultural or spiritual superiority, or simply by right of conquest as in the present case, could be compensated by generalizations about native character and society as devoid of all that stood for positive values in the alien's own society and character. Sociologies, histories, philosophies, theologies, literatures, jokes, and downright abuse could all be made to serve as the vehicle for such generalizations in a many-sided repertoire of racist discourse. One has only to look up the Board of Revenue records of the 1770s and 1780s to realize how a good deal of the sentiment and at least some of the language which go with the sport of Paki-bashing in parts of Britain today, had already been anticipated by the East India Company's administrators in their desperation to make up for the hurt they felt on being denied access to a body of indigenous knowledge they believed they had a right to use as "official intelligence." By blaming such inaccessibility on native cunning, secrecy, and deception, they merely acknowledged defeat and accepted that, as aliens, they would never qualify for initiates.

So they turned to history as ethnology's surrogate. They realized that the Indian specialist would not share his knowledge with them, and decided therefore to acquire a knowledge of precolonial conditions of the agrarian economy and property relations by a historical investigation of the Indian past. But such a recovery of the past was bound to make for a very different kind of knowledge from the one denied. The latter was of course informed by a sense of the past, but did not constitute, for the specialists, a historical past. It was, with them, a past made up of discrete moments recovered synchronically as the occasion required. In this sense the recall, for instance, by the zamindari *amla* of who owned which estate generations ago, what was collected as *abwab* and paid as *jama,* was not very different from the recall of ancestral names, kinship transactions, ritual procedures, and so forth by priests, marriage brokers, genealogists, and other traditional specialists who, too, dipped into the past ever so often for information but did not negotiate it as a diachronic flow, that is, never as history.

The British, by contrast, had to historicize the Indian past in order to have access to it. But historicization, like the formation of the colonial state, could not be achieved except by the operation of metropolitan rules and models on native material. The material which had to be historicized was of course the sum of all existing narratives like annals, chronicles, anecdotes, and folklore, but the narratology brought to bear on such material was that of contemporary European and particularly whig historiography. All three types of late eighteenth-century East India historiography mentioned above bore the marks of this operation. Take, for example, Alexander Dow's macro-political *History of Hindostan* which was fairly representative of what was common to all three types in this respect. He relied, according to his own admission, primarily on Firishtah's early seventeenth-century chronicle, but gave it, in the third volume, a narrative closure that was characteristic of the post-Renaissance historiography of Europe, a closure for want of which, as Hayden White has observed, a chronicle could never qualify as a proper historical discourse.[10]

Again, Grant's macro-economic dissertation, which announced its historiographical conceit in its title, *An Historical and Comparative Analysis of the Finances of Bengal; Chronologically arranged in different periods from the Mogul Conquest to the present time,* sought consciously to impose the discipline of the eighteenth-century European model on its unruly material gathered from a wide variety of sources ranging from Persian ledgers and genealogical tables to chronicles and oral tradition. He rejected the narrative mode of his primary sources in which concentration on detail often obscured the perspective on general issues and adopted instead the broad survey as the mode suited to "the magnitude of our present subject of inquiry." Also, in conformity to current practice, he calibrated his narrative according to the relative importance of the fiscal units and departed thus again from the absurdity of the attempt, characteristic of his primary sources, "to exhibit . . . the vast financial operations of a mighty empire . . . partially by undefined unwieldy provinces, and partly by the frittered divisions of an insignificant hamlet."[11] In local history, too, like the one that came in with a letter from Samuel Davis, Assistant on deputation to the Collector of Bhagalpur, it would be easy to see a typically eighteenth-century European notion of the past struggling with an odd assortment of folklore and genealogies and patwari accounts to produce a narrative which the senior members of the government in Calcutta might recognize as "a general historical account of the zemindars and zemindaries" of Pargana Monghyr (Munger).[12] There was no Indian history written by a British author during the late eighteenth century which did not show signs of such struggle.

We have spoken of the beginnings of colonialist historiography as a history of turbulence. Far from being a benign gift of metropolitan liberalism, it was complicit to a project that turned conquest into occupation. The issue of an ethnological encounter, its function was to aid a foreign power forcibly to exploit the resources of our land. And far from being the smooth and self-confident discourse that it grew up to be in the nineteenth century under the impact of Mill's *History of British India,* it was, during the first thirty-five years or so of Diwani, a rather awkward genre in which native content and alien form were still not at peace with each other in the body of the narrative. We wanted to emphasize this turbulence in order to remind ourselves that no colonialist knowledge had ever been anything but an intrusion even at the hour of its debut. Like every other aspect of colonialism—like a battle of Plassey or the arrival of an East Indiaman on the Hugli or the setting up of a filature in a Birbhum village—it always had to make its way through friction. Historiography, too, had to do so.

Education as an Instrument of Colonialism

It follows from what has been said so far that the early official attempt to historicize the Indian past amounted to a simple technical
exercise. Its purpose was not so much to promote the writing of history as to enable the East India Company to end its dependence on
the indigenous method of storing and retrieving information about
landed property and land management. Indeed, this historiography
was, like any other technical knowledge, instrumental in character,
a knowledge focused accurately and exclusively on the end for
which it was devised, namely, the collection of revenues. There was
hardly anything in this narrow specialization that could be expected
to generate a movement towards encouraging Indians to write their
own history. On the contrary, it was, from the Indian point of view,
an adversary knowledge which inspired some of the most obnoxious
governmental procedures such as the scrutiny of zamindari accounts and cadastral surveys and measurements. The former was
bitterly resented by the proprietors, while the peasants' resistance to
the latter developed into jacqueries in a number of districts.[13]

Where, then, should we situate the impulse for the agenda invoked at the beginning of the chapter? The answer that readily
comes to one's mind is, of course, education. By the last quarter of
the nineteenth century education had already established itself as
the most distinctive aspect of westernization in our culture.
Bankimchandra took notice of this when, in 1886, he observed,
"The term *sikshita* has now become the usual designation for those
who have been educated in the Western mode," and went on to
define the sikshita negatively as Indians who had been alienated
from traditional learning by the very nature of such education.
"They are not to be blamed for this," he remarked; "this is the
natural consequence of their education . . . Nowadays the members of the sikshita community conform to Western modes of
thinking from their very infancy, and are not acquainted with the
systems of ancient Indian thought."[14]

Ironically, however, it is by identifying *siksha* thus as antony-
mous to *vidya*, and education as a displacement of tradition, that
Bankimchandra identified himself as one of the community of the
sikshita. Since the beginning of the century, since its second decade to be precise, the latter had come to believe in education as

merely another way of thinking. This was indeed how the colonial regime itself wanted education to be thought. All its agencies, private, public and missionary, projected education exclusively in the image of a spiritual operation on the native mind. "To animate intellectual exertion and facilitate the acquirement of knowledge" was what an official of the Committee of Public Instruction described as the aim of the institutions under its control.[15]

But how true was that description? Did education have nothing other than intellectual exertion and advancement of knowledge for its content? Was it simply the code of an innocuous alternative culture? Although colonialism and the many-sided thrust of liberal politics made it out to be so, there was more to education than that. It stood not only for enlightenment but also authority—a fact which it has been the function of ideology in all its forms, including historiography, to hide from the educators and the educated alike. In other words, it was an ideological effect that made both the propagators and the beneficiaries of education look upon it as a purely cultural transaction and ignore that aspect which related it directly to power.

Taking the transactional metaphor one step further, one could say that if propagating and benefiting, giving and receiving were to be regarded as a semiosis, education would not figure in it as a denotative code of culture at all. On the contrary, it would be found, on a closer look, to have functioned at two different, though related, levels of expression, each with a different content assigned to it. At one level that content was culture, and at another, power. Education, under the historical conditions of British rule, made thus for a connotative structure of the kind in which, as Louis Hjelmslev has argued, expression and content were asymmetrically superimposed on each other to constitute a layered text. Or, one could say (following Umberto Eco's adaptation of the same structure) that education was a text whose content was a multi-levelled discourse formed by the coupling of a code of culture and a code of power.[16]

We speak of this complexity in order to demonstrate how education related to colonial dominance not only as a means of persuasion, but as an arm of its coercive apparatus as well. It is a fact of history which the ideology of liberalism, in its eagerness to display education merely in a hegemonic role, would rather forget. But there is a great deal of evidence to show that the aim of education, as conceived by the founders of the raj, was far from emancipatory.

It was designed to harness the native mind to the new state apparatus as a cheap but indispensable carrier of its administrative
burden. Philip Francis, the first of the Company's officers to grasp
the importance of education for the formation of a colonial state
and far more astute in this respect than Warren Hastings himself,
had recommended, as early as 1775, the schooling of native youths
in English as a condition for their recruitment into the bureaucracy. "If . . . the English language could be introduced into the
transaction of business, . . . it would be attended with convenience
and advantage to Government and no distress or disadvantage to
the natives," he wrote in a letter to Lord North. "To qualify themselves for employment, they would be obliged to study English
instead of Persian. If schools were established in the districts, . . .
a few years would produce a set of young men qualified for business, whose example and success would spread, and graft the
institution gradually into the manners of the people."[17]

Some fifty years later, when the raj had finally come into its own,
the Committee of Public Instruction was to pick up precisely that
state-building theme and observe that the institutions under its
superintendence, though not connected with the Fort William College, had "one object common with it—the training up of a class of
Public Officers in whose example and influence the moral and
intellectual improvement of the people [might] be confidently anticipated."[18] Francis's eighteenth-century idea was incorporated
into the vision of a postrevolutionary bourgeois state run by the
bureaucracy as a "universal class" in which efficiency would be
fruitfully wedded to virtue—power to culture.

However, under the conditions of colonial rule, that is, the rule
of a post-revolutionary bourgeoisie in a state without citizenship,
such a vision was bound to end up in a caricature of itself. And so
it did. What most of the first beneficiaries of education imbibed
from it as a code of culture was a superficial Anglicism amounting
to a mimicry of the vigorous liberalism of metropolitan England.
To say this is not to tarnish the brilliance of the fifteen or so brave
Derozians[19] who have always provided the cult of Bengal Renaissance with its quotes on reason and reform, nor to diminish the
youthful charm of their inconsequential defiance of convention
which never fails to remind us, a community of equally inconsequential intellectuals, that once we were young.

But with the exception of that illustrious minority whose whim-
sicalities are often unhistorically assimilated to the far more momentous, far more difficult, and indeed qualitatively different
struggles and achievements of Rammohun Roy and Ishwarchandra
Vidyasagar as those, respectively, of a predecessor and a successor—with our homage paid to them as is appropriate, what we are
left with is a sprawling mediocrity given to flaunt its uncritical
imitation of the West as a cultural achievement. The shallow and
purely imitative character of that culture was recognized as such
and denounced not by the troglodytes of Hindu conservatism alone,
but also by some of those who were amongst the educated themselves and had come to know that phenomenon at first hand.

How they tried to distance themselves from that Anglo-Indian
charade could be sensed, for instance, from what was evidently
Michael Madhusudan Dutt's own comment, as he put it in the
mouth of a character in his play, *Ekei Ki Bawley Sabhyota?* There a
middle-class woman explodes in utter disgust when her young and
educated husband returns home at the end of an evening of debauchery and makes a racket under the influence of alcohol. "It
seems," she says, "that the only knowledge cultivated really well by
many of the educated in Calcutta nowadays is that [of womanizing
and drinking] . . . And these shameless creatures go on boasting
that they have become cultured like the sahibs. To gorge oneself
on wine and meat and dally—is that how one becomes cultured?
Is this what you call culture?" (Act II, Sc. 2).[20]

At one point in the play, its hero, the educated debauchee, meets
his cronies at a club called "The Association of the Ocean of
Knowledge" (Jnanatarangini Sabha), but used in fact for the cultivation of carnal knowledge and consumption of liquor, and in-
augurates the evening's merriments with a little speech thus:
"Gentlemen, this country is at present like a vast prison for us; this
club house alone is our hall of liberty, our palace of freedom; you
may feel free to do whatever you like." He concludes in English
with the words, "Gentlemen, in the name of freedom, let us enjoy
ourselves," asks for drinks to be served, and calls upon the two
whores hired for the occasion to begin the nautch. "Come open the
ball, my beauties," he commands, again in English. (Act II, Sc. 1).[21]

The prison mentioned in this speech stood, of course, for Hindu
conservatism and not colonial subjection; the phrases "liberty" and

"freedom" were meant to militate only against values and relations internal to Hindu society and not against those that inhered in the power structure of the raj. Which shows how words and ideas that had been political dynamite in Europe had their critical charge doused and defused by colonialist education in our subcontinent. Indeed, what most of the nineteenth-century beneficiaries of that education imbibed from it as a code of power was unquestioning servility to the ruling power.

The Importance of English

The progress of such education as a measure of increasing middle-class acquiescence to colonialism was abundantly clear to Sivnath Shastri when he looked back on it in the early years of our century. "As the paramountcy of the English came to be more and more firmly established from year to year," he wrote, "as the legal, juridical and other institutions for governance were gradually built up, and businessmen arrived from England in large numbers and set up commercial firms in Calcutta, the native inhabitants, and especially the middle-class families of Calcutta amongst them, were increasingly seized with the urge to have their children educated in the English manner."[22] The connection between the urge for education and the consolidation of the raj, noted here by Shastri, had ideological consequences which were soon to be made explicit by the bhadralok's response to the Mutiny. The difficulty of reconciling that response with the image of our educated nineteenth-century forbears as pioneers of a freedom movement is a conundrum on which the problematic of Indian history under British rule will continue to turn for a long time yet.

In dealing with that conundrum, we who are spiritual successors to the alumni of the first colonial schools are quite understandably rather more circumspect than were the insurgents of Hamirpur in Uttar Pradesh at the outbreak of the Mutiny. There, on 14 June 1857—we quote from an eye-witness account published soon afterwards—"the sowars attended by a number of *badmashes* of the place, began to parade through the streets armed with swords and latties, and put to the sword every Christian and every Bengalee whom they could suspect of an acquaintance with English."[23] What must have been, by and large, an illiterate crowd of mutineers and small-town poor, appears thus to have acted according to a view they came to take of education as an exercise in politics by another name. It is salutary, therefore, for us to recognize that such a view, formed not by learning but by understanding born of oppression and exploitation, is corroborated by historical evidence as well.

For some of that evidence one may turn to a number of essays written by students of the Hindu College in answer to the question: "Has Europe or Asia benefited most by the discovery of the passage round the Cape of Good Hope to India?" These essays were proudly exhibited by the school authorities at a prize-giving ceremony in January 1828. Here is an excerpt from one of them.

> Of all the nations of Europe . . . the English have derived the greatest advantage by this passage . . . On the other hand it must be acknowledged, that it has also, in some measure, contributed to the good of Asia, particularly in the countries under the British sway; for in the time of the Mohammedan tyrants, nothing but luxury and oppression prevailed among the nobles; they had properly speaking, no fixed laws for the administration of justice. In fact, the Natives suffered the most mortifying proofs of their cruelties, until Providence, to avert the evil, brought them under the illustrious sway of the English, who not only freed this country from their hands, but have adopted all possible measures for its amelioration, introducing arts, sciences, schools, academies and colleges for the dissemination of knowledge.

Another student, too, concluded in much the same vein, saying that as a result of that discovery "we are safe every way, improving in literature and the sciences day by day, and shall continue to do so as long as the British patronizing sway shall rule over us."[24]

Clearly, the politics of collaboration caught the natives young. The youthful enthusiasm for Western science and literature and the institutions set up to promote these was predicated unquestioningly on an appreciation of "the illustrious sway of the English." After that there would be only one short step for the student to take before maturing into a committed loyalist as he left school for employment at a lower rung of the colonial administration or with a British mercantile firm or for a career in one of the liberal professions or simply for a life of leisure as an absentee landlord.

It was this loyalist, political aspect of education that was rudely exposed by the violence of the Hamirpur uprising. By contrast, the colonial authorities went on insisting on its sanitized, intellectual function alone, as they did when they tried to explain why the schoolboy encomia addressed to the raj were considered good enough for publication in the official journal. These were published, they said, "not with reference to any opinions they contain[ed], but solely with a view to their literary character, and to shew the progress that [had] been made by the Hindoo students in European History and Composition."[25] There is little in this apology to show that education was indeed quarantined from "opinions." The latter, understood broadly as politics, were explicit in the self-assurance with which the educators nominated the discovery of the route to India as a theme of "European History" and *not* of South Asian history.

What constituted the politics of such thematization was its attempt to persuade Indians to take pride in an event that made for their subjection to a number of Western powers culminating in the establishment of British paramountcy by an act of conquest. To teach Indians to appreciate that discovery as a triumph and an achievement, when triumph meant their own defeat and achievement the loss of independence, was clearly a lesson in power meant to educate the colonized to interpret the past not in terms of their own interests, but those of the colonizers. Education in history was thus designed as a servant's education — an education to conform undeviatingly to the master's gaze in regarding the past. It served the project of imperial dominance by annexing the past in order to pre-empt its use by the subject people as a site on which to assert their own identity. Any progress made by Indians in the study of this genre of history could only be a measure of the success with which they had been taught to acquiesce in the processes of such colonialist appropriation. There was nothing in this education, tailored meticulously to fit British imperial interests and the British point of view, to allow any distinctively Indian approach to the South Asian past. It would be in vain therefore to try and seek the impulse for an Indian historiography of India in this education.

The education we have discussed so far was anglophone education. It was the English language which functioned within that educational system as the purveyor of the knowledge it had for its content. As such, that language was complicit to both the codes, that is, the code of power and the code of culture, which gave education its meaning for colonizers and colonized in their roles, respectively, of educators and educated. To regard that complicity simply as instrumental in character would be to underestimate it. For it was, in a real sense, constitutive as well. The customary description of English as the medium of instruction would be of little help unless the medium were understood, in this instance, to have been integral to the message.

The importance of English as an emblem of power within the system of education was not the result of official sponsorship alone. Even before governmental agencies for education were set up, the schooling of Bengali boys had already begun at a number of Eurasian institutions. Thanks to that initiative, English gained recognition increasingly as a source of prestige for anyone with even a slight command of the language. Two of this first generation of scholars have been immortalized by Sivnath Shastri. Both of them went to Arratoon Petrus's school. Known as Nitai Sen the One-eyed and Advaita Sen the Cripple of Kolutola, "they could speak and write in a sort of broken English without any sense of grammar at all. Consequently," wrote Shastri, "the reputation and prestige they enjoyed in the contemporary Calcutta society knew no bounds. They used to flaunt their elevated status at *jatras* and other large festive gatherings by turning up in *kaba chapkan* (loose, flowing robes worn by aristocrats) and brocaded shoes. People used to look upon them with reverence."[26] Going by this evidence, English, as a status-marker, was obviously on a par with such insignia of social importance as courtly apparel. The latter was, for its wearers, a mark of high social standing in precolonial India. In much the same way, the language of the colonial rulers helped significantly to improve the social standing of any native who used it, even if he did so without proficiency.

English managed thus to insinuate itself into education's code of power already at this early date. But it did so only in an iconic sense. Just as their suits of kaba chapkan made the two youths of Kolutola look like noblemen, so did a smattering of English make them sound like the sahibs. Which shows that with these learners the language, as a signifying system, worked on the principle of similarity rather than on that of contiguity,[27] and had, therefore, not fully realized its potential yet as a linguistic form. One could indeed say, with V. N. Vološinov, that it was still trapped in the "process of recognition" and had not quite made it to the "process of understanding."[28]

According to him, these processes correspond respectively to the two states of a language as signal and sign. Language as signal is still not adequate to itself as a linguistic form. "Should a linguistic form remain only a signal, recognized as such by the understander, it, then, does not exist for him as a linguistic form." Signalization involves the use of words as "simply a technical means for indicating this or that object (some definite, fixed object) or this or that action (likewise definite and fixed)." It often dominates the teaching and learning of a foreign language. "In the process of mastering a foreign language," writes Vološinov, "signality and recognition still make themselves felt, so to speak, and still remain to be surmounted, the language not yet fully having become language." He illustrates this by a reference to an obviously primitive method of instruction in the Russian language: "A word extracted from context, written down in an exercise book, and then memorized together with its Russian translation undergoes signalization, so to speak."[29]

The similarity between this mode of instruction and the teaching of English in the early nineteenth-century Calcutta schools should be evident from what both Rajnarayan Basu and Sivnath Shastri had to say on the subject. To quote from the latter,

In those days, no one cared to give lessons in grammar nor teach the pupils how to construct sentences. Attention was limited primarily to the teaching of English words and their meanings. The greater the number of English words and their meanings memorized by a person, the higher was his standing and reputation as a man vastly learned in English . . . Consequently, some young lads would try and commit an entire English dictionary to memory. There were many schools where at the end of the day the pupils were made to recite English words [rhythmically] much in the same manner as they recited multiplication tables. Thus:

Philosopher — *Bijnalok*, Ploughman — *Chasha*,
Pumpkin — *Laukumro*, Cucumber — *Shosha*.[30]

But an "English education" of this kind, which "had little more than the mere language for its object"[31] (that was how the phenomenon of signalization was officially described), could not cope with the needs of power and culture in a maturing colonial state. For, although such education provided young Indians with "a sufficient command of [English] for conducting the details of official duty" and with "qualification as copyist[s] and accountant[s]," it did not prepare them for the more complex tasks which the consolidation and expansion of empire came increasingly to impose on even that lowest level of the bureaucracy where alone the natives could find employment. Nor did a mere word-book knowledge of English help them to assimilate the values and ideas of British liberalism well enough to justify any claim by the rulers that the raj was based on consent rather than force. In other words, the imperatives of both power and culture required that English, as a linguistic form, should outgrow signality and function as a truly dynamic system of signs in its role of a medium of instruction. For "the ideal of mastering a language is absorption of signality by pure semioticity and of recognition by pure understanding."[32]

Under the conditions of colonial rule still in its formative phase, any progress from signality to semioticity in the use of English for Indian education was bound to have the most momentous of political consequences. It would forge that language into a hegemonic instrument to persuade the subject population about the desirability of its own subjection. Education would unfold, therefore, as an ideological campaign with English assigned, in a variety of discursive forms, the task of committing the colonized to the notion of colonialism as a historically necessary and beneficial development.

The importance of the Hindu College in this campaign is too well-known to require elaboration. It was here that a systematic attempt was made for the first time, at an institutional level, to put "the ideal of mastering a language" by teaching based on literary texts rather than word-books, on lessons in grammar rather than spelling, on writing rather than memorizing. The aim of education at that college was, according to the *Calcutta Gazette*, "to teach [the] Bengalee youth to read and relish English literature; to store their minds with the facts of history and science, and to enable them to express just conclusions in a clear and polished style, founded upon

a comprehensive view of the constitution of society and the phenomena of nature."[33]

But the actual achievement of this program greatly exceeded
mere curricular efforts at "the extension of human knowledge and
the diffusion of European science and learning among the Native
subjects." For in addition to training the minds of the native youths,
it also benefited them spiritually, according to the authorities, by
"enlarging the sphere of their understanding, and freeing them from
the spell of prejudice, which [had] so long bound them to their
primeval notions and customs."[34] In short, education, mediated by
English, deposited Western values into the soul of the educated.

Its cumulative effect was to be described by Bankimchandra as
nothing short of a chasm that had already, by the penultimate
decade of the century, made it impossible for the new generation
of the educated and the older generation of traditional scholars to
communicate with each other.

> This community of the educated [he wrote] cannot understand
> the discourses of traditional scholarship, even if these are trans-
> lated into Bangla. Just as the pandits belonging to the traditional
> schools *(tols)* find it difficult to understand statements made by
> Europeans, even when they read these in translation, those who
> have been educated in the western mode, do not find it easy to
> grasp what the traditional eastern scholars have said, even when
> that is available in translation . . . The Western mode of thinking
> is so very different from the traditional Indian mode of thinking
> that the translation of ideas cannot be achieved simply by the
> translation of one language into another.[35]

Thanks to colonialist education, English had thus become constitutive of thought itself for the educated. It cut them off from
their own tradition. By the same token, it also made their own past
inaccessible to them as a history. Since the contemporary mode of
historicizing the past was an aspect of post-Enlightenment European thought made available to Indians solely by "Anglo-Indian
education" and English, they did not know how to think it in any
way other than did their rulers. This was particularly true of the
most recent past—the colonial past, for it was there that the texts
constructed by the ruling culture were most active in persuading
the colonized in favor of an interpretation supportive of colonial

176 Dominance without Hegemony

rule. Far from promoting any development towards a distinctively Indian historiography of colonial India, anglophone education ended up as a vehicle of ideologies that hindered it.

III. Colonialism and the Languages of the Colonized

Indigenous Languages Harnessed to the Raj

If the urge for an indigenous historiography did not come from the bonding of education and the language of the rulers, could it then be said to have issued from the other kind of bonding, namely, that of education and the indigenous languages? The importance of that connection for the making of the colonial state and its culture was at least as critical and pervasive as was the relation between English rule in the subcontinent and English. Much of what was original about the raj and distinguished it from the historic outcome of some of the other European adventures of the mercantilist era, may be traced precisely to this connection. For purposes of comparison, one could turn to that well-known instance of European expansion chronicled by Bernal Díaz in his classic account, *The Conquest of New Spain*.[36] There, the author writes of the relation between conquest and language in all its lucidity and brutality. The Spaniards, we are told, taught Spanish to some of the natives taken as prisoners and used them as interpreters in their attempt to communicate with the indigenous peoples. The object of such communication was to acquire gold. The pattern was significantly different in the case of the British conquest of Bengal. Here, the Company's mercantile operations required "investment" of the land revenues in the purchase of piecegoods and a certain amount of raw material of various kinds. Conquest was therefore not content simply with grabbing and moving on to the next raid. It coveted regularity and tenure, which showed, among other things, that there had been a sea-change in the character of mercantilism itself since the sixteenth century. It was a measure of such change that instead of having their contact with the conquered mediated by native interpreters, as the Spaniards had done in Mexico, the British chose to deal directly with the subject population by learning their languages. Indeed, in India, unlike in New Spain, a knowledge of the indigenous languages was recognized by the rulers as an essential condition for the maintenance of their rule; and the Fort William College, set up in 1800, was the first historic step they took to harness Indian languages to the construction of a colonial state apparatus.

Of all the far-reaching consequences of this shotgun wedding of language and colonialism, the one most relevant to our argument here is the development of Bangla prose and the possibility it created for the production of a modern and autonomous Indian historiography. Three of the pandits appointed to assist in teaching the language at Fort William College were our first historians. Ramram Basu's *Raja Pratapaditya Charitra* (1801), Rajiblochan Mukhopadhyay's *Maharaj Krishnachandra Rayasya Charitram* (1805) and Mrityunjoy Bidyalankar's *Rajabali* (1808) were the very first books on history to be published in a vernacular under British rule. Written in what was soon to emerge as the standard form of the prose narrative in Bangla, all three works were textual sites of a conflict between archaism and modernism at both the literary and the historiographical levels. Many of the symptoms of that conflict have been diagnosed in terms of the distribution of *tatsama* and *tadbhava* phrases, the relative incidence of Persianism and Sanskritism in the vocabulary, and the peculiarities of collocation, syntax, and other grammatical features of these writings.[37] Judgments vary about the merits of individual authors and their performances, but there is a general agreement that their imperfections were merely the signs of strain in a language as it was about to enter a formative and critical phase of its career.

Linguistic immaturity in these early works was matched by flaws at the historiographical level as well. All three have been found by literary scholars as wanting in authenticity.[38] To which one could add a number of other obvious defects to show how these writings failed to measure up to the standards of modern historical discourse in their notion of time and in narrative structure. However, any such assessment must end up in empty abstraction, unless it takes into account the contradictions through which a rationalist historiography had to force its way before establishing itself in the intellectual milieu of a colonial society like that of nineteenth-century India — unless, that is, it recognizes the scars and bruises of that difficult passage in the faulty conception and craftsmanship of these first exercises.

For the history of discursive formations parallels, in this respect, that of social formations, which are never immaculate when they make their debut. Elements of all previous social formations persist within the most recent issue of the series not only as vestiges but also as constituents. Inevitably, therefore, a society is fraught with conflict between the old and the new from the very moment of its inception. That is why no capitalist mode of production has ever triumphed in its original habitat in Europe (the case of American capitalism with its foreshortened history being an exception in this regard) without encountering, combating, overcoming, and yet in a certain sense, yielding to the resistance of the feudal mode. And there has been no bourgeois culture in the Old World which did not have its taste of victory soured by the attrition of a contest with feudal culture and the need to compromise with it to some extent. What is true of capitalism is true of all other social formations as well. Every one of them has been inadequate to its concept and caught up, one could say after Marx, in the incompleteness of its own development.[39] The striving to cope with and make up for such inadequacy and incompleteness constitutes for each of them its historic project and the condition of all its dynamism.

Much the same could be said of discursive formations. Those, too, are born of turbulence and operate as tissues of contradiction within the cultures to which they belong. As such, they have it as their function to animate those cultures by an enduring struggle between the old and the new both at the level of expression and that of content. Even the European novel had its hegemony buffeted by the tensions of that struggle and its paramountcy modified by accommodation with elements of prenovelistic forms. Epitome of mimesis and realism, it still fed liberally, in its formative stages, on myth and romance as material for its plots.[40] Child of the age of printing, it continued for a long time to use narrative strategies derived from what Walter J. Ong has described as "the old oral narrator's world."[41]

Novels and Histories

The Bangla novel, too, borrowed freely from traditional prenovelistic forms in its early stages. The impact of Bankimchandra's pioneering contribution to this genre was so comprehensive and so dramatic that many of his contemporaries regarded the publication of his first novel, in 1865, as a complete break with our literary past. "We shall never forget that day," wrote Sivnath Shastri as one of them.

> Never before had there been a novel of that kind written in the Bangla language. We had been, until then, avid readers of *Bijay Basanta, Kamini Kumar* and a few other old-style novellas modelled on the [Sanskrit romance] *Kadamvari,* and of some short stories called *Hamsarupi Rajputra, Chakmokir Baksho* and others of that kind published by the Garhasthya Pustak Prachar Sabha, supplemented by a few exotic tales such as *Arabya Upanyas.* Of all these, it was only *Alaler Gharer Dulal* which had any claim at all to novelty. However, what we found in *Durgeshnandini* was altogether unprecedented.[42]

Rabindranath Tagore himself corroborated this testimony when he referred to *Bijay Basanta, Golebkaoli,* and such other "stories meant for the distraction of children" *(chhele-bhulano katha)* as "that darkness," which ended with the advent of *The Bangadarshan* and the serialization of Bankimchandra's novels in its pages.[43]

However, even after such tribute has been paid, as is unquestionably due to that historic watershed for which these novels stand in our literary culture, it will still be true to say that their break with the past was, in some significant ways, rather less radical than the observations cited above would imply. For there is a good deal of evidence in these works to show how the author drew freely on narratological and rhetorical conventions of pre-novelistic discourse — on the conventions of classical Sanskrit drama and epic poetry for some of his descriptions of nature; on those of Baishnab lyrics for the representation of sexuality and eroticism; on those of folk comedy and burlesque for his farcical effects; on those of oral literature like the ballad for direct address to the reader in an authorial voice; on those of Hindu mythology for prophecies and other forms of providential intervention as elements of narrative action, and so on. To note these traces of traditionalism and archaism in the works of our first modern novelist is not to underestimate his achievement but rather to enhance it. For it is only by identifying such relics and their constitutive effects that we can appreciate the heroism of the struggle to establish the novel as a genre in a culture which had no linguistic, narratological or ideological preparation for it at all.

The first three Bangla works on history preceded the first novel in that language by nearly sixty years. When these were written, there was even less in the conditions of our culture to support a rationalist historiography than the little that was there to assist in the rise of the novel later on in the century. Consequently, the linguistic, narratological, and ideological obstacles to historicization were even greater than those to "novelization" (to use M. Bakhtin's term). The deficiencies of these early historical discourses were all, in varying degrees, symptomatic of their encounter with such obstacles and its still indecisive outcome. It might be correct, in a formal sense, to use such deficiencies as a measure of their failure to match the standards of the rationalist historiography of contemporary Western Europe or those of Indian historiography of a later date. But what purpose would that serve except to reiterate the obvious? It would, in any case, do little to help our understanding of these texts as the site of a contest between very different, indeed mutually antagonistic, ways of interpreting the past. For all that flaws these works as historical discourse is evidence of the ongoing and indecisive character of that contest.

Nowhere are these shortcomings more pronounced than in *Rajabali*, if only because it is more comprehensive in its scope than the other two works. Mrityunjoy Bidyalankar looks at the past as one long, aggregative story of princely lives. It begins with a notice on the installation of the first Indian king Ikshvaku by God himself at some point in time during the Satyayug, surveys that and the next two *yugs* in two short paragraphs, and concentrates, for the rest of the work, on the Kaliyug and its rulers, commencing with the reign of Yudhisthhir and ending with the regime of the Company Bahadur installed, again, by God himself, some fifty years ago. The very first attempt made in the Bangla language to span all of the northern Indian past in a single discourse, it is a vast compendium of whatever information the author had of Hindu and Muslim princes, their wars, adventures and alliances, their pomp and grandeur, their liberality and cruelty, their good deeds and bad deeds, and so on. The serially arranged dynastic accounts in which these details are deposited higgledy-piggledy, do not rely in all instances on rigorously tested evidence, but draw indiscriminately on myths and unverified local legends and folklore. The result has been to compromise the text by too easy a traffic between the secular and the supernatural, between fact and fancy. It will not qualify as an entirely authentic work of history.

It is a matter of some significance, however, that a vernacular account of the Indian past, published in 1808, should lend itself to be questioned at all on the ground of evidence and authenticity. It indicates that all was not well with the hallowed sense of the past which had been reproducing itself in Puranic discourse for a thousand years or so until as recently as the eighteenth century. A youthful pretender, contemporary with the author himself, was keen on taking over memory's old estate and knocking at the gate. History had declared war on tradition. Yet it was clear that the struggle which had been thus engaged was by no means over. In the first decade of the nineteenth century and for some time to come, every historical discourse was still to bear the marks of resistance on the part of tradition. No wonder, therefore, that mythic genealogies, sacred geographies, fantasies of divine intervention, and other Puranic material of that sort clung resolutely to the text of *Rajabali*. But even there, the narrative managed to shake off much of the incubus as it progressed from the remote to the proximate past, as if to suggest that the balance was tilted inexorably in favor of history and the latter would overcome. Henceforth, there would be no going back to Purāṇa.

In saying this we take our cue from Bakhtin's observations on the role of the novel as a solvent of epic time. That role was paralleled in our culture by historiography in its relation to Puranic time. "The epic," wrote Bakhtin, with reference to the European genre of that name, "has been from the beginning a poem about the past, and the authorial position immanent in the epic and constitutive for it (that is, the position of the one who utters the epic word) is the environment of a man speaking about a past that is to him inaccessible, the reverent point of view of a descendant."[44] With the phrase "epic" replaced by "Purāṇa," this could pass for a precise description of the latter as that generic discourse by which Indian culture had, since antiquity, constructed and cyclically reproduced the past as a sacred and ancestral time, distantiated altogether from the times and values of its authors.

This was an "absolute past," and lacked "any relativity, that is, any gradual, purely temporal progressions that might connect it with the present," and especially that present in which the authors and their audiences belonged.[45] In Europe the emergence of the novel was, according to Bakhtin, the signal of "an enormous revolution in the creative consciousness of man," precisely because it had the present "taken as a starting point and center for artistic and ideological orientation." It was the intrusion of the present which desacralized and finally destroyed the absolute past of the epic by putting it in direct contact with reality and experience.[46]

In our culture the demolition of the absolute past of the Purāṇa began with historicization rather than with novelization (although the two were soon to join forces and deliver a *coup de grace*). The first three historical works in Bangla are all witness to that beginning. Although interlarded with Puranic elements, they all have the present as their point of departure. This is documented, to some extent at least, in a letter written by William Carey soon after his appointment as head of the Bangla department of Fort William College. "When the appointment was made," says Carey, "I saw that I had a very important charge committed to me, and no books or helps of any kind to assist me. I therefore set about compiling a grammar, which is now half printed. I got Ram Boshu to compose a history of one of their kings, the first prose book ever written in the Bengali language; which we are also printing."[47]

Thus the first prose narrative about the past to be written by a Bengali in his own language was commissioned as an unmistakably secular work and designed to serve the purely secular purpose of teaching the Company's servants how to put that language to official use. The Englishman who commissioned it defined its epistemic character as history and its function as an administrative teaching manual. The author, for his part, responded to that assignment as a writer addressing the past from his situation within his own world and his own age. As such, he set out consciously to produce a history rather than yet another Puranic tale. This emerges so clearly from the rectilinear structure of his narrative and the discrimination shown in his handling of evidence that the occasional indulgence in myth notwithstanding, the character of the work as rationalist historiography is recognized by modern scholarship.[48]

It would be wrong, however, to overestimate the control these pandits had over the mythic drift of their narratives. The struggle for historicization was to continue for a while yet. In Mrityunjoy Bidyalankar's work this is fought out as a contest between historical time and Puranic time.[49] The latter is invoked at the very beginning of the text together with elements of Hindu cosmology and a sacred geography to provide what is apparently regarded by the author as an indispensable background for the mundane chronicle of the kings of Bharatbarsha which is, of course, only one of the nine Barshas of Jambudvip, which is itself only one of the Seven Islands which, taken together with the Seven Seas, constitute the world.[50] Time, we are told, is reckoned in that world according to its division made by Parameshwar the Supreme Being himself into Kalpa, Manu, Yug, and Batsar, with 432,000 Batsars adding up to a Yug, 284 Yugs to a Manu, 14 Manus to a Kalpa, and 30 Kalpas to the totality of all time. Within that temporal scheme our own time belongs to the Yug called Kali, which is the hundred-and-twelfth Yug of the seventh Manu called Baibasvat, which is a component of the Kalpa of the White Boar (Svetabaraha Kalpa).

Heady stuff, and one starts wondering what history has to do with this. However, a second glance at this mind-blowing arithmetic makes it obvious that preoccupation with such divinely ordained temporality has not prevented the author from situating himself and his discourse at a determinate point of worldly time identified as the year 1726 of the Saka Era or 1805 Anno Domini. That is his own time, a benchmark of the present from which he speaks.

But how is it possible, the reader may ask, to situate oneself at a determinate point of worldly time within so meticulously constructed an aeonic space? The answer clearly is that this cannot be done without running into an irresolvable contradiction like the one implied by Bidyalankar's horological metaphor when he refers to the movement of the wheel of time *(kalachakra)* made up of the thirty Kalpas as a clockwork *(ghatiyantrer nyay).*[51] To introduce clockwork into the mythic time of the Kalpas is to dissolve its cyclicity into linear, natural time, just as to introduce the authorial present in a discourse is to free it from thraldom to Puranic time and transpose it to historical time. It is the introjection of that "now" of the writer and the writing which historicizes the text of *Rajabali* and saves it from being swamped in the plethora of mythic matter deposited there by a sense of the past still partially bound to tradition.

Beginnings of an Indigenous Rationalist Historiography

The movement inaugurated thus by the first three historical works in Bangla prose to demythologize the Indian past, continued to gather momentum over the decades. An unexpected consequence which outweighed, in importance, the stimulus that had originated from Carey's need to have manuals written for the training of civilians, it was helped on its way by a number of factors such as the adoption of Bangla as an official medium of public instruction, the growing demand for and production of history text-books in that language, the multiplier effects of a liberal education in increasing the appetite for historical literature and of Orientalism in enhancing the value of the indigenous past, and generally, a new-found faith in the creativity of *matribhasha* (mother-tongue). Thanks to this and more, not all of which we have the time to consider here, an indigenous, rationalist historiography matured to the point when, by the middle of the century, it would feel strong enough to make decisive inroads into the Puranic past.

Let us take Nilmani Basak's *Nabanari,* published in 1852, as an instance of that development. This work is in a certain sense more representative of the author's skill as a modern historian and of the state of contemporary historiography than the three volumes of *Bharatbarsher Itihas,* for which he is better known. *Nabanari,* literally, *Nine Women,* is, as the sub-title of the book indicates, a collection of "biographical studies of nine ancient and modern women."[52] Such a characterization need not detract from its standing as a genuinely historical discourse. It is, in that respect, an altogether different kind of exercise from Ishwarchandra Vidyasagar's studies in illustrious lives, *Charitabali* (Calcutta, 1856), a difference which it is easy to overlook in view of the latter's association with Basak's work, as acknowledged by the author himself in a prefatory note.

With Vidyasagar, the *charit,* as a genre, operates at the level of morality—social morality, to be precise. That genre does not require any development in time. All it is concerned with is a particular set of moral principles as illustrated, positively or otherwise, by the protagonist's action or experience. It is thus a genre which is synchronic in concept. By contrast, *jibancharit,* as we find it in Nilmani Basak's work (and indeed in Vidyasagar's own series of

that name published in 1849), derives its form and movement from
the development of an individual's life within a concrete social and
cultural context. Diachronic in concept, it is essentially a genre
that has its place within historiography. Indeed, the correspondence between the historical and the biographical forms in the
Bangla prose narrative replicates so closely an analogous relationship within the European literary tradition that it must be recognized as yet another instance of a new orientation in our culture
brought about by the union of the indigenous languages and the
rationalist historiography of the West.

What makes Basak's *Nabanari* particularly significant for us is
that seven out of the nine women whose lives are discussed there
are figures lifted directly out of Hindu mythology.[53] But he sets out
resolutely to treat them as if they were no less real than the two
historical personages on his list. The evidential value of the Puranic
lives is, for him, as good as that of the historical ones. They refute,
he says in his preface, the baseless notion many foreigners have
about the Indian past as wanting altogether in learned and talented
women. By valorizing the mythic lives thus on a par with the real
lives he abolishes the distinction between mythic past and real past
at one stroke and provides for myth the condition it needs for
swamping history in his narrative. However, what his studies of
the seven Puranic lives end up doing, is the very opposite: they
historicize the myths. This is achieved by the use of rhetorical and
narrative devices to create such secular, rationalist effects in the
text as would make the historicity of its contents obvious to the
reader.

To start with, he desacralizes the mythic lives by the stratagem
of adopting them as biographical themes. "It has not been customary in this country," he observes, "to write any biographies."[54]
Indeed, the sanctity of myth is safe only so long as it is contained
in customary discourse. To plunder mythic material for biography
is therefore to violate custom and secularize myth at the same time.
The secularist design is made all the more explicit by the author's
claim to have compressed all of the Rāmāyaṇa and the Mahābhārata respectively into his essays on Sita and Draupadi "in order
to make this book pleasurable reading." There is no definition of
pleasure by which the story of these two lives as given in the epics
can be said to make for "pleasurable reading." Spiritually edifying,

morally uplifting—yes; but, "pleasurable?"—hardly so. Trapped in the sacred texts, Sita and Draupadi stood for ideals whose function was to teach by example. To be entertaining, they had first to be taken out of their Puranic mould and humanized. This was done in popular culture by art operating for the most part at a preliterate level. By the middle of the nineteenth century, with the novel still at an incipient stage, it was up to the relatively mature historical-biographical discourse to do that for an increasingly literate and educated culture constituted by a readership acquainted with the printed word.

Basak makes his humanizing and secularizing intention quite obvious when he says, "There is hardly any literature to inform us when the women whose biographies are given in this book, were born and how many years they lived. Consequently, reference to birth-date and age has been left out of this writing." An apology of this kind would have been quite irrelevant had the object of the writing not been regarded as historical personalities; for the bio-graphical details said to be wanting are not required for the con-struction of mythic lives, nor indeed is it necessary to support such construction by reference to any authoritative literature. The writer is apparently eager to demonstrate that he has taken care to subject his work to the kind of verification which applies to ration-alist historiography, even if his material is entirely Puranic. This is emphasized further by the claim he makes for his exercise as one based on research *(anusamdhan)* and compilation of data *(samkalan)*, neither of which is essential for the recycling of an absolute past that is simply given and inherited.

The narration itself also testifies to a historicizing strategy at work. Take, for example, the study of Sita, based, as Basak says, on the Rāmāyaṇa. Yet the cyclical time of that text has been recast by him in order to produce a linear discourse situated, like a novel, in homogeneous time. An exercise in pure diachrony, it dispenses with the procedure, adopted in the original, to use a mythic past as an aid to contextualizing the present. By contrast, the past works in this biography as an aspect of secular sub-plots which run on parallel lines to the main story and are inserted occasionally into the latter by analeptic operators such as "at that time" *(oi samaye)*, "at this time" *(ei samaye)*, "in the meantime" *(e dike)*, and so forth. The convergences brought about in this manner help to structure the narrative as a series of ordered episodes joined sequentially by diachronic markers like *anantar* (then), *tadanantar* (after that), *kiyatkalanantar* (after some time), *kiyatkal pare* (after a while), and other phrases more or less synonymous with "thereafter" in English.

It is by such devices that the author recuperates the past from mythology to invest it in historiography. But for a reference to Sita's miraculous birth in the very first paragraph of the essay—a nod in the direction of mythology without which the story could not be told at all and for which, in any case, he shrugs off responsibility by attributing it to Valmiki—and the equally obligatory mention of *vanaras* and *rakshasas* (mythic apes and monsters who figure respectively as the hero's friends and foes in the epic battle of the Rāmāyaṇa), there is nothing that makes this biography different in structure from the studies on Ahalyabai and Rani Bhabani, the two historical personages on his list of illustrious lives. Thus a rationalist discourse which enables linearity to replace cyclicity and the secular the sacred even in traditional narratives, celebrates in Nilmani Basak's *Nabanari* the coming of age of a modern historiography in Bangla. It was a decisive victory in that struggle to free the Indian past from the coils of epic time, which had begun with the works of the pandits of Fort William College some fifty years ago.

The maturation of historiography coincided with that of the Bangla language as well. A belief had begun to gain ground that if the latter could lend itself to creative use for something so complex and so radical in its break with tradition as a rationalist representation of the Indian past, it could be trusted to do anything. It would not be long before a comment[55] about that language being "ill adapted for the very stately measure and sonorous cadence of blank verse" was to provoke Michael Madhusudan Dutt to write a poem in four cantos precisely in blank verse and prove his friend, the doubter, to have grossly underestimated Bangla. *Tilottamasambhav Kavya*, Madhusudan's intervention in that famous debate which took place at Belgachia Villa on a summer evening in 1859, has found its place in literary history as an act of faith. Far less known is the fact that, in this respect, poetry had already been anticipated by historiography. For the publication of Nilmani Basak's three-volume work, *Bharatbarsher Itihas*, in 1857–1858, was also an act of faith. Writing it was, for the author, an affirmation of the claim that the Indian past could be represented more attractively and more authentically in Bangla than in English. The history of India, Basak remarked in his introduction to that work,[56] was written up mostly in English. The few books in Bangla which dealt with history were "merely translations from English" and lacked so utterly in aesthetic quality *(nirash)* that people would either not read them at all or would feel dissatisfied even if they did. As for the English works, these were, according to him, both prejudiced and ill-informed about the Hindu past. Students who read them at school were led to believe that "the religions and customs of this country were all based on falsehood and the ancient Hindus were a very stupid lot." It was "to remedy these defects," he said, that he had undertaken to write *Bharatbarsher Itihas* in Bangla.

An Ideology of Matribhasha

The critique of anglophone historiography and Nilmani Basak's resolve to overcome its inadequacy by the use of Bangla were both premised apparently on the belief that there was a special relationship between the Indian past and an indigenous language, which made of the latter a more competent and sensitive instrument for writing Indian history. For, by this time, Bangla was beginning to be recognized by its educated middle-class speakers as an index of their identity and trusted to represent truthfully that vital dimension of their existence which constituted the Indian past. A language-consciousness was allowed thus to stand in for self-consciousness so that by the end of the 1840s a sentiment about matribhasha had already crystallized into an ideology. Such an ideology had of course been prefigured in the conservative resistance to English as purveyor of a liberal culture and its traces continued, throughout the rest of the century, to mark both the gravity of denunciation by priests and pandits and the levity of folk comment registered, for instance, in Rupchand Pakshi's bilingual verses. But this fear of English as the enemy of tradition was soon exceeded by a positive concern for the prestige and potentialities of the mother language. The point of that concern was not so much to replace English as to make Bangla emulate it.

The initiative for emulation, as for so many other things, came from Rammohun Roy, when by rendering the Vedanta into Bangla he demonstrated how the latter could be made to work for the popularization of Hindu theology just as the missionaries made it work for the propagation of Christianity. It is significant that the importance of the vernacular highlighted thus by so renowned an Anglicist and liberal did not prevent the idea from being adopted even by some of the more conservative intellectuals who, on many other matters, differed with the Raja. One of them, Ishwarchandra Gupta campaigned consistently and vigorously for the promotion of Bangla in his journal *Sambad Prabhakar*. "The people of every nation cherish their *national language* and try to learn it well," he wrote in an editorial in 1848. "But it is a curious fact that the people of this country pay no attention to national education and devote most of their energies to cultivating English. The lack of interest and care on their part has, therefore, impeded the progress of Bangla."[57]

Notice the phrase "national language" *(jatiya bhasha)* in this passage. Throughout the 1850s that phrase was used in this journal interchangeably with matribhasha to indicate that the natural language of the Bengali people had already been made into an ideological marker by which the literate part of the population identified all native speakers as constituting a "nation" and distinguished them from their English-speaking rulers. The colonized would henceforth use their own language consciously and systematically as a defining element of their relationship with the colonizers.

Like all the other elements of that relationship, this too was not without its tensions. It was used, on the one hand, to signal to the rulers the complete acquiescence of the intelligentsia to their rule. The *Prabhakar* was therefore quite consistent when it anticipated the loyalism of its editorial comment on the Mutiny by advocating, for years before that event, the need to improve instruction in Bangla on the ground that it would help the colonial authorities to govern more efficiently and the colonized to propagate better "the contents of books written in English" presumably for their own good.[58] But the promotion of matribhasha for hegemonic use was only one aspect of its deployment as ideology. The relationship of dominance and subordination to which it was assimilated, was also charged with antagonism. For the subordinate language to emulate the dominant was not only to acknowledge the latter's superiority, but also to enter into rivalry with it in an attempt to achieve parity. Concern for and amelioration of the mother language became issues thus in a contest for prestige.

No contest could be more circumspect, but none more important for the development of our literature and historiography. At a time when acquiescence to British rule was parametric to middle-class notions of politics, we have here an instance which it would be wrong to designate as resistance or defiance in any sense that is explicit or otherwise pronounced. A movement, with its springs rooted deeply in that relation which man as species-being has with his natural language, it was no more than a reflex action of the will. The passions it inspired and the metaphors of motherhood used to describe it, were all evidence of its rootedness in such a primordial connection. Madhusudan Dutt based himself precisely on that connection in arguing why Bangla was suitable for blank verse while French was not. "The Bengali is born of the Sanskrit than which a more copious and elaborate language does not exist," he said.[59] Again, in a famous sonnet, he paid tribute to Bangla as the daughter who surpassed in beauty her mother, Sanskrit, born of the gods.[60]

Copious, elaborate, beautiful, divine—words of high praise such as these were a measure of the distance in time and values from those of Rammohun Roy, who had thought it fit to emphasize the poverty of that very language before proceeding to advise his readers on how to cope with its use in the prose of his *Vedanta Grantha*.[61] That was in 1815. By contrast, there was nothing defensive at all in the claim Shyamacharan Sarma Sarkar made for the language in 1850. "The Bengali," he wrote, "is a truly noble language even in its present state, able to convey almost any idea with precision, force and elegance. Words may be compounded with such facility, and to so great an extent that any scientific or technical term of any language may be rendered by an exact equivalent—an advantage which, amongst the dead and living languages of Europe, is possessed by Greek and German."[62] It was such confidence in the strength and potentiality of the language that induced Madhusudan Dutt to emulate Milton in poetry and Nilmani Basak to try and surpass all of anglophone writing in Indian historiography. For a people who, during the middle decades of the century, were forcefully and insistently reminded of their subjection, the triumph, even an imaginary triumph, of matribhasha over European languages, was no mean compensation for a battered self-respect.

It would be unfair, however, to think of this faith merely as the product of an imagination in ferment. For it was inspired, to no small extent, by an assessment of the limitations and possibilities of the language as demonstrated in practice. Such an assessment had been, for modern Bangla, especially in its prose form, a part of the process of its growing up. Its dialogic situation, which forced it constantly to enter into exchanges with English, put its resources to test in every transaction wherever it took place — on the page of an administrative document, in literary writing, in school manuals, at mercantile offices in conversations between sahibs and babus, and any number of such encounters. Every semantic slide that occurred in such exchanges was evidence not only of what Bangla could not do, but also of what it could. For every difference which, in any instance, survived the most exacting attempt at translation, was an index of its originality: it revealed a property of the matribhasha for which no other language had an equivalent to offer. That originality could, of course, be put to genuinely creative use only in autonomous exercises where the compulsion to fit the language to a foreign text or to a foreigner's want of aptitude for it, did not constrain its freedom to generate sentences according to the full measure of its competence.

It was precisely a constraint of this kind to which Basak objected when he spoke of translations from anglophone works in history as aesthetically inadequate and unreadable. He could have made the point equally well by addressing his critique to the inadequacies of historical works written by foreigners in Bangla, such as J. C. Marshman's influential and widely-read *Bharatbarsher Itihas*, published in two volumes in 1831. Sushil Kumar De has cited an extract from this work as a sample of what he calls the "pervading uniformity and general sameness" of European writing in Bangla at this time.[63] The extract is a description of the battle of Plassey, and it is indeed illuminating, as De suggests, to compare it with an account of the same event in Rajiblochan Mukhopadhyay's *Maharaj Krishnachandra Rayasya Charitram*.[64]

Of the two, Marshman's is the more straightforward reporting of the event with one sentence devoted to mobilization of the rival armies, two to their respective strengths in men and arms, and three to the actual battle and its conclusion in British victory as a result of Mir Jafar's treachery. All this is written in a terse, matter-of-fact manner intended to distance the author from the event and attest thereby to the objectivity of his report. The only comment that is his own comes at the very end where he says how this relatively minor battle in which the total number of casualties was only seventy-two, taking both the sides together, had the consequence of changing the destinies of sixty million people in a vast kingdom. It is a comment that also stands for a closure and attests to the narrative's status as a historical discourse.[65]

By contrast, Rajiblochan's account does not appear to be excessively concerned with the appearance of objectivity or narrative closure. It concludes with the statement that "Thereafter, the Nawab's troops stopped fighting and took to flight, and the English were victorious"—an episodic ending that has no pretension to being anything more decisive than what could be a pause before the beginning of another tale. This agrees with the anecdotal mode of story-telling—the mode of the Indian *akhyayika*—according to a plot that opposes Mohanlal's loyalty to Mir Jafar's betrayal. Thanks to such a plot, the event assumes the character of a drama in which the passions of its protagonists and the uncertainties of the battle are brought together to make for an experience that resists being reduced to a mere reportage like the one in Marshman's work. There can be little doubt that with all its naive, chatty and episodic air, this narrative impresses the reader as the more attractive of the two accounts of the battle, if only because it does not represent the event simply as a deployment of armies and its outcome, but as a tissue of conflicting choices objectified in the violence of a struggle for power.

The difference between these two representations shows that a historian's relation to the language he uses to write about the past has a bearing on how he writes about it. One could perhaps say with a little help from some Chomskyan notions, that compared to the European scholar who had acquired proficiency in Bangla by learning, the native speaker who had internalized its "generative grammar" had an initial advantage in using its system of rules creatively "in new and untried combinations to form new sentences and to assign semantic interpretations to new sentences."[66] But that initial advantage born of competence, that is, his intuitive "ability to associate sounds and meanings strictly in accordance with the rules of his language,"[67] would not, taken by itself, explain the superiority of the indigenous account. For actual linguistic performance involves, according to Chomsky, "a variety of factors of which the underlying competence of the speaker-hearer is only one."[68] However, the difference made by such "a variety of factors" can only be to ensure that more often than not the foreigner will take second place to the native speaker in performance as well. For the latter, speaking as he does from his situation within his own society, has a far greater access to and control over extralinguistic beliefs, cognitive structures, and a myriad other factors "that interact with underlying competence to determine actual performance."[69]

One can understand, therefore, why Rajiblochan succeeded in making his matribhasha do more work for him than Marshman managed to get out of his second language, although both had the same event to write about and nearly the same information to write it up with. It was from his European rulers that the Bengali intellectual learnt to rethink his own past according to a post-Enlightenment, rationalist view of history. It was to the impact of British rule again that he owed the beginnings of a modern Bangla prose. However, once the sense of history and the sense of prose came together in indigenous narrative practice, the outcome was a historiography which promised at once to make for a far more sensitive reading of the Indian past than any European writing in Bangla on the same subject.

IV. Historiography and the Question of Power

An Appropriated Past

It was thus that the development of modern Bangla prose provided, from its very beginning in the first decade of the nineteenth century, a necessary condition for the making of an autonomous view of the Indian past. But the promise of autonomy had not materialized even as late as 1880 when that failure seemed to

Bankimchandra obvious enough to merit his call for an Indian historiography of India. Quite clearly, the autonomy of historiography was not only a question of language. It was also a question of power. Since the Indian past had already been appropriated by colonialist discourse for reasons of state, its reclamation could only be achieved by expropriating the expropriators.

Appropriation is an exercise in proprietorship. One can say, after Hegel, that to appropriate is to put one's will into a thing and then objectify such willing by occupancy and use.[70] To appropriate a past is, therefore, to make time, dead time, into a thing before grasping it by one's will. That, of course, is no problem for the bourgeoisie, who constitute themselves into a class precisely by turning time into that ultimate and most generalized form of the thing, money—the thing which, under the rule of that class, becomes the measure and symbol of all other things. Nor is the prospect of having to do with dead time any deterrent to bourgeois appropriation of the past. For "capital is dead labour which, vampire-like, lives only by sucking living labour,"[71] that is, by making the surplus labor-time of the past congealed in its constant part absorb the greatest possible amount of surplus labor-time which is actually present at any point of a process of production in the form of surplus labor. That is why the objectification of the past as a thing to seize and possess comes as easily to the capitalist in the sphere of culture as in that of commodity production. And where, in the nineteenth century, was dead time easier for masters of capital to come by than in the continents of frozen time made up of the so-called archaic societies?

It was quite in order, therefore, that the bourgeoisie who came from the West to rule over South Asia, the most grasping of all the bourgeoisie of that period, should have the will to appropriate the Indian past and realize that will objectively by conquest and use: conquest—to make the act of will recognizable by others, because without such recognition the will remains trapped in its concept;[72] and use—in order to convert dominance, acquired by conquest, into hegemony. But, says Hegel, "The use of the thing is my need being externally realized through the change, destruction, and consumption of the thing."[73]

Change, destruction, consumption: the purpose of these moments of use is to ensure that "the thing is reduced to a means of the satisfaction of my need."[74] It was to satisfy Britain's imperial need to get its conquest and dominion recognized as the triumph of a historic will and realization of a historic destiny that the Indian past was appropriated and used for the construction of British Indian history. However, it is not possible to appropriate a people's past without imposing the appropriator's will on their will, without ousting them from the site of an autochthonous occupancy, without violating the traditions of a pre-existing right of use. In other words, appropriation of another people's past amounts to expropriation. Nilmani Basak's grievance about the falsification of the Indian past in anglophone historiography indicated how the "change, destruction and consumption" brought about by the violence of colonialist appropriation did not fail to register on the sensitivities of the expropriated.

It was only through the hardening of such sensitivity into resistance that the expropriators could be expropriated. That would mean, of course, questioning Britain's right to appropriate our past, its right to annex Indian history as "a portion of the British history" according to Mill's notorious formula. But that right, as the more vigorous amongst the ideologues of the raj never failed to remind the subject people, followed from the right of dominion acquired by conquest. To assert the autonomy of Indian historiography amounted, therefore, to challenging that right — Britain's right to rule India. In other words, no historiography of colonial India would be truly Indian except as a critique of the very fundamentals of the power relations which constituted colonialism itself. If with all the help it had from a maturing Bangla prose, historiography in that language still continued to be tied to the colonialist model, it was because of its failure to develop a critique of colonialism in any fundamental sense.

Conformity to that model was characteristic of both the principal varieties of indigenous writing on the history of British rule. One of these was made up of manuals used for teaching at schools. It is not possible to exaggerate their importance as the means of propagating a rationalist view of the past among the youth. It was these text-books which, more than anything else, helped history to establish itself as a normal knowledge — normal in a Kuhnian sense — within a culture still largely anchored to the Puranic tradition. The narrative, in all of these, adhered scrupulously to a standard schema according to which Indian history, since 1757, was simply a record of governor-generalships consisting, for the most part, of two kinds of facts—namely, geopolitical events relating to wars and alliances by which the British incorporated various parts of the subcontinent into a growing empire, and administrative measures by which that empire was made secure and governable.

Turn, for instance, to such popular manuals as Krishna Chandra Ray's *Bharatbarsher Itihas: Ingrejdiger Adhikarkal* (the author was a student of E. B. Cowell and a member of Ishwarchandra Gupta's literary circle) or to Kantichandra Rarhi's *Bharatbarshe Ingraj Rajatwer Samkshipta Itihas* or to Rajkrishna Mukhopadhyay's *Pratham Siksha Bangalar Itihas* (praised by Bankimchandra as invaluable though short—"a fistful of gold" he called it), and you can see the uniformity of the pattern in which chapter headings inscribed with the names of governors, wars, and legislations follow one another from Clive to Dalhousie, from the conquest of Bengal to the annexation of Nagpur, from Pitt's India Act to the India Bill of 1853.[75] The pattern, originally designed by Mill for his *History* and adopted by most British authors in text-books written for use in the subcontinent, was evidence of the resoluteness with which the conquerors had taken over the Indian past since Plassey and stuffed it with the grandeur of their own dominance as its principal content. The colonized could not be more completely expropriated. By conforming to that pattern, Indian historiography merely acquiesced to such expropriation.

That acquiescence might have been produced under duress to some extent. For the standard narrative structure of the manuals was officially induced and authors could expect no governmental approval for them unless they conformed. They had to be careful, said Tagore, not to overstep the boundaries marked out for them according to the canon of loyalism and the wisdom of the text-book societies.[76] No such consideration applied, however, to the second variety of historical literature in Bangla, and yet that too was equally conspicuous by its silence on the fundamental question of power—the question of Britain's right to rule India. Strictly speaking, it was as complicit to British rule as was the other kind. Unlike the schoolbooks, however, it was not addressed primarily to children but to adult readers. The literary quality and craft which distinguished it, in its most accomplished form, put it on a par with the best of contemporary Indian histories written in English. It combined description with reflection according to the standard mode of modern European historiography and had more use for criticism than did the manuals. But the limits which such criticism imposed on itself were a true measure of its failure to develop into a critique of colonialism in a fundamental sense.

Failure in this respect was exemplified even in the best specimens of the genre, such as Rajanikanta Gupta's *Sipahi Juddher Itihas* (1880; Bengali Year 1286) and Akshaykumar Maitreya's *Sirajuddowla* (1898; Bengali Year 1304).[77] Each of these was recognized by contemporaries for its historiographical skill and erudition—the first by Romesh Chunder Dutt and the second by Rabindranath Tagore, among others.[78] Each was commended as an exercise in fearless criticism. Maitreya's book marked, for Rabindranath, "the inauguration of an age of freedom in Bengali historiography," while Ramendrasundar Tribedi saw in Gupta's work the first signs of an "independent critical attitude" towards British historians of India.[79] Much of this praise was deserved. There was, indeed, an attempt made in both of these to break away from the habit, developed by indigenous authors almost into a convention, of recycling the chauvinistic, racist and factually unsubstantiated rubbish produced by a good deal of Anglo-Indian writing in the form of histories, dissertations, diaries, reminiscences and novels. By confronting these critically on the ground of evidence and the no less important ground of sentiment, Gupta and Maitreya steered indigenous historiography in a genuinely healthy, skeptical direction.

Healthy, though not so original as the encomium seemed to imply. For, the questioning and refutation of certain kinds of British writing on the Mutiny and on Sirajuddowla relied, in both of these works, on an empirical-critical approach which had already established itself firmly within British historiography itself. It was very conspicuous indeed in the growing volume of dissent which had, since the 1860s, set itself up in opposition to the chauvinism of official and non-official accounts of the Mutiny as well as in the indictment of the East India Company's early transactions that had increasingly gained in authority during the hundred years between Burke's speech at the trial of Warren Hastings and Beveridge's articles on Hastings serialized in the *Calcutta Review* in 1877–1886. Quite a few of the references in Gupta's and Maitreya's books make it obvious that they owed much to these sources for their information, and indeed, not a little of what has been called their courage. Tribedi lauded Gupta's work as "an act of daring." But in spite of the irritation that it might have caused in some official circles, it did not take a lot of daring to say, even in 1880, what had been openly and elaborately argued by English writers themselves during the past two decades.

More to the point than either originality or courage was the symbolic value of these writings as an assertion of self-respect. Or, to put the same thing in another way, the originality and courage attributed to these authors consisted less in what they said—for what they said was derivative—than in their saying it at all. As Rabindranath observed, not without bitterness, in a review of Maitreya's monograph,

> The English are hardly aware that the innumerable abuses addressed to the Oriental character and Oriental principles of government briefly or elaborately, vaguely or explicitly, relevantly or irrelevantly, in books written in the English language, generate a grievance, born of a sense of humiliation, in the minds of the educated [Indian] readers.
>
> Yet during the first phase of our education, we used to revere the works of English authors as sacred texts on a par with the Vedas. However much they hurt, we could not bring ourselves to believe that it was possible for us to dissent, that it was within our means to verify their contents by the use of evidence and criticism. We felt obliged to bow down to such insult in mute self-deprecation and regard it as the very truth about ourselves.
>
> If under such circumstances, an able, skillful and powerful writer of our country succeeds in breaking our mental bonds and sets an example in rescuing us from blind imitation, he deserves the gratitude of our people.[80]

Despite some reservations, Rabindranath welcomed the book as a blow struck for self-respect, and Tribedi, too, expressed his appreciation of the other work for exactly the same reason. But the self-respect at issue here was that of a subject people reconciled to subjection. As such, it was not predicated on political independence, but on recognition within the framework of colonial dependence. The fight for prestige engaged in these works was one to clear our name as a people by disproving the aspersions about cowardice and treachery cast on our princes, peasants, sepoys—in general, on us in our collective designation as a nation. In other words, it was prestige coveted by the servant in the form of recognition from the master. If this was a blow for self-respect, the self concerned was one that had not learnt to reach out for mastery yet.

That was why the urge for self-respect did nothing to mark or modify the abject, abundant and explicit loyalism of these texts. Loyalist assumptions and loyalist professions were so well integrated in their argument that colonialism features in both these histories as an unquestioned and unquestionable necessity. That is why, after showing beyond dispute that the destruction of Sirajuddowla and his kingdom was brought about by chicanery, deceit and venality on the part of Clive and the Company, and by perfidy and intrigue on the part of their native collaborators, Maitreya found it fit to conclude thus: "In view of the happiness and peace which characterize the new conditions of life in contemporary India, it must be admitted that . . . poison has produced ambrosia and a new India has been brought to life—an auspicious outcome which could have hardly been possible without the help of the English merchants!"[81] And this image of a new India was consistent with his view of its power structure, as he wrote: "England is for our good, and we are for England's glory. We, the two great nations, stand together under the protection of a single monarchy; we share each other's weal and woe; arm in arm, we have stepped into a glorious new age! Let this companionship in arms grow stronger, let this eternal friendship contribute to our mutual happiness . . .!"[82]

The fate of Sirajuddowla was merely a matter of academic interest when Maitreya wrote about it in 1898. By contrast, the memory of the Mutiny was still fresh in people's minds as well as within the administration when Gupta came out with his history. At that point, barely two decades after that massive clash of arms between the rulers and the ruled, their relationship could hardly be perceived as one of companionship in arms. Gupta had, therefore, little use for "eternal friendship," and went on professing, on behalf of his compatriots, an enduring loyalty to Britain, a loyalty that triumphed over all British atrocities, insults, innuendoes and plain denunciation of Indians as wanting in the gratitude they owed to their colonial masters.

The theme of loyalty was made to weave through most of his narrative as a connecting thread and its importance for his argument was put beyond doubt by the long, concluding section of the very last chapter of his four-volume work. In this section, called "Bharatbashidiger Rajbhakti" ("Indian Loyalty to the State"), he cited thirteen outstanding instances—these were in addition to those already mentioned in the rest of the book—to illustrate how widespread loyalty to the raj was among all strata of the population from landlords and princes to soldiers, peasants and nannies employed in European households.[83] All this was evidence for him of the support natives gave the British whenever the latter were in trouble. "In the event," he wrote, "the rebellion was limited to sepoys alone . . . Indians, as a whole, were not seized by the madness of insurgency. Educated Indians, in particular, had nothing to do with it,"[84] and he had, of course, a special word of commendation for Bengalis who, he said, "were never lacking in loyalty . . . The Bengalis never allowed anything to blemish their loyalty to the raj."[85]

The Theme of Kalamka

Gupta's book was published in 1880, the year Bankimchandra came out with his agenda for an Indian historiography in the *Bangadarshan*. Quite clearly, there was little in indigenous historical writings yet to provide that agenda with its most indispensable condition, namely, a critique to put in question the necessity of colonialism itself. And judging by Maitreya's work, such a critique would not be forthcoming even as late as 1898. Was it this deficiency—the failure of historiography to use the already adequate resources of the language for the construction of an autonomous discourse—that prompted Bankimchandra to formulate his agenda? Did he consider such a critique as its *sine qua non?*

It is possible to elicit an answer to this question from a number of his essays written over a period of nearly twenty years on history and historiography. As Rakhaldas Bandyopadhyay has observed, these fall roughly into two classes—one concerned primarily with the ethno-cultural origins of the Bengali people and the other with the refutation of what the author regarded as historical slander *(kalamka)* against Indians in general and Bengalis in particular.[86] It is the second of these two groups which is more relevant for our present discussion. What was particularly striking about these writings was their polemical and defensive character. The need for an Indian historiography derived, in them, from the need to correct the misrepresentations to which, in Bankimchandra's opinion, the Indian past, and especially the Bengali past, had been subjected by foreign authors. Our past, written up as history by those foreigners, was, according to him, no history at all. For that past had been misappropriated and falsified. It was not our true past, and the discourse which claimed to represent it, was, therefore, not true history. "In our view," he wrote, "there is not a single work in English that is a true history *(prakrita itihas)* of Bengal . . . [What has been written] is not the history of Bengal, not even the merest fragment of it. It has got nothing at all to do with the history of Bengal. There is no history of the Bengali nation in it. A Bengali who accepts this kind of writing as the history of Bengal, is not a true Bengali."[87]

Strong stuff. This reiterative denial of historiographical status to what he called foreign writings on the Bengali past was the author's way of defining the true past as one for which Bengalis alone could be their own historians. Conversely, a true history of Bengal could only be a representation of their own past by Bengalis themselves. In other words, misrepresentation by foreigners was to be combated and overcome by self-representation. An indigenous historiography was the means of such self-representation. Hence, the urgency of that call: "There is no history of Bengal . . . There has to be a history of Bengal . . . Who is to write it? . . . Anyone, who is a Bengali, has to write it."[88] A call for an autonomous historiography, it insisted on self-representation as the very condition of that autonomy. But the right of self-representation was not for a subject people to claim: it was not supposed to represent itself and was there merely to be represented. To insist on self-representation, if only in terms of its past, was, therefore, for such a people already a signal of its impatience with the state of subjection. Considered thus, the urge for an autonomous historiography could be understood as the symptom it really was of an urgent, insistent, though incipient nationalism.

It was to be expected, therefore, that the cry, "We don't have a history. We must have a history!" should echo the other cry, "We are not yet a nation. We must become a nation!" The reciprocities of lack and desire in one corresponded so directly to those in the other that the energies and ideas invested in the project of historiography were easily assimilated to those meant for the project of nationhood—*jatipratishtha* (nation formation)—a theme of central concern to the author. The foreigner was, for each of these projects, the Other in terms of which it defined itself negatively. The polemic against kalamka was so important for Bankimchandra precisely because it marked the presence of the Other who had appropriated our past and falsified it.

Appropriation always leaves its mark on what is appropriated. "When I grasp a thing or form it," says Hegel, "this also means in the last resort that I mark it, and mark it for others, in order to exclude them and show that I have put my will into the thing."[89] Kalamka, taken in both its visual sense as stigma and its verbal sense as slander was the mark an alien will had left on the purloined indigenous past. To remove the stigma was therefore crucial to the struggle for the recovery of that past. Hence the pride of place Bankimchandra assigned to this theme in his articles on history contributed to *Bangadarshan* and *Prachar*. He made it a point to address this question in both of his inaugural essays published in these journals, at an interval of twelve years, as "Bharat-kalamka" ("India Slandered") in one and "Bangalar Kalamka" ("Bengal Slandered") in the other. As he wrote in the opening paragraph of the latter: "When *Bangadarshan* was first published, the very first article of its first issue was devoted to the refutation of a long-standing slander about India. That was an act of ritual meant to ensure prosperity *(mangalacharan)* for the journal. *Prachar* is now emulating that example by undertaking to refute a long-standing slander about Bengal in the first article of its very first number as well. May God and all the children of Bengal help us."[90]

We invoke these words to underscore not only the polemical function of that theme in Bankimchandra's agenda, but also the high seriousness, amounting to a quasi-religious fervor, with which he approached it. He was entirely consistent with himself in doing so. For he had already endowed the past with the sanctity of an ancestral time, as witness some of those key passages,[91] where *purbamahatmya* (former glory) was assimilated to *amadiger purbapu-rushdiger gourob* (the glory of our forefathers) and the recovery of the past as history prescribed as a filial duty to redeem the family name. Rhetoric of this sort was the sign of an ideological operation by which historiography, in its turn, was assimilated to national-ism—a sign, indeed, of the times when sentiments, obligations and notions related to the natural family would be transferred increas-ingly to a larger, ideal family, constructed by political culture as the nation.

Bahubol and Its Objects

Kalamka, the mark of the Other on a past appropriated by foreign-ers, was supposed to have been the work of both British and Musalman historians. But between the two, it was the latter who, according to Bankimchandra, were more to blame, because the British relied on them for much of their source material.[92] Of the strings of uncomplimentary phrases he used for the Muslim writ-ers two sets were particularly revealing—one of which (made up of the phrases *satyabhita* and *mithyabadi*) characterized them as liars, and the other (made up of *paradharmadveshi* and *hindudveshi*) described them generally as intolerant towards other religions and particularly as Hindu-haters.[93] The past, falsified by foreign writ-ers, was identified thus as a Hindu past.

In what sense was that past falsified? It was falsified, he argued, by the failure of European and Musalman historians to acknow-ledge the former glory of the Bengali people. Of the two kinds of glory he mentioned in this connection, one was spiritual and intel-lectual, and his list of allegedly unacknowledged achievements in that category included the religious doctrines of Chaitanya, the logic of the Navyanyaya school, and the poetry of Jaydeb, Vidya-pati, and others.[94] What however was particularly significant was the emphasis he put on the denial of yet another kind of glory—the glory of physical prowess, bahubol, literally, the strength of arms. He dwelt so obsessively on this aspect of the kalamka, so persistent and indeed so passionate was his attempt to disprove it, that the slander, as he called it, appeared primarily to refer to this one imputed weakness. The importance of bahubol for his idea of an alternative historiography could therefore be hardly overstated.

Its significance lay, in the first place, in its originality. For this notion clearly set him apart, as a liberal thinker, from many of his distinguished contemporaries. From Nilmani Basak, for instance. The failure of anglophone historiography to notice the intellectual achievements of ancient India was deplored by him as well. But his complaint on this score, like that of many others, was not inconsistent with the liberal values propagated by the colonial system of education. Nor was any dissent to British dominance presupposed in it. On the contrary, Basak's concern in this regard, like Bankimchandra's, could be considered as a derivative of that Orientalist element of the ruling culture which had taught the Indian intelligentsia to appreciate the wonder that India had been in the past. However, Bankimchandra's sense of loss, unlike Basak's, extended beyond the question of intellectual achievement to that of physical prowess and shifted the complaint about foreigners—and about foreign rule by implication—to a political level where acquiescence to colonialism was only one of two possible choices, the other being antagonism. Whether that other choice was, in the event, made operative at all within the liberal intelligentsia's attitude to colonial rule, hence in historiography, is a question we shall soon take up for discussion. Suffice it to note, at this point of the argument, that the notion of bahubol gave to Bankimchandra's agenda a rather different orientation from that of any other liberal Indian effort of this period at rewriting our history.

That orientation hinged critically on the function of bahubol as a conceptual link between historiography and power. Not an easy link to forge under the best of conditions, it was all the more difficult to do so during the last quarter of the century, when, with the Mutiny crushed and most of the wars of annexation fought and won, the raj was more secure than ever in its paramountcy. This was no time for a disarmed subject population to flaunt its strength, past or present. On the contrary, it would be opportune now to slide cosily into introspection and sublimate despair by self-improvement and character-building. A time to propagate *charitrabol* rather than bahubol. The former had, of course, its attraction for Bankimchandra, as witness his fabrication of an ideal character in Krishna, and above all, his labors at that school of character-building he had set up under the sign of Anushiland-harma. But inwardness, with him, unlike Vidyasagar, was never quite so hermetically sealed. It was indeed one of the many paradoxes of that paradox-ridden age. For his individualism with all its religiosity and other-worldly tendencies was still more open, in a sense, to worldly intrusion than was the secular, but hard-baked, bourgeois individualism of the illustrious lives packed into his older contemporary's *Jibancharit* and *Charitabali.*

The concept of bahubol stood, in Bankimchandra's thought, for that rat-hole which allowed history to flood into what would otherwise have been a banked-up and interiorized nationalism. That concept was, by definition, predicated on an object. Power of arms was power only in the sense and to the extent that it had an object for its exercise. It was in terms of such objectification and the values assigned to it that a historiography of India would henceforth be tested for any claim to autonomy. For such autonomy required a critique of the fundamental power relation of colonialism, that is, a critique of the necessity of colonialism itself, as its indispensable condition. In other words, a historiography of colonial India would qualify as genuinely Indian and autonomous if and only if it allowed bahubol to operate as a decisive element of that critique. This was what made Bankimchandra's agenda so original and so pregnant with possibilities. It problematized historiography at a higher level of politics than had been done so far by any other tendency in liberal historical thinking. Above all, it armed Indian historiography with a principle that would enable it to expropriate the expropriators by making the Indian people, constituted as a nation, the subject of their own history.

The irony of it all was that having gone as far as he did to formulate such a principle Bankimchandra turned back precisely at the point where he was called upon to practice it by the logic of his own discourse. This can be clearly seen from the manner in which bahubol was used in his writings on the theme of kalamka. In all the five essays[95] dealing with this question between "Bharat-kalamka" (1873) and "Bangalar Kalamka" (1885) his defense of ancestral reputation consisted primarily in an effort to prove that the Hindus did not lack in strength of arms. Indeed, his emphasis on this aspect so completely outweighed his incidental references to spiritual achievement—and even these were absent from the two key articles, the first and the last, of the series—that the slander he had set out to answer appeared entirely to be a matter of aspersions about physical weakness and want of fighting quality. The recovery of past glory meant, therefore, setting the record right for bahubol and putting history to work to that end if it was to be a genuine history *(prakrita itihas)* —a national history.

The five essays, taken together, stand for his own contribution to such a history. However, the evidence he put forward there in support of his case against misrepresentation by foreign authors makes it obvious that the exercise of bahubol was, for him, primarily a demonstration of the martial superiority of Hindus to Musalmans. Bahubol, in the form of wars and armed raids, was invoked, on a rough count, twenty-five times in these essays. Excluding three references to Hindu colonization abroad (Simhal, Java and Bali) and six to Hindus fighting amongst themselves,[96] we are left with sixteen instances, only three of which have Europeans as the object of bahubol and the rest, that is, thirteen—Musalmans. Since the Hindus figure in each of these instances as the principal and victorious agent of bahubol, the latter may be said to have been objectified by Bankimchandra, for the greater part of his argument—covering eighty percent of the cases mentioned—as a protracted trial of strength with the verdict pronounced decisively in favor of the Hindus. Insofar as this verdict was his own contribution to the recovery of a glorious past, there could be no doubt about his faith in the Hindu character of that past. And, insofar as that verdict was his answer to defamation of the Indian national character, there could be no doubt either about the purely Hindu identity of that nationhood. Any historiography, constructed in these terms, was bound to be inadequate for the agenda formulated by the author himself, if only because the contradiction that governed the deployment of bahubol in it did not have colonialism as one of its terms. There would be nothing in it, therefore, to constitute that critique of colonialism without which no historiography could be truly autonomous.

Another look at those instances of bahubol may help to clarify this point further. Of the sixteen citations which were strictly relevant to Bankimchandra's argument, all but one were about demonstrations of physical prowess in the precolonial period. Two out of the three references to Europeans as the object of bahubol concerned Alexander's invasion of Panjab in 327 B.C. The only case of an armed encounter with Europeans in colonial times was taken from the Second Anglo-Sikh War of 1848–49, and although the valor of Sikh resistance at Ramnagar and Chilianwala was promptly assimilated to the record of Hindu glory, the decisive character of British victory did not allow for the nomination of this event as the most convincing example of bahubol.

For all practical purposes, therefore, the importance of bahubol, for Bankimchandra, was limited to its exercise in the precolonial history of India. By choosing not to extend it into the period of British paramountcy in spite of the large incidence of armed conflict between the raj and the people with which to illustrate it (the first and the last essays of the kalamka series were written respectively within sixteen and twenty-eight years of the Mutiny), he failed to explore the power of that concept to its full extent, that is, its power to objectify the most significant contradiction of the colonial era — the contradiction between colonizer and colonized, as one which could not be resolved except by recourse to arms. Since an objectification of that order was indispensable for the autonomy of historiography, if it were to develop a fundamental critique of colonialism in the only way it was possible to do so, namely, in terms of a critique by arms, the excision of colonial rule from the history of bahubol, hence the exclusion of bahubol from the history of colonial rule, prevented the agenda for an alternative historiography from being put into effect even as it was formulated and urged with such fervor.

But if Bankimchandra had no use for bahubol as an element of the power relations of colonialism, why did he posit that concept in the first place? For by doing so and limiting its deployment to precolonial India, he certainly got himself into a tangle of his own making, as should be easy to demonstrate by considering bahubol together with the notion of jatipratishtha, which was no less germane to his historical thinking. He connected these two ideas in the very first article of the kalamka series, "Bharat-kalamka," which had all of its concluding part taken up by a discussion of jatipratishtha.[97] The latter had never been a part of the Indian historical experience in precolonial times except on three occasions, according to him. The Aryans had constituted themselves as a nation or nationality (these two English phrases were used by him synonymously with *jati*) in the Vedic and the immediate post-Vedic period; and subsequently, the Marathas and the Sikhs, too, had done the same, each for a short while, under their respective leaders, Sivaji and Ranjit Singh. Excluding these three instances, the precolonial past, he argued, had been conspicuous by the absence of nationhood, because it lacked in both of the conditions without which a people could never form itself into a nation. The first of these was a positive condition consisting of a sense of unity *(aikyajnan)* — a threefold unity of common counsel, common opinion, and common action. The second condition, a negative one, he wrote in a Machiavellian vein, required that the interests of one's own nation had to be promoted, if necessary — and it was necessary in most cases — by harming those of other nations, even if that meant putting them down *(parajatipiran)* by force, that is, by bahubol.

It was Bankimchandra's view that neither of these conditions obtained in the precolonial polity. For one thing, the diversities of Indian life — territorial, linguistic, ethnic, and religious — combined to defeat the sense of unity not only at the all-India level, but regionally as well. "The Bengalis do not have a sense of unity as a Bengali nationality, the Sikhs do not have a sense of unity as a Sikh nationality," he deplored. And since there was no nationhood, there was nothing to defend by force. "*Jatipratishtha* disappeared from India long ago for a variety of reasons . . . Precisely because it disappeared, rulers of all other nationalities were installed as rulers of the Hindu kingdoms by the [Hindu] society itself without a fight. That is why Hindu society never lifted a finger to defend its own independence." The sum of the argument was, therefore, to say that barring three solitary instances, there was no jatipratishtha in precolonial India because there was no sense of unity *(aikyajnan)*, and since there was no nationhood to fight for, there was no bahubol.

What a glaring inconsistency! The theory of jatipratishtha demolished in effect the construction of Hindu prowess in precolonial India by the concept of bahubol. The inconsistency is further aggravated by Bankimchandra's acknowledgment, in the concluding lines of the same seminal essay, "Bharat-kalamka," that love of independence and nation-formation, which had been unknown to the Hindus, were intellectual gifts bestowed on us by our "great benefactors" *(paramopakari)*, the English. Why, one is tempted to ask, were these gifts not used by the author to develop a critique of colonial rule which, too, was bestowed on us by the same "great benefactors?" How is it, one wonders, that he came so tantalizingly close to identifying British dominance as the proper object both of his theory of jatipratishtha and his concept of bahubol and yet missed it?

We puzzle about such questions because there is enough evidence to suggest that Bankimchandra was not altogether unaware of the bearing of these concepts on the power relations of colonialism. Confronted with it from time to time by the logic of his own discourse, he would respond with a quick defensive gesture that was eloquent with the anxieties which stimulated it. Thus, when the rigor of his argument in a well-known essay forced on him the question, "Are independence and dependence then equivalent to you?" his riposte was to say, "Our submission to those who speak thus is that we are not engaged in debating such issues. We are a dependent nation and shall remain in a state of dependence for a long time yet. It is not for us to debate such issues."[98] An evasive reply, it did more to reveal than hide the censoring mechanism he used to muzzle himself when it came to addressing critically the question of power under the conditions of colonial rule. The same kind of self-censorship was at work again when the author, speaking in the voice of the Chikitsak, stopped Satyananda from exercising bahubol against the British, although he had just used it convincingly to defeat the Musalmans at the battle of Anandamath.

All of which goes to show how the need for a critique of colonialism pressed itself again and again on Bankimchandra's work in both its discursive forms — that is, the essay and the novel, and how he evaded that critique. However, in thinking, as in writing, the outcome of such games of evasion does not always favor the player. Slippages occur. As the psychopathology of everyday life demonstrates so well, phrases we are so careful not to utter, may suddenly give us the slip, and a slip of the tongue can expose what is repressed more amply than an entire affidavit. There is an instance of such a parapraxis which managed to defy the vigilance of Bankimchandra's self-censorship. This occurred in the course of one of his many obsessive references to the sack of Nabadwip by

Bakhtyar Khilji and his horsemen, and his equally obsessive attempt to prove that this was a lie invented by a Muslim chronicler. "The history of Bengal abounds in such [misrepresentations]," he wrote. "According to such history, a handful of English and Telinga troops are said to have destroyed thousands of native soldiers to win a spectacular victory at the battle of Plassey. This is mere fiction. No real battle was fought at Plassey. It was all a farce."[99]

A chain of associations by which the battle of Plassey substituted for the sack of Nabadwip and the English for the Musalman in this parapraxis, rendered the censorship of a conscious will inoperative for a moment and enabled a hitherto repressed idea to manifest itself by assigning the colonizers, for once, as the object of bahubol in a historically decisive battle for power. It is easy therefore to see, in the light of this slippage, how, conversely, the force of ideology had brought about a series of displacements to make the Musalman rather than the British the object of bahubol and the remote precolonial past rather than the recent colonial past its temporal site. The inconsistency, noticed above, between Bankimchandra's theory of jatipratishtha and his notion of bahubol was a symptom precisely of this displacement. By putting bahubol in the wrong place in Indian history, that is, by displacing it to the precolonial period, it denied the concept of its true historical function as an indispensable element of that critique without which the formation of nationhood, hence the writing of its history, would not be possible in the era of imperialism.

V. A Failed Agenda

It was thus that elements of rationalist thought imbibed from a Western-style education, the development of a vernacular prose, and above all, an incipient nationalism converged on Bankimchandra's genius to produce the nineteenth-century agenda for an Indian historiography of India. But there was nothing in liberal ideology yet to enable the Indian intellectual to put that agenda into effect. For the critique of the fundamental power relations of colonialism, the critique which would question the very necessity of colonialism itself and without which that agenda could not be effectuated into historiography, was still beyond the ken of liberal politics.

It would not be until the first decade of the twentieth century that a nationalist view of the past would arm itself with such a critique and act upon that agenda to produce the first truly Indian historiography of India. In doing so, it would fire itself by the militancy of the less conciliatory tendencies within the Swadeshi campaign and above all, by the uncompromising anti-imperialist stance of the revolutionary-terrorist movements. It would derive much of its passion from a symptomatic reading of Bankimchandra's historiographical essays and historical novels and exploit the slippages and inconsistencies of his discourse to recuperate the suggestions of a radical critique which he had himself taken so much care to excise and suppress by self-censorship and evasion. The thresholds set up by the cautious and calculating loyalism of nineteenth-century liberal thought would henceforth be ignored by a new patriotic historiography which made up by its vigor for what it lacked in finesse and discrimination characteristic of some of the best colonialist and loyalist writings. But with all its crudity, this still predominantly petty-bourgeois discourse would use its prides and prejudices to stake out for the first time a claim to the entire period of colonial rule as an Indian past, hence as a proper subject for an autonomous Indian historiography.

This struggle for expropriating the expropriators of the recent Indian past was, of course, not eligible for official patronage. An unauthorized alternative to colonialist discourse, pitted against the latter from its inception, it would have no place for a long time yet in class-rooms and curricula. Far from being promoted as an aid to the education of the young, it was destined to be classified as forbidden reading for all—young and old. Some of this new historical literature would be identified not only as a misguided deviation from the rulers' own view of the record of the raj, but more gravely, as a threat to the security of the raj itself. Not a few exercises in this genre of historiography, of which Sakharam Ganesh Deuskar's *Desher Katha* was one, entered the dreaded list of seditious books and pamphlets. Produced in secrecy by small backstreet printers, often at much risk to their persons and properties, these publications circulated among a clandestine readership, passing from hand to hand, until the relay would be disrupted by a dawn raid and the last reader, usually a schoolboy or some unemployed youth in a mufassil town, taken to the local police station together with the offending object, an exhibit in support of the Crown's case against a member or sympathizer of some militant nationalist *samiti*. That was the price that Indian historiography had to pay as it moved into the twentieth century to act upon Bankimchandra's agenda by defying him and using his concept of bahubol to develop a critique not only of the administrative performance of the colonial rulers, but of their right to rule.

Notes
Glossary
Index

Notes

1. Colonialism in South Asia

1. Hayden White, *Metahistory* (Baltimore: Johns Hopkins University Press, 1983), pp. 21–22.

2. Aristotle, *The Politics* (Harmondsworth: Penguin Books, 1974), p. 34.

3. M. I. Finley, *Ancient Slavery and Modern Ideology* (Harmondsworth: Penguin Books, 1983), p. 119.

4. Perry Anderson, *Passages from Antiquity to Feudalism* (London: New Left Books, 1975), p. 23.

5. Ibid.

6. See, for instance, R. C. Majumdar, "Ideas of History in Sanskrit Literature," and A. L. Basham, "The Kashmir Chronicle" both in C. H. Philips, ed., *Historians of India, Pakistan and Ceylon* (London: Oxford University Press, 1961).

7. *Rājataraṅgiṇī*, translated by Ranjit Sitaram Pandit (New Delhi: Sahitya Akademi, 1968), I:13–15.

8. Ibid., I:7.

9. D. D. Kosambi, *An Introduction to the Study of Indian History* (Bombay: Popular Prakashan, 1975), 2nd rev. ed., p. 365.

10. Majumdar, "Ideas of History," p. 23; Basham, "Kashmir Chronicle," p. 62.

11. Basham, "Kashmir Chronicle," pp. 62–63.

12. Majumdar, "Ideas of History," p. 21.

13. Ibid., p. 23.

14. *Rājataraṅgiṇī*, I:9–10.

15. Ibid., n. 324.

16. Basham, "Kashmir Chronicle," p. 62.

17. *Rājataraṅgiṇī*, I:9–10. For a discussion of the errors in Bühler's reading of this verse and its correct interpretation, see the translator's note in ibid., pp. 7–9, and Majumdar, "Ideas of History," p. 21.

18. Montesquieu, *De l'Esprit des Lois* (Paris: Garnier, n.d.), I:260; and Montesquieu, *The Spirit of the Laws*, trans. and ed. by A. M. Cohler, B. C. Miller, and H. S. Stone (Cambridge: Cambridge University Press, 1989), p. 252.

19.   G. W. F. Hegel, *Lectures on the Philosophy of World History. Introduction: Reason in History*, trans. H. B. Nisbet (Cambridge: Cambridge University Press, 1982), p. 54.

20.   Majumdar, "Ideas of History," p. 23.

21.   Basham, "Kashmir Chronicle," p. 64.

22.   Karl Marx, *Grundrisse* (Harmondsworth: Penguin Books, 1973), p. 408.

23.   Ibid., p. 539.

24.   Ibid., p. 540.

25.   Ibid., p. 409.

26.   Ibid., pp. 409–410.

27.   Ibid., p. 410.

28.   Bertrand Russell, *History of Western Philosophy* (London: George Allen & Unwin, 1965), p. 578.

29.   Karl Marx, *Capital* (Chicago: Charles H. Kerr, 1909), 3:910. Emphasis added.

30.   Marx, *Grundrisse*, p. 884. Much of the section "Bastiat and Carey" on pp. 883–893 of this work is taken up with that question.

31.   Karl Marx and Frederick Engels, *Collected Works* (London: Lawrence & Wishart, 1975–1994), 8:161.

32.   Ibid., p. 162.

33.   Marx and Engels, *Collected Works*, 7:294–295.

34.   Hegel, *Lectures on the Philosophy of World History*, pp. 72–73.

35.   Ibid., p. 71.

36.   Thomas Hobbes, *Leviathan* (Harmondsworth: Penguin Books, 1975), p. 272.

37.   For an informative note on Gramsci's use of the word "hegemony" *(egemonia)* interchangeably with "leadership" *(direzione)* and occasional exceptions to that practice, see Antonio Gramsci, *Prison Notebooks* (London: Lawrence & Wishart, 1976), pp. 55–57. A passage cited in that note illustrates a characteristic use of these terms synonymously with as well as in opposition to the notion of dominance in his writings: "a class is dominant in two ways, i.e. 'leading' and 'dominant'. It leads the classes which are its allies, and dominates those which are its enemies . . . there can and must be a 'political hegemony' even before the attainment of government power, and one should not count solely on the power and material force which such a position gives in order to exercise political leadership or hegemony." Quite a few such instances will also be found in Antonio Gramsci, *Selections from Cultural Writings* (London: Lawrence & Wishart, 1985).

38.   Ranajit Guha, *A Rule of Property for Bengal: An Essay on the Idea of Permanent Settlement* (Durham and London: Duke University Press, 1996), p. 155.

39. Veena Talwar Oldenburg, *The Making of Colonial Lucknow, 1856–1877* (Princeton: Princeton University Press, 1984).

40. Dinesh Chandra Sen, *Vanga Sahitya Parichaya* (Calcutta: University of Calcutta, 1914), pp. 1430–1432.

41. The information on Kumaun used here is taken from Ramachandra Guha's essay, "Forestry and Social Protest in British Kumaun, c. 1893–1921," in *Subaltern Studies IV* (Delhi: Oxford University Press, 1985).

42. This question has been discussed at length in Ranajit Guha, "Neel-Darpan: the Image of a Peasant Revolt in a Liberal Mirror," *Journal of Peasant Studies*, 2:1 (October 1974), pp. 1–46.

43. Amalendu Guha, *Planter Raj to Swaraj: Freedom Struggle and Electoral Politics in Assam, 1826–1947* (New Delhi: Indian Council of Historical Research, 1977), pp. 41–42.

44. Jan Gonda, *Ancient Indian Kingship from the Religious Point of View* (Leiden: E. J. Brill, 1966), p. 22.

45. The source of my citations from that text is *The Laws of Manu*, ed. G. Bühler, *Sacred Books of the East Series* (Oxford: Clarendon Press, 1886), vol. 25.

46. Charles Drekmeier, *Kingship and Community in Early India* (Stanford, Calif.: Stanford University Press, 1962), p. 10.

47. Asa Briggs identifies this period of English history as 1783–1867 in *Age of Improvement* (London: Longmans, 1959), the best general survey. Elie Halévy's classic work, *The Growth of Philosophical Radicalism* (London: Faber and Faber, 1928), is still unsurpassed as an exposition of the ideological issues involved in the idea of Improvement.

48. Briggs, *Age of Improvement*, pp. 6–7.

49. W. K. Firminger, ed., *The Fifth Report from the Select Committee of the House of Commons on the Affairs of the East India Company* (Calcutta: R. Cambray, 1917), 2:510–515, 527–543. Hereafter, *Fifth Report*.

50. For some discussions on this point, see Guha, *A Rule of Property*, pp. 178–185.

51. *Fifth Report*, 2:542.

52. Ibid., p. 541.

53. *The Correspondence of Lord William Cavendish Bentinck*, 1:207. C. H. Philips, ed. (Oxford: Oxford University Press, 1977). Hereafter, *Bentinck Correspondence*.

54. The reference is to John Rosselli's authoritative work, *Lord William Bentinck: The Making of a Liberal Imperialist* (London: Chatto & Windus, 1974).

55. Ibid., pp. 182–183.

56. *Bentinck Correspondence*, p. 203.

57. See *Bankim Rachanabali* (Calcutta: Sahitya Samsad, Bengali Year 1363–1371), 1:787, for the point on positivist knowledge, and for its assimilation to Hinduism, his *Dharmatattva*, especially ch. 22, in ibid., 2:584–679. In Bankim-

chandra's usage, *bahirbishayak jnan* stands for positivist knowledge, *hitabad* for Utilitarianism, and *anushilan dharma* for Hindu spiritual culture.

58. Max Weber, *The Religion of India* (New York: Free Press, 1958), p. 147; Drekmeier, *Kingship and Community*, p. 8.

59. Gonda, *Ancient Indian Kingship*, pp. 128–131; Drekmeier, *Kingship and Community*, pp. 21, 67 nn. 138, 297; Weber, *Religion of India*, p. 145.

60. D. D. Kosambi, *The Culture and Civilisation of Ancient India* (Delhi: Vikas Publishing House, 1972), p. 165. How the term "dharma" has evolved in meaning has been discussed by P. V. Kane, *History of Dharmaśāstra* (Poona: Bhandarkar Oriental Research Institute, 1968), 1:1–6.

61. *Rabindra Rachanabali* (Calcutta: Paschim Banga Sarkar, 1961), centenary ed., 12:919. There are numerous statements to this effect in Tagore's writings of this period. Many other examples occur in ibid., pp. 673–1099.

62. M. K. Gandhi, *Economic and Industrial Life and Relations*, ed. V. B. Kher (Ahmedabad: Navajivan Publishing House, 1957),1:37, 38. Reproduced from *Harijan*, 30 October 1949.

63. M. K. Gandhi, *Trusteeship* (Ahmedabad: Navajivan Publishing House, 1960), p. 5. Reproduced from *Harijan*, 3 June 1939.

64. The source of this and the other excerpts from Gandhi's writings in the next two paragraphs is his *Young India* (5 December 1929) article, "Zamindars and Talukdars," in M. K. Gandhi, *The Collected Works of Mahatma Gandhi* (New Delhi: Publications Division, Government of India, 1958–1984), 42:239–240.

65. "The Duty of Capitalists," in *Young India* (19 December 1929) in Gandhi, *Collected Works*, 42:294.

66. Halévy, *Philosophical Radicalism*, p. 140.

67. Asa Briggs in "Introduction" to Samuel Smiles, *Self-Help* (London: John Murray, 1958), centenary ed., p. 15.

68. Samuel Smiles, *Duty* (London: John Murray, 1908), pp. 4, 7, 9.

69. See Briggs, "Introduction," p. 9, commenting on J. S. Mill's words used as an epigraph to the first chapter of Smiles, *Self-Help:* "the worth of a State, in the long run, is the worth of the individuals composing it."

70. Smiles, *Duty*, pp. 3, 4, 11.

71. Ibid., pp. 11, 31, 46, 295.

72. Briggs, "Introduction," p. 12.

73. Smiles, *Duty*, pp. 3, 48, 209, 295.

74. For these names and the observation quoted here, see ibid., pp. 93–97.

75. I owe my awareness of this ceremonial aspect of loyalism to some of the researches and publications of Bernard S. Cohn. See especially "Representing Authority in Victorian India," in B. S. Cohn, *An Anthropologist Among the Historians and Other Essays* (Delhi: Oxford University Press, 1987), pp. 632–682.

76. D. G. Tendulkar, *Mahatma* (New Delhi: Publications Division, Government of India, 1960), new ed., 1:53.

77. Gandhi, *Collected Works*, 3:137.

78. Excerpts taken from Gandhi, *Collected Works*, 2:113–114, 119–120, 129, 141, 143, 147–148. Emphasis added.

79. Gandhi, *Collected Works*, 3:137.

80. Kosambi, *Culture and Civilisation*, pp. 208–209.

81. Sushil Kumar De, *Early History of the Vaiṣṇava Faith and Movement in Bengal* (Calcutta: K. L. Mukhopadhyay, 1961), 2nd ed., p. 372.

82. Ibid., pp. 370–372.

83. Ibid., p. 372.

84. F. R. Allchin, "Introduction" to Tulsi Das, *The Petition to Ram* (London: George Allen & Unwin, 1966), p. 59.

85. See, for instance, hymn nos. 27–29, 144, 152, 163–166, 215, 253 in Tulsi Das, *Petition*.

86. *Uttarakāṇḍa*:119 as quoted in Allchin, "Introduction," p. 59.

87. De, *Early History*, p. 408. Hazari Prasad Dwivedi, the eminent authority on Hindi literature, concurs with this view: "The worshippers of Kṛṣṇa say that the pacific sentiment is the lowest." Quoted in Allchin, "Introduction," p. 58.

88. De, *Early History*, p. 379.

89. Ibid, p. 398.

90. Ibid, p. 379.

91. Allchin, "Introduction," p. 58.

92. See Akshaykumar Datta's *Bharatbarshiya Upasak Sampraday* (Calcutta: Pathabhaban, Bengali Year 1376) for some valuable information on this point.

93. De, *Early History*, p. 408.

94. The source of my citations from this work is *Dharmatattva*, ch. X, in *Bankim Rachanabali*, 2:615–620 unless otherwise mentioned.

95. *Bankim Rachanabali*, 2:813, 814.

96. "Loyalty Lotus arthat Rajbhakti Satadal" in *Dinabandhu Rachanabali* (Calcutta: Sahitya Samsad, 1967), pp. 437–438. For some observations on this text, see R. Guha, "Neel-Darpan."

97. Halévy, *Philosophical Radicalism*, pp. 130–131, 136.

98. Ibid., p. 137.

99. Mahābhārata: Śāntiparva, 57.41. References to the epic in this paragraph are to translations by Manmatha Nath Dutt, published as *The Mahābhārata: Shanti Parva* (Calcutta: Elysium Press, 1903), and ibid.: *Anushasana Parva* (Calcutta: Elysium Press, 1905).

100. Gonda, *Ancient Indian Kingship*, p. 130.

101. Mahābhārata: Śāntiparva, 90.39.

102. Jacques Lacan, "The Function and Field of Speech and Language in Psychoanalysis" in *Ecrits* (London: Tavistock, 1980), p. 59.

103. Montesquieu, *De l'Esprit des Lois*, book 3, chaps. 9 and 10, pp. 31–33; *The Spirit of the Laws*, pp. 28–30.

104. *De l'Esprit des Lois*, book 4, ch. 3, pp. 37–38; *The Spirit of the Laws*, pp. 34–35.

105. *De l'Esprit des Lois*, book 3, ch. 10, p. 32; *The Spirit of the Laws*, p. 29.

106. As we have already said earlier, the word "hegemony" in our use of the word stands for *conditions of Dominance (D), such that, in the organic composition of the latter Persuasion (P) outweighs Coercion (C)*.

107. Niccolò Machiavelli, *The Prince* (Harmondsworth: Penguin Books, 1975), p. 99.

108. Henry Dodwell, *A Sketch of the History of India from 1858 to 1918* (London: Longmans, Green, 1925), pp. 12, 13, 221.

109. Ibid., pp. 221, 248.

110. E. P. Thompson, *Whigs and Hunters: The Origin of the Black Act* (London: Allen Lane, 1975), p. 265.

111. Ibid., pp. 258–269, and especially pp. 265–267.

112. The five essays in this series used for the present argument are "Ingrajer Atamka" (1300), "Raja O Proja" (1301), "Prasanga Katha" (1305), "Rajkutumba" (1310), and "Ghushaghushi" (1310). The figures in parenthesis indicate dates of publication according to the Bengali calendar. Our citations are all from *Rabindra Rachanabali*, 12:838–868, 887–897.

113. Ibid., p. 888.

114. Ibid., pp. 850–851, 856, 857.

115. Ibid., p. 856.

116. Ibid., p. 892.

117. Gandhi, *Collected Works*, 23:115.

118. Ibid.

119. Ibid., p. 116.

120. Ibid., p. 117.

121. Ibid., pp. 117–118

122. Kosambi, *Culture and Civilisation*, p. 51.

123. Marx and Engels, *Collected Works*, 5:59.

124. Hegel, *Lectures on the Philosophy of World History*, p. 136.

125. Alexander Dow, *The History of Hindostan* (London: J. Murray, 1792), 3rd ed., 1:i. Emphasis added.

126. Alexander Bain, *James Mill: A Biography* (New York: A. M. Kelley, 1967), p. 178.

127. Hegel, *Lectures on the Philosophy of World History*, p. 134.

128. Ibid., pp. 136–137.

129. Ibid., p. 145.

130. Ibid., p. 136.

131. James Mill, *The History of British India* (London: J. Madden, 1840), 4th ed., 2:67.

132. Ibid., 1:152–153.

133. Ibid., 1:2.
134. Bain, *James Mill,* p. 176.
135. Mill, *History,* 1:2–3. Emphasis added.
136. Ibid., 2:479.
137. Ibid., 2:484.
138. Ibid., 2:485.
139. Ibid., 2:517.
140. Ibid., 1:2. Emphasis added.
141. Ibid.
142. Guha, *A Rule of Property,* p. 165.
143. H. H. Dodwell, *India* (Bristol: Arrowsmith, 1936), pp. 188–189, and generally ch. 7.
144. Anil Seal, *The Emergence of Indian Nationalism* (Cambridge: Cambridge University Press, 1968), p. 16.
145. Anil Seal, "Imperialism and Nationalism in India" in John Gallagher, Gordon Johnson, and Anil Seal, *Locality, Province and Nation* (Cambridge: Cambridge University Press, 1973), p. 6 and n. 4.
146. David Washbrook, "Introduction" in C. J. Baker and D. A. Washbrook, *South India: Political Institutions and Political Change, 1880–1940* (Delhi: Macmillan, 1975), p. 1.
147. Ibid. For a number of claims made for the superiority of Cambridge historiography, see Washbrook, "Introduction," pp. 1–19 as well as D. A. Washbrook, *The Emergence of Provincial Politics: The Madras Presidency, 1870–1920* (New Delhi: Vikas Publishing House, 1977), pp. 1–8.
148. Seal, "Imperialism and Nationalism," p. 8.
149. John Gallagher, "Congress in Decline: Bengal 1930 to 1939," in Gallagher et al., *Locality, Province and Nation,* p. 270.
150. "Imperialism built a system which interlocked its rule in locality, province and nation; nationalism emerged as a matching structure of politics." (Seal, "Imperialism and Nationalism," p. 27). "Imperialism devours its own children. Nationalism destroys its own parents." (Gallagher, "Congress in Decline," p. 325).
151. At least six times in Seal, "Imperialism and Nationalism."
152. Seal, "Imperialism and Nationalism," pp. 12, 13, 15.
153. Ibid., pp. 6, 12, 13, 14.
154. Seal, *Indian Nationalism,* pp. 12–14.
155. Seal, "Imperialism and Nationalism," p. 5. Also see ibid., p. 27, where he speaks of arguments of a different kind as "probably significant, possibly crucial, but certainly not general."
156. Ibid., p. 3.
157. Ibid.
158. Washbrook, "Introduction," pp. 1, 2; and "Political Change in a Sta-

ble Society: Tanjore District 1880 to 1920" in Baker and Washbrook, *South India,* p. 20.

159. Washbrook, "Political Change in a Stable Society," p. 28.

160. Washbrook, "Introduction," p. 8.

161. Washbrook, *Provincial Politics,* pp. 286–287.

162. Partha Chatterjee, *Bengal 1920–1947* (Calcutta: K. P. Bagchi, 1984); Gyan Pandey, "Rallying Round the Cow: Sectarian Strife in the Bhojpuri Region, c. 1888–1917" in Ranajit Guha, ed., *Subaltern Studies II* (Delhi: Oxford University Press, 1983), pp. 60–129.

163. Washbrook, *Provincial Politics,* p. 287.

164. Ibid.

165. For an elaborate discussion of Indian historiography of that period see Chapter 3 below.

166. My understanding of this aspect of Indian nationalism has been greatly enhanced by Partha Chatterjee's monograph, *Nationalist Thought and the Colonial World—A Derivative Discourse?* (London & Delhi: Zed Books, 1986).

167. This question is discussed at length in Chapter 3 below.

2. Discipline and Mobilize

1. This question has been discussed at length in Chapter 1 above.

2. Karl Marx and Frederick Engels, *Collected Works* (London: Lawrence & Wishart, 1975–1994), 5:60.

3. The critical importance of collaboration for neo-colonialist historiography has been discussed in Chapter 1 above.

4. For our definition of "hegemony" as used herein see Chapter 1 above.

5. For these tendencies, see Bimanbehari Majumdar, *Militant Nationalism in India* (Calcutta: General Printers, 1966), p. 75, and Sumit Sarkar, *The Swadeshi Movement in Bengal* (New Delhi: People's Publishing House, 1973), ch. 2.

6. Cited in Majumdar, *Militant Nationalism,* p. 70.

7. M. K. Gandhi, *The Collected Works of Mahatma Gandhi* (New Delhi: Publications Division, Government of India, 1958–1984), 18:18, 19, 31, 102; and 21:60, 195. On the question of prestige, also see ibid., 18:114, where Gandhi writes: "It is adding insult to injury to bring the Prince and through his visit to steal honours and further prestige for a Government that deserves to be dismissed with disgrace."

8. Ibid., 18:102.

9. Ibid. Emphasis added.

10. These two are L. F. Rushbrook Williams, *India in 1922–1923* (Calcutta: Superintendent Government Printing, 1923), p. 272, and "Report of the Civil Disobedience Enquiry Committee" in *The Indian Annual Register 1922–1923*

(Calcutta: Annual Register Office, 1923), pp. 65–67, 72–73. Citations in the next four paragraphs are all taken from these two texts.

11.   An English translation of this novel was published by Macmillan (London) in 1919 as *Home and the World* and has gone through a number of reprints. In recent years, Satyajit Ray's film based on and named after the novel has translated it visually for speakers of all languages.

12.   National Archives of India (New Delhi): *Memorandum showing how far the boycott agitation has gone beyond the advocacy of mere boycott of British goods in the interest of native industries.* Home Dept. Pol. Deposit: October 1909, no. 25. References to this document by page could be misleading. Our references are therefore to its district rubrics, for instance, *Memo.*/Burdwan, with some of the district names given in their anglicized form as in the original.

13.   "Sadupay," in *Rabindra Rachanabali* (Calcutta: Pashchim Banga Sarkar, Bengali Year 1368), centenary ed., 12:830.

14.   See the preliminary note, unsigned but identified as "Home Department. D.C.I. u/o No. 5864 of 30.9.[0]9."

15.   *Memo.*/Pabna, Dacca, Backergunge.

16.   *Memo.*/Dacca.

17.   *Memo.*/Tippera.

18.   *Memo.*/Faridpur.

19.   *Memo.*/Midnapore.

20.   *Memo.*/Mymensingh.

21.   *Memo.*/Dacca.

22.   Surendranath Banerjee was reported 10 times from 8 districts as advocating social boycott, and Aswinikumar Datta 4 times from 3 districts: *Memo.*/Backergunge, Birbhum, Burdwan, Calcutta, Dacca, Hoogly, Midnapore, Nadia. For Aurobindo Ghosh as an advocate of this measure, see n. 31 below.

23.   For the most part, social boycott managed to evade the law and no more than the tip of an iceberg has been made visible for us by our source, the Home Department compilation. Even there, out of the total number of reported instances, only 50 from 18 districts specify the professional and/or ritual agencies withdrawn to enforce boycott, as shown in Table 1.

24.   A total of 18 cases, 13 involving lawyers and 5 doctors, as shown in Table 1.

25.   "Sadupay," published originally in *Probasi* (July-August 1908) and reproduced in *Rabindra Rachanabali*, 12: 826–833.

26.   *Rabindra Rachanabali*, 12: 831–833 and throughout the essay "Sadupay."

27.   Ibid., p. 830.

28.   Cited in Sarkar, *Swadeshi Movement*, pp. 316–317.

29.   *Rabindra Rachanabali*, 12:828. The sentence in the Bangla original reads: "Kramasa loker sammatike joy koria loibar bilambo amra sohite parilam na."

30. Ibid., p. 831.

31. Some of the most representative of Aurobindo Ghosh's contributions to this debate were published in the *Bande Mataram* and have been reproduced in his collected works, *Complete Works: Sri Aurobindo* (Pondicherry: Sri Aurobindo Birth Centenary Library, 1970–1972). See, for instance, 1:111–112, 113–114, 121, 124–125, 127; and 2:144, 182–185.

32. For these interventions, see Gandhi, *Collected Works*, 18:75–76, 352; 19:82–83, 367–368; 20:96, 119–120; 21:533; 22:380.

33. Gandhi, *Collected Works*, 25:75, 352; 19:19, 83, 367.

34. See especially two articles, both called "Social Boycott" written for *Young India* (8 December 1920; 16 February 1921) in Gandhi, *Collected Works*, 19:82–83, 367–368, as well as "My Notes" in ibid., 29:119–120, written originally for *Navajivan* (22 May 1921).

35. Gandhi, *Collected Works*, 20:119–120.

36. Ibid., 19:83, 367.

37. Ibid., 20:119, 120.

38. Ibid., 19:368.

39. Ibid., 20:119.

40. For Gandhi's insistence on dealing with a question of principle in what he thought was an exaggeration of this kind, see ibid., 19:82–83.

41. Some cases of social boycott in Kheda district are mentioned by David Hardiman in *Peasant Nationalists of Gujarat* (Delhi: Oxford University Press, 1981), pp. 144, 155–156.

42. Gandhi, *Collected Works*, 21:484.

43. Even in his case it is difficult to assert with any degree of confidence that, in the balance, his approval of certain aspects of casteism throughout the rather ardently "Hindu" phase of his literary career in the last two decades of the nineteenth century did not weaken, if not cancel out, the force of his objection to caste sanctions during the Swadeshi Movement.

44. Gandhi, *Collected Works*, 20:96–97.

45. Ibid., 22:256.

46. Ibid., 19:82.

47. Ibid., 21:533.

48. Ibid., 19:368.

49. Ibid., 19:82–83.

50. Antonio Gramsci, *Selections from the Prison Notebooks* (London: Lawrence & Wishart, 1971), p. 57.

51. Gandhi, *Collected Works*, 41:537.

52. *Selected Works of Jawaharlal Nehru* (New Delhi: Orient Longmans, 1972–1982), 10:3. Emphasis added.

53. Ibid., 8:417–418.

54. Gandhi, *Collected Works*, 41:350.

55.   Nehru, *Selected Works,* 8:309, 418; 10:309.

56.   Ibid., 10:35.

57.   Ibid., 10:324.

58.   K. Marx's marginal note on "universality" in *The German Ideology,* Marx and Engels, *Collected Works,* 5:60–61.

59.   Gandhi, *Collected Works,* 41:539.

60.   Nehru to Jinnah, 14 December 1939 in Nehru, *Selected Works,* 10:400.

61.   Marx and Engels, *Collected Works,* 5:60–61.

62.   When two persons were accidently injured in a crowd that had turned out to greet Nehru on his arrival at the Howrah railway station in Calcutta in May 1937, the incident prompted him to cite it as "a lesson for the people who must realise that enthusiasm, although in itself a good thing, must be kept within limits." Nehru, *Selected Works,* 8:92. In November that year he warned some Kanpur workers who had gone on strike of the danger of acting "in a fit of temporary enthusiasm" (ibid., 8:352) and admonished a local Congress *mandal* for "enthusiasm" in assuming the role of adjudicators in a neighborhood dispute (ibid., 8:367).

63.   Gandhi, *Collected Works,* 18:361.

64.   Ibid., 18:240, 274.

65.   Ibid., 18:274–275.

66.   The information used in this and the previous two paragraphs and the citations are taken from ibid., 18:80, 273, 274, 360, 361, 381; 20:106; 21:139, 140. The word "mobocracy" appears in the title of an important article in *Young India* (8 September 1920), "Democracy Versus Mobocracy," reproduced in Gandhi, *Collected Works,* 18:240–244, and in sentences such as this: "With a little forethought this *mobocracy,* for such it was, could have been changed into a splendidly organized and educative demonstration." Ibid., p. 274. Emphasis added.

67.   Gandhi, *Collected Works,* 18:240, 241, 242, 275.

68.   Ibid., p. 361; 20:107, 490. Emphasis added.

69.   Ibid., 18:361.

70.   Ibid., p. 242.

71.   Ibid., p. 275.

72.   Ibid., p. 241.

73.   Ibid., p. 275.

74.   Ibid., p. 429.

75.   Ibid., p. 242.

76.   Ibid., 20:107.

77.   Ibid., 18:240, 241, 273. Emphasis added. Gandhi's observation on the behavior of volunteers and crowds is confirmed by his secretary, Krishnadas, in *Seven Months with Mahatma Gandhi* (Madras: S. Ganesh, 1928), vol. 1. To quote an instance: "He [Gandhi] came to the public meeting [at Kumbhakonam]. But what sort of a meeting was this? . . . The noise and rush not abating even when

Mahatmaji had begun to speak, he could not proceed. Then Maulana Azad Sobhani tried his best to get the crowd under control, but all in vain. For each one among the hearers felt it his duty to call upon everybody else to keep the peace. The cry of *Shattam podadey, Shattam podadey* (Silence, silence!) was on everybody's lips, and so there was a horrible din instead of a calm." Ibid., p. 187.

78. Gandhi, *Collected Works*, 18:242–244, 244–245, 381–382; 21:50–52.

79. Ibid., 18:242.

80. Ibid., 18:242–244.

81. Ibid., 18:284.

82. Ibid., 18:406.

83. Ibid., 20:490.

84. Ibid., 22:374.

85. Ibid., 21:20–21.

86. Ibid., 21:112–113.

87. Ibid., 21:44.

88. Ibid., 21:21, 44; 22:205.

89. *Gandhijino Aksharadeha* (Ahmedabad: Navajivan Prakasan Mandir, 1971),20:105.

90. Gandhi, *Collected Works*, 20:55.

91. Ibid., 20:113.

92. Ibid., 20:71–72.

93. Ibid., 21:465.

94. Our reservation on this point derives not only from the persistence of social boycott, albeit in an attenuated form, throughout Non-cooperation as documented above, but also from the fact of its continued use later on, as, for instance, in the Bardoli Satyagraha of 1928. According to Mahadev Desai, *The Story of Bardoli* (Ahmedabad: Navajivan Publishing House, 1957), even Vallabhbhai Patel "maintained the people's right to use peaceful weapons like social boycott and excommunication" (p. 117) against village Patels and Vethias (p. 115) as well as against those members of the community whose support for the campaign showed signs of weakening under official pressure (p. 116).

3. An Indian Historiography of India

1. This question has been discussed at length in Chapter 2.

2. Bankimchandra Chattopadhyay, *Bankim Rachanabali* (Calcutta: Sahitya Samsad, Bengali Year 1363–1371), 2:337.

3. Cited by Walter Kelly Firminger, "Historical Introduction to the Bengal Portion of the *Fifth Report*," p. cxx, in *The Fifth Report from the Select Committee of the House of Commons on the Affairs of the East India Company, dated 28th July, 1812*, ed. Walter Kelly Firminger (Calcutta: R. Cambray, 1917), 3 vols. Hereafter, *Fifth Report*.

4. *Fifth Report*, 2:159.

5. Ibid., 2:160.

6. These opinions were expressed by James Grant in his letter of 27 April 1786 to the Governor-General, John Macpherson, enclosing his work, *An Historical and Comparative Analysis of the Finances of Bengal*. It was in recognition of his expertise that the Governor-General and Council "created the office of Chief Sheristadar in favour of Mr Grant" on 19 July 1786. Firminger, "Historical Introduction," in *Fifth Report*, 1:xxx, n.3.

7. Ibid., 1:166.

8. For an elaborate discussion of Alexander's Dow's work see Ranajit Guha, *A Rule of Property for Bengal: An Essay on the Idea of Permanent Settlement* (Durham, N.C.: Duke University Press, 1996), ch. 2, especially pp. 13–36.

9. Grant, *Finances of Bengal*, in *Fifth Report*, 2:168.

10. On this point, see Hayden White, "The Value of Narrativity in the Representation of Reality," in *The Content of the Form* (Baltimore: Johns Hopkins University Press, 1987), pp. 21–23.

11. *Fifth Report*, 2:169.

12. Ibid., 2:146–155.

13. For an account of one such jacquerie provoked by an English landlord's insistence on resurveying peasant holdings within his estate in the Bengal district of Sandwip in 1870, see Suprakash Ray, *Bharater Krishak Bidroha O Ganatantrik Samgram* (Calcutta: Bidyodoy Library, 1966), pp. 413–415.

14. *Bankim Rachanabali*, 2:680.

15. Anil Chandra Das Gupta, ed., *The Days of the John Company: Selections from Calcutta Gazette 1824–1832* (Calcutta: West Bengal Government, 1959), p. 229. Hereafter, *Calcutta Gazette*.

16. For the concepts used in this paragraph, see Louis Hjelmslev, *Language, An Introduction* (Madison: University of Wisconsin Press, 1970), pp. 97–114, and Umberto Eco, *A Theory of Semiotics* (London: Macmillan, 1977), pp. 48–58.

17. Quoted in Guha, *A Rule of Property*, pp. 164–165.

18. *Calcutta Gazette*, pp. 226–227.

19. This figure has been worked out on the basis of Sushobhan Sarkar's authoritative list in his *Bengal Renaissance and Other Essays* (New Delhi: People's Publishing House, 1970), p. 119.

20. *Madhusudan Granthabali* (Calcutta: Sahitya Samsad, 1971), p. 254.

21. Ibid., pp. 250–251.

22. Sivnath Shastri, *Ramtanu Lahiri O Tatkalin Bangasamaj* (Calcutta: New Age Publishers, Bengali Year 1362), p. 72.

23. W. H. Carey, *The Mahommedan Rebellion* (Roorkee: The Directory Press, 1857), p. 189.

24. *Calcutta Gazette*, pp. 273–281.

25. Ibid., pp. 280–281.

26. Shastri, *Ramtanu Lahiri*, p. 74.

27. For a discussion of similarity and contiguity as aspects of the relation between signs and their objects, see Roman Jakobson, "Visual and Auditory Signs" in his *Selected Writings II: Word and Language* (The Hague: Mouton, 1971), pp. 334–337.

28. This distinction and the arguments which follow from it are based on V. N. Vološinov, *Marxism and the Philosophy of Language* (Cambridge, Mass.: Harvard University Press, 1986). The direct quotations are also taken from this work unless otherwise mentioned.

29. Ibid., p. 69 and n. 3.

30. Shastri, *Ramtanu Lahiri*, p. 74.

31. *Calcutta Gazette*, p. 273.

32. Vološinov, *Marxism and the Philosophy of Language*, p. 69.

33. *Calcutta Gazette*, p. 273.

34. Ibid., p. 276.

35. *Bankim Rachanabali*, 2:680.

36. Bernal Díaz, *The Conquest of New Spain* (Harmondsworth: Penguin Books, 1963).

37. Sisir Kumar Das, *Early Bengali Prose* (Calcutta: Bookland, 1966), chaps. iv–v, and Susil Kumar De, *Bengali Literature in the Nineteenth Century* (Calcutta: K. L. Mukhopadhyay, 1962), 2nd ed., pp. 144–206, are among the best assessments of these questions.

38. Both Das and De have cited instances of such inauthenticity.

39. Karl Marx: "just like the rest of Continental Western Europe, we suffer not only from the development of capitalist production, but also from the incompleteness of that development." *Capital* (Harmondsworth: Penguin Books, 1976), 1:91.

40. Robert Scholes and Robert Kellogg, *The Nature of Narrative* (New York: Oxford University Press, 1966), ch. 6.

41. Walter J. Ong, *Orality and Literacy. The Technologizing of the Word* (London: Methuen, 1982), pp. 148–149.

42. Shastri, *Ramtanu Lahiri*, pp. 252–253. Shastri is obviously in error when he mentions 1864 as the date of publication of *Durgeshnandini*. It should be 1865.

43. *Rabindra Rachanabali* (Calcutta: Pashchim Banga Sarkar, Bengali Year 1368), centenary ed., 13:891.

44. M. M. Bakhtin, *The Dialogic Imagination* (Austin: University of Texas Press, 1986), p. 13.

45. Ibid., pp. 15–16.

46. Ibid., pp. 38–39.

47. Carey to Ryland (15 June 1801), cited in Eustace Carey's *Memoir of William Carey* (Boston: Gould, Kendall and Lincoln, 1836), pp. 453–454.

48. There is a general agreement on this point among such scholars as Nikhilnath Ray, Jadunath Sarkar, Sushil Kumar De, and Sisir Kumar Das. See, for instance, De, *Bengali Literature*, pp. 146–154 and Das, *Early Bengali Prose*, pp. 78–82.

49. Our references to this work, *Rajabali*, are all to its third edition published in Serampore in 1822.

50. Ibid., pp. 1–2.

51. Ibid., p. 1.

52. References to this work, in this essay, are all to its sixth edition, published posthumously in Calcutta in 1884 as *Nabanari Arthat Prachin O Adhunik Noy Narir Jibancharit [Mrita] Nilmani Basak Kartrik Samgrihita.*

53. These are Sita, Savitri, Shakuntala, Damayanti, Draupadi, Lilavati, and Khana. The only non-mythical lives included in the collection are those of Ahalyabai and Rani Bhabani.

54. All citations in this paragraph are from the author's preface to *Nabanari*.

55. Cited in the editor's introduction to *Madhusudan Rachanabali.*

56. Cited in Brajendranath Bandyopadhyay, *Nilmani Basak [and] Harachandra Ghosh* (Calcutta: Bangiya-Sahitya-Parishat, Bengali Year 1351), pp. 20–22.

57. Benoy Ghosh (ed.), *Samayik Patre Banglar Samajchitra* (Calcutta: Bengal Publishers, 1962), 1:297. Emphasis added.

58. Ibid., pp. 226–236, 297–299, 322.

59. Cited in editor's introduction to *Madhusudan Rachanabali*, p. 26.

60. "Bhasha" in Ibid., pp. 175–176.

61. See "Anushthhan" in *Vedanta Grantha* in Rammohan Ray, *Rammohan Granthabali* (Calcutta: Bangiya-Sahitya-Parishat, n.d.). Originally published in 1815.

62. Author's preface to *Introduction to the Bengalee Language, Adapted to Students Who Know English. By a Native.* (Calcutta, 1850). The "native" is identified as Shyamacharan Sarma Sarkar in Brajendranath Bandyopadhyay, *Shyamacharan Sarma Sarkar [and] Ramchandra Mitra* (Calcutta: Bangiya-Sahitya-Parishat, Bengali Year 1350), p. 21. Sarkar makes a similar observation in his *Bangla Vyakaran* published in 1852. See Bandyopadhyay, ibid., p. 23.

63. De, *Bengali Literature*, p. 224.

64. For this comparison, I have used the extract from Marshman's *Bharatvarsher Itihas*, vol. 1, as reproduced in De, *Bengali Literature*, p. 225, and the corresponding extract from Rajiblochan Mukhopadhyay's *Maharaja Krishnachandra Rayasya Charitram*, in Dinesh Chandra Sen's *History of Bengali Language and Literature* (Calcutta: University of Calcutta, 1954), 2nd ed., pp. 750–751.

65. For a discussion of closure as a condition of historicality, see White, "The Value of Narrativity," p. 16, 17, 21.

66. Noam Chomsky, "Implications for Language Teaching" in J. P. B. Allen and Paul Van Buren (eds.), *Chomsky: Selected Readings* (London: Oxford University Press, 1971), p. 156.

67. Noam Chomsky, *Language and Mind* (New York: Harcourt Brace Jovanovich, 1968, 1972), p. 116.

68. Noam Chomsky, *Aspects of the Theory of Syntax* (Cambridge, Mass.: MIT Press, 1975), p. 4. The same point is made also in his *Language and Mind*, p. 117, and *Rules and Representation* (Oxford: Basil Blackwell, 1980), p. 222.

69. Chomsky, *Language and Mind*, p. 116.

70. See *Hegel's Philosophy of Right* (London: Oxford University Press, 1967), First Part: Abstract Right, (i) Property, pp. 40–57, and Addenda to paras. 44, 51, 59, 65.

71. For the concepts of "dead labor" and "surplus labor-time" used here, see Karl Marx, *Capital* (Harmondsworth: Penguin Books, 1979), 1:325, 342.

72. "A person puts his will into a thing—that is just the concept of property, and the next step is the *realization* of this concept. The inner act of will which consists in saying that something is mine, must also be recognizable by others." Hegel, *Philosophy of Right*, p. 237.

73. Ibid., p. 49.

74. Ibid., p. 239.

75. The editions of these works consulted by us are: (l) Krishnachandra Ray, *Bharatvarsher Itihas. Ingreidiger Adhikarkal* (Calcutta, 1868), 7th ed.; (2) Kantichandra Rarhi, *Bharatvarshe Ingraj Rajatwer Samkshipta Itihas* (Calcutta, 1874); and (3) Rajkrishna Mukhopadhyay, *Pratham Siksha Banglar Itihas* (Calcutta, 1875). The author of (l) was mentioned as a pupil of Ishwarchandra Gupta in a letter to the editor of *Sambad Prabhakar* of 23 May 1857 (Ghosh, *Samayik Patre*, 1:222). Bankimchandra's words of praise for (3) occur in his review of the book in *Bangadarshan* (Bengali Year 1281) and reproduced in *Bankim Rachanabali*, 2:331. One third of the book (pp. 69–100), a general history of Bengal, is devoted to "Ingrej Shasankal" (period of British rule), written up in thirty-one sections.

76. *Rabindra Rachanabali*, 13:472.

77. Our references to these works are to recent reprints as follows: Rajanikanta Gupta, *Sipahi Juddher Itihas* (Calcutta: Nabapatra Prakashan, 1981–1982), 4 parts, and Akshaykumar Maitreya, *Sirajuddowla* (Calcutta: Samakal Prakashani, 1983).

78. See Romesh Chunder Dutt, *Cultural Heritage of Bengal* (Calcutta: Punthi Pustak, 1962), 3rd rev. ed., p. 152, and *Rabindra Rachanabali*, 13:473.

79. *Rabindra Rachanabali*, 13:476. For Tribedi's comments cited here and later on, see his essay "Rajanikanta Gupta," included in Gupta, *Sipahi Juddher Itihas*, pt. 1.

80. *Rabindra Rachanabali*, 13:475.

81. Maitreya, *Sirajuddowla*, p. 295.
82. Ibid., p. 296.
83. Gupta, *Sipahi Juddher Itihas*, pt. 4, pp. 217–224.
84. Ibid., p. 220.
85. Ibid., p. 222.
86. See editor's introduction ("Sahitya Prasanga") to *Bankim Rachanabali*, 2:22.
87. Ibid., 2:336.
88. Ibid., 2:337.
89. Hegel, *Philosophy of Right*, p. 239.
90. *Bankim Rachanabali*, 2:333.
91. See, for instance, the opening paragraphs of the essays "Bangalar Itihas Sambandhey Koyekti Katha." Ibid., 2:336.
92. Ibid., 2:234, 337.
93. Literally, these four phrases translate as follows: *satyabhita*, "afraid of the truth"; *mithyabadi*, "liar"; *paradharmadveshi*, "those who hate the religion of others"; *hindudveshi*, "those who hate Hindus."
94. Ibid., 2:330, 336.
95. These essays, with the date of publication shown for each of them in paranthesis according to the Bengali year, are as follows: "Bharat-kalamka" (1279), "Bangalar Itihas" (1281), "Bangalar Itihas Sambandhe Koyekti Katha" (1287), "Bangalar Itihaser Bhagnangsha" (1289), and "Bangalar Kalamka" (1291). All are included in *Bankim Rachanabali*, 2.
96. These six citations are used by the author to illustrate the military superiority of the Hindus of Bengal to those of Bihar, Orissa, and southern India. However, these have no bearing on the dispute about Hindu prowess in general. Since the sides involved in each of these trials of *bahubol* were both Hindus, the weakness of the latter as the vanquished canceled out their strength as victors.
97. *Bankim Rachanabali*, 2:239–241, is our source for the summary of Bankimchandra's argument in this and the next paragraph as well as for all direct quotations not otherwise identified.
98. This exchange occurs in the concluding paragraph of the essay "Bharatbarsher Swadhinata ebam Paradhinata," in *Bankim Rachanabali*, 2:245.
99. Ibid., 2:337.

Glossary

abwab Miscellaneous cesses, imposts and charges levied by landlords and public officials in addition to rent.

ācāra Conduct prescribed by the Hindu shastras.

adharma Opposed to or inconsistent with dharma (q.v.).

adivasi Aborigine; autochthonous tribal people. (Lit., original inhabitant.)

ākhyāikā A form of Sanskrit prose narrative belonging to the same genre as kathā (q.v.).

amla Officials employed by landlords or governmental agencies.

Arthaśāstra An ancient Indian knowledge system which deals with politics in the broadest sense of that word.

atideśa A linguistic operation in Sanskrit grammar and poetics which allows for the metonymic extension of a phenomenon beyond its original scope.

ātma, ātman Self; ego.

ātmaśakti One's own strength; used by Tagore as a general term for self-reliance in Swadeshi (q.v.) ideology.

ātmaśuddhi Self-purification.

Ayurvedic Relating to Āyurveda, an ancient Indian science of medicine.

babu An honorific title designating a male Hindu as a person of importance. Used also generically to describe educated middle-class men in Bengal who came to be distinguished by their dress, speech, and generally their urbanity since the advent of colonial rule. According to *Hobson-Jobson,* "it is often used with a slight savour of disparagement, as characterizing a superficially cultivated, bit too often effeminate, Bengali."

badmash Villain; scoundrel.

bahubol Physical strength.

Baishnab From the Sanskrit Vaiṣṇava, meaning an individual or sect devoted to the cult of Viṣṇu or Krishna.

batsar A mythic span of time corresponding to a secular year. Vernacular for the Sanskrit *vatsara.*

bhadralok Lit., the gentle folk. A collective designatiion for the three elite castes of Bengal, namely, Baidya, Brahman, and Kayastha.

bhakti Attitude of devotion to a deity or any other superior.

Bhakti A Hindu devotional cult based on the worship of the god Krishna (vernacular for the Sanskrit Kṛṣṇa) and his consort Radha (Sanskrit: Rādhā).

Bhangi A caste of sweepers stigmatized as polluting, hence untouchable, by Brahmans and some of the other Hindu castes.

bilati Foreign; generally, Western.

caraṇāmṛta Water consecrated by contact with the feet of a holy man and drunk as nectar.

Chamar A caste stigmatized as polluting and untouchable by Brahmans and some of the upper castes.

charitrabol Strength of character.

charka A spinning wheel.

dada Elder brother; a man regarded as an elder brother because of his seniority in age or status.

dakṣiṇā A gift offered to priests as part of a Hindu ritual.

Daṇḍa Punishment; the god of punishment.

darbar Persian for royal court. This term was adopted by the British in colonial India as a name for assemblies convoked to allow members of the indigenous elite to meet central, provincial, or local government officials in an atmosphere marked by pomp and ceremony.

darsan Sanctifying sight of a divine image or a holy and venerable person.

dāsya Bondage, servitude; the aesthetics (rasa) of servitude in one's relationship with the deity according to the Bhakti cult.

dhamma Pāli for dharma (q.v.) A term often used in ancient Buddhist texts.

dharma A comprehensive term embracing all aspects of Hindu way of life, used also to denote any of its particular moments such as morality, conduct, duty, religion, ritual, custom, tradition, and so forth.

Dharmaśāstra, Dharmashastra The authoritative corpus of doctrinal literature which deals with dharma (q.v.) in all its most important aspects.

dharna A traditional form of protest by which a person sits indefinitely at the door of another against whom he or she has a grievance and threatens to fast unto death if no redress is obtained.

Diwani The office of Diwan under the Nawab of Bengal, Bihar, and Orissa entrusted with the duties of the chief collector of land revenues, and the head of the branch of judicial administration concerned with litigation over landed property.

hartal A general cessation of all public activities as a form of protest.

Itihāsa An ancient genre of Sanskrit literature in which the past is represented ideally by narratives rich in moral and spiritual lessons.

jai Lit., "Long live," "Viva." Often used as an expression in collectively shouted patriotic slogans: thus, "Mahatma Gandhijiki jai," or "Long live Mahatma Gandhi."

jajman An individual or family for whom a purohit (q.v.) serves as an officiant at a Hindu ritual occasion.

jama Persian term for the total amount of rent or revenue payable by a peasant cultivator to the landlord or by the latter to the state.

jati Caste; nation; generally, any class of entities.

jatipratishtha Nation formation.

jatra A traditional form of dramatic performance.

kaba chapkan A suit of clothes worn usually by aristocrats and men of high official standing in precolonial India.

kalamka Stigma; slander.

Kaliyug The Age of Kali, the last of the four ages (q.v. yug) according to the Puranic (q.v. Purāṇa) concept of time.

kalpa A measure of mythical time.

karmi A social or political activist.

kathā A form of Sanskrit prose narrative belonging to the same genre as ākhyāy-ikā (q.v.).

khadi Cotton yarn spun by hand on a spindle or a charka (q.v.); fabrics made out of such yarn.

kisan sabha A peasant association.

Lakshmi The Hindu goddess of wealth and prosperity.

lambardar A village official.

lattie An anglicized form of the word "lathi," meaning a heavy stick or bludgeon made usually of a long piece of bamboo.

ma-baap Lit., father and mother. A traditional expression by which the patron's role in his relation to a client was conceptualized as parental, this phrase was often used by representatives of the raj to claim a parental role for their relationship with the colonized and especially the peasantry amongst them.

mahāpātaka Grave sin; the category of pātaka (q.v.) which calls for the highest sanction against an offender, according to the Dharmashastras (q.v.).

mangalacharan A ritual utterance or activity meant to sanctify a beginning and wish it well.

Manu The most authoritative of ancient Hindu law-givers; a mythic span of time.

manushyatva Humanity; humanism; the condition of being human.

matribhasha Mother tongue.

mufassil The countryside or stations in the countryside, as opposed to the *sadar* or provincial station or town. Its most usual application in Bengal under colonial rule was to the countryside in general as distinct from Calcutta.

mutsuddi A scribe or clerk employed by some official agency.

naudhobi bandh The withdrawal of the services of barbers and washermen used as a caste sanction against an offender.

nazrana A quasi-feudal levy, tribute, or cess extracted by a landlord from his tenants, or a prince from his subjects, but idealized as a gift or present from a person of inferior status to a superior.

nīti Corpus of works on Hindu moral conduct.

pahari Person or people of the hills.

pandal A traditional tent-like structure used for large assemblies.

parajatipiran Oppression of or violence against people of another caste, nation, or faith.

pātaka Sin.

patwari A village accountant specializing in dealing with landed property.

prāyaścitta Ritual expiation.

pralaya The mythic concept of the dissolution of everything in a final cosmic catastrophe.

proja A king's subjects; a landlord's tenants.

projabidroha The revolt of the proja (q.v.).

purāṇa, Purāṇa Generic name for a body of mythic accounts composed in Sanskrit verse.

purohit A Brahman whose function was to act as an officiant at Hindu rituals.

rājabhakti, rajbhakti Loyalty to the king.

rakhi A colored twine worn around the wrist to mark the ritual affirmation of solidarity or affection amongst Hindus during a calendrical festival.

Ramrajya The rule of the mythic king Rāma invoked as a virtuous Golden Age or millennium. Mahatma Gandhi wrote and spoke of this as a moral and political ideal for Indian nationalism.

rasa Aesthetics; a sentiment which has been aestheticized.

ryot Legally recognized tenant-cultivator; peasant.

sakhya Friendship; the name of the aestheticized sentiment or rasa (q.v.) of friendship between Krishna and his devotees in Vaishnava theology.

samaj Society; caste association.

samiti Association; club.

samkirtan A mode of Baishnab devotional singing in public.

samrajya Empire.

saṃsarga Contact; association.

sanatan Orthodox; traditional.

sānta Name of a rasa (q.v.) in Bhakti theology.

Sarkar Government; state; bureaucracy.

sati A Hindu custom of widow-burning.

satyagraha Passive resistance as enunciated and practiced by Mahatma Gandhi.

shastra The corpus of doctrinal and theoretical writings in Sanskrit, especially those relating to religion. From the Sanskrit, Śāstra.

siksha, sikshita Education; educated.

sishya Disciple of a guru or some other spiritual mentor.

smṛti Doctrines and discourses on the traditional Hindu code of behavior.

sowar A native cavalry soldier of the British army in India.

śṛṇgāra The erotic rasa (q.v.) in Bhakti theology.

Sudra The lowest category of castes in the varṇa (q.v.) hierarchy.

swaraj Self-rule; self-determination.

tadbhava A word of Sanskritic origin which has been modified in the course of its circulation first in Prākṛta and subsequently in Bangla.

tādrūpya The rule of analogy in Sanskrit grammar and poetics.

talukdar A category of big landlords.

tapas Ascetical austerities practiced for spiritual reasons.

tapascaryā The practice of tapas (q.v.).

tatsama A word of Sanskritic origin which has been in circulation in Bangla without any modification.

tol A school for teaching courses in traditional learning from Sanskrit texts.

ulgulan Rebellion; uprising.

Vaishya, Vaisya A category of castes in the varṇa (q.v.) hierarchy. A generic term for merchants, traders, moneylenders, and craftsmen.

varṇa A classificatory category used in the Hindu sociology of castes.

Varsha A unit of mythic space in Puranic geography.

vatsalya A rasa (q.v.) of Baishnab (q.v.) theology according to which Krishna's relation to his devotees is conceptualized as that between parents and children.

vidya Learning. Used by some nineteenth-century writers to distinguish the traditional learning of precolonial India from Western-style siksha (q.v.) of the colonial period.

yajña The ritual of sacrifice.

yug A mythic measure of time; epoch; aeon.

zamindar A category of big landlords.

Index

Other books in the *Convergence* series: